GOD'S LOVE

Dr. Maxwell Shimba

Shimba Publishing, LLC
Printed in the United States of America

First Printing Edition 2024

TABLE OF CONTENTS

INTRODUCTION

The message of God's love is the heart of the Christian faith. From the very beginning, the Bible tells a story of a loving Creator who seeks a relationship with His creation. This love is not limited or conditional; it is universal and all-encompassing, extending to every person regardless of their background, status, or wealth. As Jesus taught, the greatest commandments are to love God with all our heart, soul, and mind, and to love our neighbors as ourselves (Matthew 22:37-40). These principles form the foundation of a life lived in alignment with God's will.

In "God's Love in Action: Living Out the Greatest Commandment," we explore the depth and breadth of God's love and its profound implications for our lives. Understanding this love calls us to reflect it in our actions, attitudes, and relationships. This book delves into the biblical teachings on love, examining how Jesus' life and ministry provide the ultimate example of serving others with compassion and selflessness. Through His actions, Jesus demonstrated that love is not just an emotion but a deliberate choice to act in the best interests of others, even at great personal cost.

We begin by exploring the nature of God's universal love, as illustrated in John 3:16 and other foundational scriptures. We discuss the steadfast, enduring, and unconditional qualities of this love and how it serves as the basis for our relationship with God and others. The narrative of the Prodigal Son, among other parables, vividly portrays God's readiness to embrace and restore anyone who turns to Him, emphasizing that His love is not dependent on material wealth or success.

The book then addresses practical ways to embody God's love in everyday life. Chapters on embracing all people, living generously, practicing forgiveness, and prioritizing relationships provide concrete steps for putting love into action. We also discuss the importance of cultivating humility and recognizing that our worth and identity are found in God's grace, not in our achievements or possessions.

In the section on serving others, we draw inspiration from Jesus' example of healing the sick, feeding the hungry, and comforting the brokenhearted. We examine the call to serve, not as an obligation but as a joyful response to the love we have received. Practical guidance on meeting physical and emotional needs, using our gifts and talents, and volunteering our time illustrates how serving others can transform lives, build community, and reflect Christ's love.

Finally, we reflect on the transformative power of living out the greatest commandment. Embracing a lifestyle of love and service leads to a fulfilling and spiritually rich life, grounded in the unchanging nature of God's love. This approach fosters unity, compassion, and a deep sense of purpose, inviting others to experience the same transformative love.

"God's Love in Action: Living Out the Greatest Commandment" aims to inspire and equip believers to live out the profound truth of God's love in practical, everyday ways. By understanding and embracing this love, we can make a meaningful impact on our world, one act of love at a time.

DR. MAXWELL SHIMBA

PART I

THE NATURE OF GOD'S LOVE

CHAPTER 1

GOD IS LOVE

"God is Love" is one of the most profound and essential truths in Christian theology. This declaration, found in 1 John 4:8, encapsulates the very nature of God and reveals the core of His character. Understanding why love is one of God's attributes provides deep insight into His essence and the way He interacts with His creation. This chapter delves into the theological, biblical, and practical dimensions of God's attribute of love, exploring its implications for believers and the world.

The Bible repeatedly affirms that love is intrinsic to God's nature. In 1 John 4:7-8, the apostle John writes, "Dear friends, let us love one another, for love comes from God. Everyone who loves has been born of God and knows God. Whoever does not love does not know God, because God is love." This passage not only asserts that God is love but also connects this attribute to the identity of believers, emphasizing that knowing God means embodying love.

To understand why love is one of God's attributes, we must consider the theological concept of God's essence. In Christian theology, God is described as omniscient, omnipotent, omnipresent, holy, and immutable. Love is not merely one of many attributes but is central to who God is. It is foundational to His nature and informs all His other attributes.

1. God's Holiness and Love: God's holiness, His perfect purity and separation from sin, does not conflict with His love. Rather, it is His holiness that makes His love pure and selfless. God's love is not tainted by selfish desires or ulterior motives but is genuinely and purely for the good of His creation.

2. God's Omnipotence and Love: God's omnipotence means He has unlimited power. His love ensures that this power is used benevolently. Unlike human power, which can corrupt, God's power is exercised in love, aiming to bring about good and redemptive outcomes.

3. God's Omniscience and Love: God's omniscience means He knows everything, including the depths of human sinfulness and the needs of His creation. His love motivates Him to act with compassion and grace, providing for our needs and offering forgiveness.

The Bible provides numerous examples of how God's love is manifested in His actions and interactions with humanity.

1. Creation: The very act of creation is a testament to God's love. He created the universe and everything in it out of love, desiring to share His goodness and glory. Genesis 1 recounts the creation of the world, emphasizing that everything God made was "very good" (Genesis 1:31).

2. Covenants: Throughout the Old Testament, God establishes covenants with His people, which are rooted in His steadfast love. The covenant with Abraham (Genesis 12:1-3), the giving of the Law to Moses (Exodus 20), and the promises to David (2 Samuel 7:12-16) all demonstrate God's commitment and love toward His chosen people.

3. Incarnation: The ultimate manifestation of God's love is found in the incarnation of Jesus Christ. John 3:16 declares, "For God so loved the world that he gave his one and only Son, that whoever believes in him shall not perish but have eternal life." The life, death, and resurrection of Jesus are the clearest expressions of God's sacrificial love for humanity.

4. Redemption: God's love is also demonstrated in His redemptive work. Romans 5:8 states, "But God demonstrates his own love for us in this: While we were still sinners, Christ

died for us." This sacrificial love offers redemption and reconciliation with God, despite human sinfulness.

5. Sanctification: God's love continues in the process of sanctification, where He works within believers to transform them into the image of Christ. Philippians 1:6 affirms, "being confident of this, that he who began a good work in you will carry it on to completion until the day of Christ Jesus."

Understanding that God is love has profound practical implications for believers.

1. Relationship with God: Recognizing God's love invites believers into a deeper, more intimate relationship with Him. It encourages trust, knowing that God's actions are motivated by love. Romans 8:38-39 assures us that nothing can separate us from the love of God in Christ Jesus.

2. Imitating God's Love: Believers are called to imitate God's love in their relationships with others. Jesus commands in John 13:34-35, "A new command I give you: Love one another. As I have loved you, so you must love one another. By this everyone will know that you are my disciples, if you love one another." Reflecting God's love through actions, words, and attitudes is a primary way to witness to the world.

3. Transforming Communities: God's love has the power to transform communities. When believers embody and extend God's love, they can impact their families,

workplaces, and society positively. Acts of kindness, justice, and mercy reflect God's love and can bring healing and reconciliation.

4. Hope and Assurance: Knowing that God is love provides hope and assurance in times of difficulty. It assures believers that God's intentions are always good, even when circumstances are challenging. Romans 8:28 reminds us, "And we know that in all things God works for the good of those who love him, who have been called according to his purpose."

God's love is universal, extending to all of creation and every individual. This universality is evident in the inclusive nature of the Gospel. 1 Timothy 2:4 states that God "wants all people to be saved and to come to a knowledge of the truth." This inclusive desire reflects God's love for every person, regardless of race, nationality, status, or past actions.

The Great Commission (Matthew 28:19-20) further emphasizes the universal scope of God's love, calling believers to "go and make disciples of all nations." This command underscores that God's love and the message of salvation are for everyone.

"God is Love" is a profound truth that lies at the heart of the Christian faith. It reveals the essence of God's character and shapes the way believers relate to Him and to each other.

God's love is manifested in His creation, covenants, incarnation, redemption, and sanctification, demonstrating His commitment and compassion. This love calls believers into a deeper relationship with God, invites them to imitate His love, transforms communities, and provides hope and assurance.

Understanding that God's love is universal and unconditional helps us embrace all people and extend the message of the Gospel to every corner of the world. As we live out this truth, we reflect the very nature of God, who is love, and fulfill our calling to love others as He has loved us. May we continually seek to know and share the boundless love of God, allowing it to transform our lives and the lives of those around us?

At the core of many religious teachings is the belief that God's love is unconditional and all-encompassing. This profound truth asserts that His love is not earned by deeds or status but is freely given to all, regardless of their circumstances. This chapter delves into the nature of God's unconditional love, exploring its biblical foundations, implications for humanity, and the transformative power it holds.

God's unconditional love means that His affection and care for us are not based on our actions, achievements, or worthiness. Instead, His love is rooted in His character and nature. It is a love that exists independently of human behavior, one that is constant, unwavering, and eternal.

1. Intrinsic to God's Character: God's love is intrinsic to who He is. 1 John 4:8 declares, "Whoever does not love does not know God, because God is love." This statement identifies love as an essential aspect of God's identity, indicating that everything He does is motivated by love.

2. Unchanging and Eternal: Unlike human love, which can be fickle and conditional, God's love is unchanging and eternal. Psalm 136 repeatedly affirms, "His love endures forever." This enduring nature of God's love ensures that it is always present and never fades.

3. Inclusive and Sacrificial: God's love is inclusive, extending to every individual regardless of their social or economic standing. John 3:16 encapsulates this truth: "For God so loved the world that he gave his one and only Son, that whoever believes in him shall not perish but have eternal life." This verse highlights the sacrificial nature of God's love, as He gave His Son for the salvation of humanity.

The Bible is replete with verses that affirm God's unwavering love for humanity. These scriptures provide a comprehensive understanding of the depth and breadth of His love.

1. Old Testament Affirmations:

- Creation: God's love is evident from the very beginning of creation. He created the world and everything in it out of love, desiring to share His goodness with His creation. Genesis 1:31 says, "God saw all that he had made, and it was very good."

- Covenants: Throughout the Old Testament, God establishes covenants with His people, which are acts of His steadfast love. For instance, God's covenant with Abraham (Genesis 12:1-3) and His promise to David (2 Samuel 7:12-16) are expressions of His enduring commitment and love.

2. New Testament Affirmations:

- Jesus' Ministry: The life and ministry of Jesus Christ are the ultimate expressions of God's love. Jesus' teachings, miracles, and compassion for the marginalized reveal God's inclusive love. In Luke 15, the parables of the Lost Sheep, the Lost Coin, and the Prodigal Son emphasize God's relentless pursuit of and joy over the return of the lost.

- The Cross: The crucifixion of Jesus is the pinnacle of God's sacrificial love. Romans 5:8 states, "But God demonstrates his own love for us in this: While we were still sinners, Christ died for us." This act of love was not based on humanity's righteousness but on God's desire to redeem and restore.

Understanding that God's love is unconditional has profound implications for how we view ourselves, others, and our relationship with God.

1. Self-Perception: Recognizing that we are loved unconditionally by God transforms our self-perception. We are no longer defined by our failures or achievements but by the fact that we are beloved children of God. This realization brings freedom from the need to earn God's approval and the assurance that we are accepted and valued.

2. Relationships with Others: God's unconditional love serves as a model for how we should love others. Jesus commands in John 13:34-35, "A new command I give you: Love one another. As I have loved you, so you must love one another. By this everyone will know that you are my disciples, if you love one another." Embracing God's love enables us to extend grace, forgiveness, and compassion to others, fostering healthy and loving relationships.

3. Relationship with God: God's unconditional love invites us into a deeper relationship with Him. It encourages us to approach Him with confidence, knowing that His love is not contingent on our behavior. Hebrews 4:16 urges, "Let us then approach God's throne of grace with confidence, so that we may receive mercy and find grace to help us in our time of need."

God's love has the power to transform lives, communities, and the world. It brings healing, restoration, and hope to those who embrace it.

1. Healing and Restoration: God's love heals the wounds of rejection, shame, and brokenness. Psalm 147:3 declares, "He heals the brokenhearted and binds up their wounds." When we accept God's love, we experience emotional and spiritual healing.

2. Empowerment for Service: Understanding God's love empowers us to serve others selflessly. 1 John 4:19 states, "We love because he first loved us." This love motivates us to engage in acts of kindness, justice, and mercy, reflecting God's love to a hurting world.

3. Hope and Assurance: God's unconditional love provides hope and assurance, especially in difficult times. Romans 8:38-39 assures us, "For I am convinced that neither death nor life, neither angels nor demons, neither the present nor the future, nor any powers, neither height nor depth, nor anything else in all creation, will be able to separate us from the love of God that is in Christ Jesus our Lord." This unwavering love gives us the confidence to face life's challenges with hope.

God's love is unconditional and all-encompassing, reaching every individual regardless of their circumstances. It is a love that is intrinsic to His character, unchanging, and eternal. The Bible affirms this love through numerous passages, illustrating its depth and breadth.

Understanding and embracing God's unconditional love transforms our self-perception, relationships with others, and relationship with God. It brings healing, empowers us to serve, and provides hope and assurance. As we continue to grow in our understanding of God's love, may we reflect this love in our lives, extending it to those around us and embodying the essence of the divine love that transcends all barriers.

CHAPTER 2

WEALTH AS AN ASPECT OF GOD'S GRACE AND LOVE

Wealth is often viewed in various lights within religious contexts. In Christianity, it can be understood as one of the many blessings that God bestows upon His followers. As an expression of His abundant grace, wealth manifests in various forms, including health, wisdom, and material prosperity. This chapter explores the concept of wealth as an aspect of God's grace and love, examining biblical examples, theological implications, and practical applications for modern believers.

The Bible contains numerous accounts where wealth is depicted as a blessing from God, reflecting His grace and favor.

1. Abraham: Abraham's story is a prime example of wealth as a divine blessing. God called Abraham to leave his homeland and promised to bless him abundantly. Genesis 24:35 illustrates the fulfillment of this promise: "The Lord has

blessed my master abundantly, and he has become wealthy. He has given him sheep and cattle, silver and gold, male and female servants, and camels and donkeys." Abraham's wealth was a sign of God's covenant and favor, indicating a deep relationship between divine blessing and material prosperity.

2. Solomon: King Solomon's wisdom and wealth were direct blessings from God. When Solomon asked for wisdom to govern Israel, God granted his request and added wealth and honor as well. 1 Kings 3:13 records God's promise: "Moreover, I will give you what you have not asked for—both wealth and honor—so that in your lifetime you will have no equal among kings." Solomon's prosperity was a testament to God's generous grace.

3. Job: Job's story also highlights wealth as a sign of God's blessing. After enduring severe trials and remaining faithful, Job's fortunes were restored and even doubled. Job 42:10 states, "After Job had prayed for his friends, the Lord restored his fortunes and gave him twice as much as he had before." Job's restored wealth was a manifestation of God's grace and favor.

Understanding wealth as an aspect of God's grace involves recognizing it as a gift rather than an entitlement. This perspective has several theological implications:

1. Grace and Stewardship: Wealth is a manifestation of God's grace, and it comes with the responsibility of stewardship. Believers are called to manage their resources wisely and use them for God's purposes. 1 Peter 4:10 advises, "Each of you should use whatever gift you have received to serve others, as faithful stewards of God's grace in its various forms." This principle emphasizes that wealth is entrusted to individuals for the benefit of others and the advancement of God's kingdom.

2. Gratitude and Humility: Recognizing wealth as a gift from God fosters gratitude and humility. Deuteronomy 8:18 reminds believers, "But remember the Lord your God, for it is he who gives you the ability to produce wealth." This acknowledgment shifts the focus from personal achievement to divine provision, encouraging a humble and thankful attitude.

3. Purpose of Wealth: Wealth is given not just for personal enjoyment but for fulfilling God's purposes. Proverbs 3:9-10 advises, "Honor the Lord with your wealth, with the first fruits of all your crops; then your barns will be filled to overflowing, and your vats will brim over with new wine." Honoring God with wealth involves supporting His work, helping the needy, and fostering community well-being.

Applying the concept of wealth as an aspect of God's grace involves practical actions and attitudes that reflect this understanding.

1. Generosity: Believers are encouraged to be generous with their wealth, sharing it with those in need and supporting charitable causes. 2 Corinthians 9:7 instructs, "Each of you should give what you have decided in your heart to give, not reluctantly or under compulsion, for God loves a cheerful giver." Generosity is a tangible expression of God's love and grace.

2. Ethical Financial Practices: Managing wealth ethically reflects a commitment to God's principles. This includes honesty in financial dealings, avoiding exploitation, and ensuring fair treatment of employees and partners. Proverbs 11:1 emphasizes, "The Lord detests dishonest scales, but accurate weights find favor with him."

3. Investing in God's Kingdom: Supporting church activities, missions, and ministries is a way to invest in God's kingdom. By contributing financially to these endeavors, believers help advance the gospel and serve communities. Philippians 4:17-18 highlights the value of such support: "Not that I desire your gifts; what I desire is that more be credited to your account. I have received full payment and have more than enough. I am amply supplied, now that I have received

from Epaphroditus the gifts you sent. They are a fragrant offering, an acceptable sacrifice, pleasing to God."

4. Contentment and Trust: Cultivating contentment and trusting in God's provision are essential attitudes. Hebrews 13:5 advises, "Keep your lives free from the love of money and be content with what you have, because God has said, 'Never will I leave you; never will I forsake you.'" Trusting in God's faithfulness alleviates anxiety about wealth and fosters peace.

While wealth can be a blessing, it is essential to maintain a balance between material prosperity and spiritual health.

1. Avoiding Materialism: The pursuit of wealth should not overshadow one's relationship with God. Matthew 6:24 warns, "No one can serve two masters. Either you will hate the one and love the other, or you will be devoted to the one and despise the other. You cannot serve both God and money." Keeping God at the center ensures that wealth does not become an idol.

2. Spiritual Riches: True prosperity includes spiritual riches such as love, joy, peace, and righteousness. Ephesians 1:3 praises God, "who has blessed us in the heavenly realms with every spiritual blessing in Christ." These spiritual blessings are the foundation of a fulfilling and meaningful life.

3. Eternal Perspective: Maintaining an eternal perspective helps prioritize spiritual over material wealth. Matthew 6:19-20 instructs, "Do not store up for yourselves treasures on earth, where moths and vermin destroy, and where thieves break in and steal. But store up for yourselves treasures in heaven, where moths and vermin do not destroy, and where thieves do not break in and steal." Focusing on eternal treasures aligns one's life with God's purposes.

Wealth, as an aspect of God's grace and love, is a multifaceted blessing that reflects His favor and generosity. The Bible provides numerous examples of individuals who experienced material prosperity as a sign of God's grace. Understanding wealth as a gift from God emphasizes the importance of stewardship, gratitude, and purposeful use of resources.

Modern believers can apply these principles by practicing generosity, ethical financial management, and investing in God's kingdom. Maintaining a balance between material and spiritual wealth ensures that one's relationship with God remains paramount. By recognizing and embracing wealth as an expression of God's grace, believers can live in a way that honors Him and benefits others, reflecting the true nature of divine prosperity.

CHAPTER 3

WEALTH AND DIVINE FAVOR

The concept of wealth as a sign of divine favor is woven throughout the fabric of biblical narratives. It is not confined to the story of Abraham but is evident in the lives of many biblical figures who were blessed with material prosperity as an indication of God's favor. This chapter explores the relationship between wealth and divine favor, examining key biblical examples and their implications for understanding the nature of God's blessings.

The Bible presents several examples where wealth is a clear sign of divine favor. These instances highlight the principle that God can and does bestow material blessings on those who are faithful to Him.

1. King Solomon: Solomon's story is a quintessential example of wealth as a sign of divine favor. Known for his wisdom, Solomon was also incredibly wealthy. When Solomon asked God for wisdom to govern the people of Israel, God granted his request and added wealth and honor to it. 1 Kings 3:13 records God's promise: "Moreover, I will

give you what you have not asked for—both wealth and honor—so that in your lifetime you will have no equal among kings." Solomon's wealth was a direct result of God's blessing and favor, reflecting his special relationship with God.

2. Job: Job's narrative also underscores the connection between divine favor and wealth. Initially, Job was a wealthy man with vast possessions, which were considered signs of God's favor. After a period of intense suffering and testing, Job's faithfulness was rewarded by God, who restored his fortunes and blessed him with even greater wealth than before. Job 42:10 states, "After Job had prayed for his friends, the Lord restored his fortunes and gave him twice as much as he had before." Job's wealth, both before and after his trials, was an expression of divine favor.

3. Joseph: The story of Joseph, the son of Jacob, illustrates how divine favor can lead to prosperity even in adverse circumstances. Despite being sold into slavery and unjustly imprisoned, Joseph remained faithful to God. His unwavering faith and God-given ability to interpret dreams led to his rise to power in Egypt. As a result, Joseph amassed significant wealth and influence. Genesis 41:41-42 describes Pharaoh's elevation of Joseph: "So Pharaoh said to Joseph, 'I hereby put you in charge of the whole land of Egypt.' Then Pharaoh took his signet ring from his finger and put it on

Joseph's finger. He dressed him in robes of fine linen and put a gold chain around his neck."

4. David: King David, a man after God's own heart, was also blessed with wealth as a sign of divine favor. His victories in battle and the establishment of his kingdom were accompanied by material prosperity. 2 Samuel 8:6 notes, "The Lord gave David victory wherever he went," indicating that his success and subsequent wealth were blessings from God.

The relationship between wealth and divine favor must be understood within the broader context of biblical theology. Several key principles emerge from the biblical narrative:

1. God's Sovereignty in Bestowing Wealth: Wealth is ultimately a gift from God and a manifestation of His sovereign will. Deuteronomy 8:18 reminds believers, "But remember the Lord your God, for it is he who gives you the ability to produce wealth." This perspective acknowledges that all material blessings originate from God's gracious hand.

2. Wealth as a Tool for God's Purposes: While wealth can be a sign of divine favor, it is also a tool for fulfilling God's purposes. Those who are blessed with wealth are called to use it responsibly and in ways that honor God. Proverbs 3:9-10 instructs, "Honor the Lord with your wealth, with the firstfruits of all your crops; then your barns will be filled to overflowing, and your vats will brim over with new wine."

3. Faithfulness and Obedience: The biblical narrative often links divine favor and wealth with faithfulness and obedience to God. Deuteronomy 28:1-2 promises blessings for obedience: "If you fully obey the Lord your God and carefully follow all his commands I give you today, the Lord your God will set you high above all the nations on earth. All these blessings will come on you and accompany you if you obey the Lord your God."

4. Humility and Gratitude: Recognizing wealth as a sign of divine favor fosters humility and gratitude. It shifts the focus from personal achievement to divine grace, encouraging a thankful attitude towards God. 1 Timothy 6:17 advises, "Command those who are rich in this present world not to be arrogant nor to put their hope in wealth, which is so uncertain, but to put their hope in God, who richly provides us with everything for our enjoyment."

Understanding wealth as a sign of divine favor has several practical implications for modern believers:

1. Stewardship: Believers are called to be good stewards of the wealth entrusted to them. This involves managing resources wisely, giving generously, and using wealth to further God's kingdom. 1 Peter 4:10 encourages, "Each of you should use whatever gift you have received to

serve others, as faithful stewards of God's grace in its various forms."

2. Generosity: Those who recognize their wealth as a sign of divine favor are encouraged to be generous, supporting those in need and contributing to charitable causes. 2 Corinthians 9:11 emphasizes, "You will be enriched in every way so that you can be generous on every occasion, and through us your generosity will result in thanksgiving to God."

3. Contentment and Trust: Understanding that wealth is a gift from God fosters contentment and trust in His provision. Philippians 4:12-13 teaches, "I know what it is to be in need, and I know what it is to have plenty. I have learned the secret of being content in any and every situation, whether well fed or hungry, whether living in plenty or in want. I can do all this through him who gives me strength."

4. Avoiding Materialism: Recognizing wealth as divine favor helps guard against materialism and the love of money. Believers are reminded to prioritize their relationship with God over the pursuit of wealth. Matthew 6:24 warns, "No one can serve two masters. Either you will hate the one and love the other, or you will be devoted to the one and despise the other. You cannot serve both God and money."

Maintaining a balance between appreciating wealth as divine favor and nurturing spiritual health is crucial. While wealth can be a blessing, it should not overshadow one's spiritual journey.

1. Spiritual Riches: True prosperity includes spiritual riches such as love, joy, peace, and righteousness. Ephesians 1:3 praises God, "who has blessed us in the heavenly realms with every spiritual blessing in Christ." These spiritual blessings are the foundation of a fulfilling and meaningful life.

2. Eternal Perspective: Keeping an eternal perspective helps prioritize spiritual over material wealth. Matthew 6:19-20 advises, "Do not store up for yourselves treasures on earth, where moths and vermin destroy, and where thieves break in and steal. But store up for yourselves treasures in heaven, where moths and vermin do not destroy, and where thieves do not break in and steal." Focusing on eternal treasures aligns one's life with God's purposes.

3. Holistic Prosperity: Understanding divine favor involves a holistic view of prosperity that includes physical, emotional, and spiritual well-being. 3 John 1:2 expresses this sentiment: "Dear friend, I pray that you may enjoy good health and that all may go well with you, even as your soul is getting along well."

Wealth as a sign of divine favor is a recurring theme throughout the Bible, illustrating God's generosity and grace towards those who are faithful to Him. Figures such as

Solomon, Job, Joseph, and David exemplify how material prosperity can reflect God's blessings and favor. However, this understanding comes with responsibilities and calls for stewardship, generosity, and humility.

Modern believers can apply these principles by managing their wealth ethically, giving generously, and maintaining a balanced perspective that prioritizes spiritual health. Recognizing wealth as a gift from God fosters contentment and trust, guarding against materialism and the love of money. Ultimately, understanding wealth as divine favor invites believers to live in a way that honors God, benefits others, and reflects the true nature of divine blessings.

CHAPTER 4

THE PURPOSE OF WEALTH IN GOD'S PLAN

Wealth, while often seen as a sign of God's blessing, serves a much broader purpose within the framework of God's divine plan. It is not intended solely for personal enjoyment but is meant to be used for the greater good, acting as a tool for stewardship. Through responsible management and generous sharing, wealth can contribute to the well-being of others and further God's work on earth. This chapter explores the purpose of wealth in God's plan, drawing from biblical teachings and practical applications for modern believers.

The Bible provides clear guidance on the intended use of wealth, emphasizing stewardship, generosity, and the advancement of God's kingdom.

1. Stewardship and Responsibility: The Parable of the Talents (Matthew 25:14-30) is a key biblical teaching on the

purpose of wealth. In this parable, a master entrusts his servants with different amounts of money (talents) before going on a journey. The servants who invest and multiply their master's money are rewarded, while the one who buries his talent is punished. This parable underscores the principle that wealth should be used responsibly and productively. It teaches that God expects us to be good stewards of the resources He entrusts to us, using them to generate positive outcomes.

2. Generosity and Support for the Needy: The Bible repeatedly calls for generosity and support for those in need. Proverbs 19:17 states, "Whoever is kind to the poor lends to the Lord, and he will reward them for what they have done." This verse highlights that using wealth to help others is a way of honoring God and fulfilling His commandments.

3. Advancing God's Kingdom: Wealth can also be used to support the work of the church and the spread of the Gospel. In Philippians 4:15-18, Paul thanks the Philippians for their financial support, which enabled him to continue his ministry. He describes their gifts as "a fragrant offering, an acceptable sacrifice, pleasing to God." This passage illustrates how financial resources can be instrumental in furthering God's mission on earth.

Wealth, in the context of stewardship, involves managing God's resources wisely and using them to serve His purposes. This concept includes several key principles:

1. Wise Management: Being a good steward means managing wealth prudently. This involves budgeting, saving, investing wisely, and avoiding debt. Proverbs 21:20 advises, "The wise store up choice food and olive oil, but fools gulp theirs down." Responsible financial management ensures that resources are available for future needs and opportunities to serve others.

2. Multiplication and Growth: Like the servants in the Parable of the Talents, we are called to multiply the resources God gives us. This could mean investing in ways that generate returns, starting businesses that create jobs, or funding initiatives that have long-term positive impacts. The goal is to use wealth in ways that produce growth and further God's work.

3. Accountability: Stewards are accountable to God for how they use His resources. Romans 14:12 reminds us, "So then, each of us will give an account of ourselves to God." This accountability encourages us to make decisions that align with God's values and purposes.

Generosity is a central aspect of the purpose of wealth. It reflects God's character and allows believers to participate in His work of caring for creation.

1. Supporting the Poor and Needy: One of the primary purposes of wealth is to support those in need. Acts 20:35 quotes Jesus saying, "It is more blessed to give than to receive." Generosity towards the poor is a tangible expression of God's love and compassion.

2. Funding Ministry and Missions: Financial resources can significantly impact the spread of the Gospel and the work of the church. Supporting missionaries, funding church activities, and contributing to Christian organizations are ways to use wealth to advance God's kingdom.

3. Building Community and Relationships: Generosity fosters community and strengthens relationships. By sharing resources, believers can support one another and create a sense of unity and mutual care. Hebrews 13:16 encourages, "And do not forget to do good and to share with others, for with such sacrifices God is pleased."

Wealth can be a powerful tool to further God's work on earth. This includes addressing social injustices, promoting education, and supporting initiatives that align with God's principles.

1. Social Justice and Advocacy: Using wealth to address social injustices reflects God's heart for justice and

righteousness. Isaiah 1:17 urges, "Learn to do right; seek justice. Defend the oppressed. Take up the cause of the fatherless; plead the case of the widow." Financial support for organizations and movements that promote justice can help create a more equitable society.

2. Education and Empowerment: Investing in education and empowerment initiatives helps individuals and communities thrive. Proverbs 16:16 states, "How much better to get wisdom than gold, to get insight rather than silver!" Supporting educational programs and scholarships can equip people with the knowledge and skills needed to improve their lives.

3. Environmental Stewardship: Caring for the environment is part of God's mandate to steward creation. Genesis 2:15 instructs, "The Lord God took the man and put him in the Garden of Eden to work it and take care of it." Using wealth to support environmental conservation and sustainable practices honors this responsibility.

To align the use of wealth with God's plan, believers can take several practical steps:

1. Prayerful Planning: Seek God's guidance through prayer when making financial decisions. James 1:5 encourages, "If any of you lacks wisdom, you should ask God,

who gives generously to all without finding fault, and it will be given to you."

2. Regular Giving: Establish a habit of regular giving to support the church, charitable organizations, and those in need. 2 Corinthians 9:6-7 teaches, "Remember this: Whoever sows sparingly will also reap sparingly, and whoever sows generously will also reap generously. Each of you should give what you have decided in your heart to give, not reluctantly or under compulsion, for God loves a cheerful giver."

3. Ethical Investing: Choose investments that align with biblical values and support causes that promote God's principles. This includes avoiding investments in industries that harm people or the environment.

4. Living Modestly: Embrace a lifestyle of modesty and contentment. Philippians 4:12-13 reflects on contentment: "I know what it is to be in need, and I know what it is to have plenty. I have learned the secret of being content in any and every situation, whether well fed or hungry, whether living in plenty or in want. I can do all this through him who gives me strength."

5. Engaging in Service: Use wealth to create opportunities for service and community building. This can include funding community centers, supporting volunteer programs, or providing resources for outreach activities.

Wealth, within the context of God's plan, is a powerful tool for stewardship, generosity, and advancing His kingdom. The Bible provides clear guidance on the responsible and purposeful use of wealth, emphasizing the importance of managing resources wisely, sharing generously, and investing in initiatives that align with God's values.

By understanding the broader purpose of wealth, believers can use their financial resources to contribute to the well-being of others and further God's work on earth. This approach not only honors God but also brings fulfillment and joy, knowing that one's wealth is being used for a greater good. As we seek to align our financial practices with God's plan, may we be inspired by the biblical principles of stewardship, generosity, and service, using our resources to reflect His love and grace in the world.

In conclusion, the nature of God's love is vast and unconditional, encompassing all aspects of life, including wealth. Wealth, when viewed through the lens of divine grace, is an expression of God's abundant love and favor. However, it also comes with responsibilities and is meant to be used for the greater good. Understanding wealth as a facet of God's love encourages a balanced perspective, where prosperity is seen not just as a personal blessing but as an opportunity for stewardship and service. As we delve deeper into this book, we will explore how this understanding shapes the lives of the prosperous and their relationship with God.

PART II

BIBLICAL PERSPECTIVES ON PROSPERITY

ABRAHAM: A COVENANT OF BLESSING

The story of Abraham is one of the most prominent examples of prosperity in the Bible, illustrating God's covenant of blessing. God's promises to Abraham encompassed both spiritual and material blessings, marking him as a pivotal figure in biblical history. This chapter explores the nature of God's covenant with Abraham, the fulfillment of His promises, and the implications of Abraham's blessings for understanding divine favor and prosperity.

God's covenant with Abraham is foundational to understanding the biblical narrative of blessing and prosperity. This covenant, established in Genesis, includes a series of profound promises that reveal God's intentions and relationship with humanity through Abraham.

1. The Call of Abraham: The covenant begins with God's call to Abraham to leave his homeland and go to a land that God would show him. Genesis 12:1-3 records this call and the accompanying promises: "The Lord had said to

Abram, 'Go from your country, your people and your father's household to the land I will show you. I will make you into a great nation, and I will bless you; I will make your name great, and you will be a blessing. I will bless those who bless you, and whoever curses you I will curse; and all peoples on earth will be blessed through you.'"

2. Promises of Blessing: The covenant promises Abraham several key blessings:

- A Great Nation: God promises to make Abraham the father of a great nation, indicating numerous descendants.

- A Great Name: Abraham's name would be renowned, signifying honor and respect.

- Blessing and Protection: God pledges to bless those who bless Abraham and curse those who curse him, providing divine protection.

- Universal Blessing: Through Abraham, all peoples on earth would be blessed, pointing to a broader redemptive purpose.

Throughout Abraham's life, God's promises are fulfilled in tangible and significant ways, demonstrating the reality of the covenant blessings.

1. Material Prosperity: Abraham's wealth is a clear sign of God's favor. Genesis 13:2 states, "Abram had become very wealthy in livestock and in silver and gold." This material

prosperity includes extensive livestock, silver, and gold, marking Abraham as a prosperous individual blessed by God.

2. Land and Legacy: The promise of land is central to God's covenant with Abraham. In Genesis 13:14-17, God reiterates His promise of land to Abraham: "The Lord said to Abram after Lot had parted from him, 'Look around from where you are, to the north and south, to the east and west. All the land that you see I will give to you and your offspring forever. I will make your offspring like the dust of the earth, so that if anyone could count the dust, then your offspring could be counted. Go, walk through the length and breadth of the land, for I am giving it to you.'" This promise establishes Abraham's descendants in the land of Canaan, securing their future inheritance.

3. Descendants and Nationhood: Despite initial barrenness, God's promise of numerous descendants is fulfilled through Isaac, the child of the promise. Genesis 21:1-3 records the birth of Isaac: "Now the Lord was gracious to Sarah as he had said, and the Lord did for Sarah what he had promised. Sarah became pregnant and bore a son to Abraham in his old age, at the very time God had promised him. Abraham gave the name Isaac to the son Sarah bore him." Isaac's birth is a testament to God's faithfulness in fulfilling His promises, paving the way for the nation of Israel.

Beyond material prosperity, Abraham's covenant blessings encompass profound spiritual significance, impacting both his personal faith journey and the broader narrative of redemption.

1. Faith and Righteousness: Abraham's relationship with God is characterized by faith and obedience. Genesis 15:6 highlights this pivotal aspect: "Abram believed the Lord, and he credited it to him as righteousness." Abraham's faith sets a precedent for understanding righteousness through faith, a theme later expounded upon in the New Testament.

2. Covenant and Sacrifice: The covenant is further solidified through the practice of sacrifice, symbolizing commitment and devotion. In Genesis 15, God instructs Abraham to prepare a sacrificial offering, leading to a profound covenantal experience. This act of sacrifice signifies the seriousness and sanctity of the covenant relationship.

3. Blessing to the Nations: One of the most significant aspects of Abraham's blessing is its universal scope. God's promise that "all peoples on earth will be blessed through you" points to the coming of the Messiah, Jesus Christ, through Abraham's lineage. Galatians 3:8-9 reflects this fulfillment: "Scripture foresaw that God would justify the Gentiles by faith, and announced the gospel in advance to Abraham: 'All nations will be blessed through you.' So those

who rely on faith are blessed along with Abraham, the man of faith."

Abraham's covenant of blessing offers valuable insights into the nature of divine favor and prosperity, with several key implications for modern believers.

1. Prosperity as a Sign of Favor: Abraham's material wealth and success are clear signs of God's favor. However, these blessings are tied to his faith and obedience, illustrating that divine favor encompasses both spiritual and material dimensions.

2. Stewardship of Blessings: The blessings given to Abraham come with the responsibility of stewardship. Abraham is called to use his wealth and influence to further God's purposes and bless others. Modern believers can learn from this principle, recognizing that prosperity should be used for the greater good.

3. Faith as the Foundation: Abraham's story emphasizes that faith is the foundation of receiving and understanding God's blessings. His faith in God's promises sets an example for believers to trust in God's provision and timing.

4. Universal Blessing and Mission: The promise that all nations would be blessed through Abraham highlights the inclusive nature of God's plan. This universal blessing points

to the mission of spreading the gospel and extending God's love to all people.

Practical Applications for Modern Believers

Applying the lessons from Abraham's covenant of blessing involves embracing principles of faith, stewardship, and mission.

1. Cultivating Faith: Believers are encouraged to cultivate a deep and abiding faith in God's promises, trusting in His provision and guidance. Hebrews 11:8-10 commends Abraham's faith, providing a model for modern believers.

2. Practicing Generosity: Like Abraham, believers are called to use their blessings to support others and further God's work. This includes financial giving, acts of kindness, and supporting community and global initiatives.

3. Embracing God's Mission: Understanding the universal scope of Abraham's blessing inspires believers to participate in God's mission of sharing the gospel and serving others. This involves both local and global outreach, reflecting God's heart for all nations.

4. Living as Stewards: Recognizing that all blessings come from God, believers are called to live as stewards, managing their resources wisely and responsibly. This includes ethical financial practices, wise investments, and intentional acts of service.

Conclusion

Abraham's story is a powerful testament to God's covenant of blessing, encompassing both spiritual and material prosperity. Through faith and obedience, Abraham received abundant blessings that extended far beyond his lifetime, impacting the course of history and the destiny of nations. His story underscores the principles of divine favor, stewardship, and mission, offering valuable lessons for modern believers.

By embracing these principles, believers can understand the true purpose of wealth and blessings within God's plan, using their resources to honor God, support others, and further His kingdom. Abraham's covenant of blessing serves as a timeless reminder of God's faithfulness, generosity, and overarching redemptive purpose for all humanity.

CHAPTER 06

JOSEPH: FROM SLAVE TO RULER

The story of Joseph is a powerful testament to how divine favor can lead to prosperity, even in the face of extreme adversity. Joseph's journey from being sold into slavery to becoming the second most powerful man in Egypt highlights the transformative power of God's favor. Despite facing numerous challenges, including betrayal, slavery, and imprisonment, Joseph remained faithful to God. His unwavering faith and integrity ultimately led to his remarkable rise to power. This chapter explores Joseph's story, the lessons it teaches about divine favor and faithfulness, and its implications for modern believers.

Joseph's story begins with his early life as the favored son of Jacob. This favoritism, symbolized by the gift of a richly ornamented coat, caused envy and resentment among his brothers.

1. Joseph's Dreams: Joseph had prophetic dreams that hinted at his future prominence, where his brothers and even

his parents would bow down to him. Genesis 37:5-8 recounts one of these dreams: "Joseph had a dream, and when he told it to his brothers, they hated him all the more. He said to them, 'Listen to this dream I had: We were binding sheaves of grain out in the field when suddenly my sheaf rose and stood upright, while your sheaves gathered around mine and bowed down to it.'"

2. Betrayal and Slavery: Joseph's brothers' envy culminated in a plot to kill him, but they ultimately sold him into slavery instead. Genesis 37:28 describes this betrayal: "So when the Midianite merchants came by, his brothers pulled Joseph up out of the cistern and sold him for twenty shekels of silver to the Ishmaelites, who took him to Egypt."

In Egypt, Joseph was sold to Potiphar, an officer of Pharaoh. Despite his status as a slave, Joseph's faithfulness and integrity quickly became evident.

1. God's Favor in Potiphar's House: Joseph's diligent service earned him Potiphar's trust, and he was put in charge of Potiphar's household. Genesis 39:2-4 details his rise: "The Lord was with Joseph so that he prospered, and he lived in the house of his Egyptian master. When his master saw that the Lord was with him and that the Lord gave him success in everything he did, Joseph found favor in his eyes and became his attendant. Potiphar put him in charge of his household, and he entrusted to his care everything he owned."

2. False Accusation and Imprisonment: Despite his success, Joseph faced false accusations from Potiphar's wife, who tried to seduce him. When Joseph resisted, she falsely accused him of attempted rape, leading to his imprisonment. Genesis 39:20 recounts, "Joseph's master took him and put him in prison, the place where the king's prisoners were confined."

Even in prison, Joseph's faith and integrity did not waver, and God's favor continued to be evident.

1. God's Presence in Prison: The Lord was with Joseph in prison, granting him favor with the prison warden. Genesis 39:21-23 describes this favor: "But while Joseph was there in the prison, the Lord was with him; he showed him kindness and granted him favor in the eyes of the prison warden. So the warden put Joseph in charge of all those held in the prison, and he was made responsible for all that was done there. The warden paid no attention to anything under Joseph's care, because the Lord was with Joseph and gave him success in whatever he did."

2. Interpreting Dreams: Joseph's ability to interpret dreams became known in prison when he accurately interpreted the dreams of Pharaoh's cupbearer and baker. Genesis 40 recounts these interpretations and their fulfillment, demonstrating Joseph's God-given gift.

Joseph's faithfulness and God's favor eventually led to his dramatic rise to power in Egypt.

1. Pharaoh's Dreams: Two years after interpreting the dreams of the cupbearer and baker, Pharaoh had two troubling dreams that none of his wise men could interpret. The cupbearer remembered Joseph and recommended him to Pharaoh. Genesis 41:14-16 describes Joseph's summoning: "So Pharaoh sent for Joseph, and he was quickly brought from the dungeon. When he had shaved and changed his clothes, he came before Pharaoh. Pharaoh said to Joseph, 'I had a dream, and no one can interpret it. But I have heard it said of you that when you hear a dream you can interpret it.' 'I cannot do it,' Joseph replied to Pharaoh, 'but God will give Pharaoh the answer he desires.'"

2. Interpretation and Promotion: Joseph interpreted Pharaoh's dreams as a divine revelation of seven years of abundance followed by seven years of severe famine. He also proposed a plan to store surplus grain during the abundant years to prepare for the famine. Impressed by Joseph's wisdom, Pharaoh appointed him as the second most powerful man in Egypt. Genesis 41:41-43 records this promotion: "So Pharaoh said to Joseph, 'I hereby put you in charge of the whole land of Egypt.' Then Pharaoh took his signet ring from his finger and put it on Joseph's finger. He dressed him in robes of fine linen and put a gold chain around his neck. He

had him ride in a chariot as his second-in-command, and people shouted before him, 'Make way!' Thus he put him in charge of the whole land of Egypt."

Joseph's leadership during the years of abundance and famine not only saved Egypt but also led to a poignant family reconciliation.

1. Effective Leadership: Joseph's administration during the seven years of abundance ensured that Egypt had sufficient grain during the famine. Genesis 41:48-49 highlights his effective management: "Joseph collected all the food produced in those seven years of abundance in Egypt and stored it in the cities. In each city he put the food grown in the fields surrounding it. Joseph stored up huge quantities of grain, like the sand of the sea; it was so much that he stopped keeping records because it was beyond measure."

2. Reconciliation with His Brothers: The famine affected the entire region, including Canaan, where Joseph's family lived. His brothers came to Egypt to buy grain, not recognizing Joseph. Through a series of interactions, Joseph eventually revealed his identity and forgave his brothers. Genesis 45:4-5 recounts this emotional moment: "Then Joseph said to his brothers, 'Come close to me.' When they had done so, he said, 'I am your brother Joseph, the one you sold into Egypt! And now, do not be distressed and do not be

angry with yourselves for selling me here, because it was to save lives that God sent me ahead of you.'"

Joseph's journey from slave to ruler offers several profound lessons about faith, integrity, and divine favor.

1. Faithfulness in Adversity: Joseph remained faithful to God despite facing severe trials. His unwavering faith and integrity, even in the darkest times, demonstrate the importance of trusting God's plan and timing.

2. God's Sovereignty and Favor: Joseph's rise to power illustrates how God's favor can transform dire circumstances into positions of influence and prosperity. It highlights God's sovereignty in orchestrating events for His purposes.

3. Forgiveness and Reconciliation: Joseph's forgiveness of his brothers and the subsequent reconciliation emphasize the power of grace and mercy. It shows how God can bring healing and restoration even from painful situations.

4. Leadership and Wisdom: Joseph's effective leadership during the years of abundance and famine underscores the value of wisdom, strategic planning, and stewardship. His ability to interpret dreams and implement solutions was a direct result of his faith and God's guidance.

The story of Joseph provides valuable insights and applications for modern believers:

1. Trust in God's Plan: Believers are encouraged to trust in God's plan, even when circumstances seem bleak. Romans 8:28 assures, "And we know that in all things God works for the good of those who love him, who have been called according to his purpose."

2. Maintain Integrity: Upholding integrity, as Joseph did, is crucial in all situations. Proverbs 11:3 teaches, "The integrity of the upright guides them, but the unfaithful are destroyed by their duplicity."

3. Seek God's Guidance: Like Joseph, believers should seek God's guidance in decision-making. James 1:5 encourages, "If any of you lacks wisdom, you should ask God, who gives generously to all without finding fault, and it will be given to you."

4. Practice Forgiveness: Joseph's forgiveness of his brothers serves as a powerful example. Ephesians 4:32 instructs, "Be kind and compassionate to one another, forgiving each other, just as in Christ God forgave you."

Joseph's story is a compelling example of how divine favor can lead to prosperity and transformation, even in the face of immense challenges. From being sold into slavery to becoming the second most powerful man in Egypt, Joseph's journey underscores the power of faith, integrity, and God's sovereignty. His life teaches valuable lessons about trusting

God, maintaining integrity, seeking divine guidance, and practicing forgiveness. As modern believers reflect on Joseph's story, they can find inspiration and guidance for navigating their own journeys, trusting in God's favor and purpose for their lives.

CHAPTER 07

SOLOMON: WISDOM AND WEALTH

King Solomon's reign is frequently cited as the epitome of wisdom and wealth granted by God. His story is a powerful testament to how divine favor can manifest in both intellectual and material abundance. When Solomon asked for wisdom to govern his people, God was pleased with his request and granted him not only unparalleled wisdom but also immense wealth and honor. This chapter explores the story of Solomon, the nature of his wisdom and wealth, and the lessons that can be drawn from his life.

Solomon's ascent to the throne of Israel was marked by his profound recognition of the need for divine wisdom to govern his people effectively.

1. The Context of Solomon's Request: Solomon became king after the death of his father, David. Recognizing the immense responsibility of ruling Israel, Solomon sought

God's guidance. In a dream, God appeared to Solomon and offered to grant him whatever he asked. Solomon's response, recorded in 1 Kings 3:7-9, reveals his humility and awareness of his need for divine assistance: "Now, Lord my God, you have made your servant king in place of my father David. But I am only a little child and do not know how to carry out my duties. Your servant is here among the people you have chosen, a great people, too numerous to count or number. So give your servant a discerning heart to govern your people and to distinguish between right and wrong."

2. God's Response: God was pleased with Solomon's request for wisdom rather than long life or wealth. In response, God granted Solomon unparalleled wisdom and added wealth and honor. 1 Kings 3:12-13 details God's promise: "I will do what you have asked. I will give you a wise and discerning heart so that there will never have been anyone like you, nor will there ever be. Moreover, I will give you what you have not asked for—both wealth and honor—so that in your lifetime you will have no equal among kings."

Solomon's wisdom became evident through his judicial decisions, writings, and leadership, earning him a reputation that extended far beyond Israel.

1. Judicial Wisdom: One of the most famous demonstrations of Solomon's wisdom is the judgment involving two women who claimed to be the mother of the

same child. Solomon's suggestion to divide the living child in two revealed the true mother, as recorded in 1 Kings 3:16-28. His decision not only resolved the dispute but also demonstrated his profound understanding of human nature and justice, earning him the respect and awe of his people.

2. Proverbs and Writings: Solomon's wisdom is also reflected in his contributions to biblical literature. He is credited with writing most of the Book of Proverbs, Ecclesiastes, and the Song of Solomon. These writings contain profound insights into life, morality, and the human condition, showcasing his God-given wisdom. Proverbs 1:1-3 introduces his proverbs: "The proverbs of Solomon son of David, king of Israel: for gaining wisdom and instruction; for understanding words of insight; for receiving instruction in prudent behavior, doing what is right and just and fair."

3. Leadership and Administration: Solomon's wisdom extended to his leadership and administrative abilities. He organized Israel into efficient administrative districts, built a powerful army, and established trade alliances with neighboring nations. His reign brought about a period of unprecedented peace and prosperity in Israel, reflecting his wise governance.

Solomon's wealth was legendary, encompassing vast amounts of gold, silver, precious stones, and other riches. This wealth was a visible sign of God's abundant blessings.

1. Construction Projects: One of Solomon's most significant projects was the construction of the Temple in Jerusalem, a magnificent structure that became the center of Israelite worship. The details of its construction, as described in 1 Kings 6 and 7, highlight the use of vast quantities of gold, cedar wood, and fine stone. Solomon also built a grand palace for himself, further demonstrating his wealth and the prosperity of his reign.

2. Trade and Commerce: Solomon's strategic alliances and trade relationships contributed significantly to his wealth. He established trade routes and partnerships with nations such as Egypt and Tyre, importing goods like gold, silver, ivory, and exotic animals. 1 Kings 10:22 describes these ventures: "The king had a fleet of trading ships at sea along with the ships of Hiram. Once every three years it returned, bringing gold, silver and ivory, and apes and baboons."

3. Tribute and Gifts: Solomon received tributes and gifts from other kings and dignitaries who visited to hear his wisdom and see his prosperity. The visit of the Queen of Sheba, as recorded in 1 Kings 10:1-10, exemplifies this. She brought a large quantity of gold, spices, and precious stones,

acknowledging Solomon's wisdom and the blessings he had received from God.

Solomon's wisdom and wealth had a profound impact on Israel and its surrounding nations. His reign is often seen as a golden age in Israelite history.

1. Peace and Prosperity: Under Solomon's rule, Israel enjoyed a period of peace and prosperity unparalleled in its history. 1 Kings 4:20-21 reflects this era: "The people of Judah and Israel were as numerous as the sand on the seashore; they ate, they drank and they were happy. And Solomon ruled over all the kingdoms from the Euphrates River to the land of the Philistines, as far as the border of Egypt. These countries brought tribute and were Solomon's subjects all his life."

2. Cultural and Religious Influence: Solomon's wealth and wisdom elevated Israel's cultural and religious standing among the nations. The Temple in Jerusalem became a center for worship and pilgrimage, symbolizing the nation's spiritual and cultural pinnacle. Solomon's wisdom, encapsulated in his proverbs and writings, influenced not only Israel but also neighboring cultures.

3. Legacy and Lessons: Solomon's reign left a lasting legacy of wisdom and prosperity, but also a cautionary tale about the potential pitfalls of wealth and power. Despite his wisdom, Solomon's later years were marked by compromises

in his faith, influenced by his many foreign wives and their idols, leading to spiritual decline. 1 Kings 11:4-6 narrates this turning point: "As Solomon grew old, his wives turned his heart after other gods, and his heart was not fully devoted to the Lord his God, as the heart of David his father had been. He followed Ashtoreth the goddess of the Sidonians, and Molek the detestable god of the Ammonites. So Solomon did evil in the eyes of the Lord; he did not follow the Lord completely, as David his father had done."

The life of Solomon offers several valuable lessons for modern believers about wisdom, wealth, and the importance of staying true to God's commandments.

1. Value of Wisdom: Solomon's story emphasizes the importance of seeking wisdom above all else. His request for wisdom over wealth and power pleased God and brought about both. James 1:5 encourages believers to seek wisdom: "If any of you lacks wisdom, you should ask God, who gives generously to all without finding fault, and it will be given to you."

2. Stewardship of Wealth: Solomon's wealth was a blessing from God, intended to be used for good purposes such as building the Temple. Modern believers are called to be good stewards of their resources, using them to honor God and serve others. 1 Timothy 6:17-19 advises, "Command those who are rich in this present world not to be arrogant

nor to put their hope in wealth, which is so uncertain, but to put their hope in God, who richly provides us with everything for our enjoyment. Command them to do good, to be rich in good deeds, and to be generous and willing to share."

3. Faithfulness to God: Solomon's decline serves as a warning about the dangers of turning away from God. Despite his wisdom, Solomon's alliances and marriages led him astray. Believers are reminded to stay faithful to God and avoid influences that can lead them away from Him. Proverbs 3:5-6 advises, "Trust in the Lord with all your heart and lean not on your own understanding; in all your ways submit to him, and he will make your paths straight."

Solomon's story provides practical insights for modern believers on how to integrate wisdom and wealth into their lives in a way that honors God.

1. Seek Divine Wisdom: Believers should prioritize seeking divine wisdom in all aspects of life, including personal, professional, and spiritual matters. Regular prayer, study of Scripture, and seeking godly counsel are essential practices.

2. Manage Wealth Responsibly: Like Solomon, believers should use their resources to further God's kingdom, support the church, and help those in need. This involves budgeting, saving, and giving generously.

3. Maintain Spiritual Integrity: It is crucial to remain faithful to God, especially when blessed with wealth and success. Regular self-reflection, accountability, and adherence to God's commandments help maintain spiritual integrity.

4. Invest in Eternal Treasures: Believers are encouraged to invest in eternal treasures by focusing on spiritual growth, supporting missions, and living out the principles of the Gospel. Matthew 6:19-21 teaches, "Do not store up for yourselves treasures on earth, where moths and vermin destroy, and where thieves break in and steal. But store up for yourselves treasures in heaven, where moths and vermin do not destroy, and where thieves do not break

in and steal. For where your treasure is, there your heart will be also."

King Solomon's reign is a powerful example of how divine wisdom and wealth can coexist as blessings from God. His life teaches valuable lessons about the importance of seeking wisdom, the responsible management of wealth, and the necessity of remaining faithful to God. While Solomon's wisdom and wealth brought unparalleled prosperity to Israel, his later years also serve as a cautionary tale about the dangers of turning away from God.

By applying the lessons from Solomon's life, modern believers can strive to seek divine wisdom, manage their resources responsibly, and maintain their spiritual integrity. In doing so, they can use their blessings to honor God, serve others, and build a legacy that reflects the true essence of divine favor and wisdom. Solomon's story remains a timeless reminder of the profound impact that wisdom and wealth, when aligned with God's purposes, can have on individuals and nations.

CHAPTER 08

JOB: RESTORATION AND PROSPERITY

The story of Job is a profound narrative that delves into themes of suffering, faith, and ultimate restoration. Despite losing everything—his wealth, health, and family—Job remained steadfast in his faith. His journey through immense trials and eventual restoration provides a powerful testament to God's ability to restore and bless abundantly. Job's story underscores that enduring faith and righteousness can lead to divine favor and prosperity, even after significant trials. This chapter explores Job's life, his trials, his unwavering faith, and his ultimate restoration and prosperity.

Before his trials, Job was a man of considerable wealth and influence, known for his righteousness and piety.

1. Job's Wealth and Righteousness: Job was a prosperous man, blessed with extensive possessions and a large family. Job 1:1-3 introduces him: "In the land of Uz there lived a man whose name was Job. This man was blameless and upright; he feared God and shunned evil. He

had seven sons and three daughters, and he owned seven thousand sheep, three thousand camels, five hundred yoke of oxen and five hundred donkeys, and had a large number of servants. He was the greatest man among all the people of the East."

2. Job's Piety and Family Life: Job was deeply committed to his family and his faith. He regularly offered sacrifices on behalf of his children, concerned for their spiritual well-being. Job 1:4-5 describes his devotion: "His sons used to hold feasts in their homes on their birthdays, and they would invite their three sisters to eat and drink with them. When a period of feasting had run its course, Job would make arrangements for them to be purified. Early in the morning, he would sacrifice a burnt offering for each of them, thinking, 'Perhaps my children have sinned and cursed God in their hearts.' This was Job's regular custom."

Job's faith was severely tested through a series of devastating trials, which were permitted by God but instigated by Satan.

1. Loss of Wealth and Children: In a short span, Job lost all his wealth and his children. Job 1:13-19 recounts these calamities: "One day when Job's sons and daughters were feasting and drinking wine at the oldest brother's house, a messenger came to Job and said, 'The oxen were plowing and

the donkeys were grazing nearby, and the Sabeans attacked and made off with them. They put the servants to the sword, and I am the only one who has escaped to tell you!' While he was still speaking, another messenger came and said, 'The fire of God fell from the heavens and burned up the sheep and the servants, and I am the only one who has escaped to tell you!' While he was still speaking, another messenger came and said, 'The Chaldeans formed three raiding parties and swept down on your camels and made off with them. They put the servants to the sword, and I am the only one who has escaped to tell you!' While he was still speaking, yet another messenger came and said, 'Your sons and daughters were feasting and drinking wine at the oldest brother's house, when suddenly a mighty wind swept in from the desert and struck the four corners of the house. It collapsed on them and they are dead, and I am the only one who has escaped to tell you!'"

2. Loss of Health: Following these tragedies, Job was afflicted with painful sores all over his body. Job 2:7-8 describes his condition: "So Satan went out from the presence of the Lord and afflicted Job with painful sores from the soles of his feet to the crown of his head. Then Job took a piece of broken pottery and scraped himself with it as he sat among the ashes."

3. Job's Response to Suffering: Despite his immense suffering, Job did not curse God. Instead, he mourned deeply

but continued to worship God. Job 1:20-22 shows his response: "At this, Job got up and tore his robe and shaved his head. Then he fell to the ground in worship and said: 'Naked I came from my mother's womb, and naked I will depart. The Lord gave and the Lord has taken away; may the name of the Lord be praised.' In all this, Job did not sin by charging God with wrongdoing."

During his trials, Job's friends came to comfort him, but their conversations often turned accusatory, suggesting that Job's suffering was due to some hidden sin.

1. Friends' Accusations: Job's friends, Eliphaz, Bildad, and Zophar, believed that his suffering must be a punishment for sin. They argued that if Job repented, he would be restored. Job, however, maintained his innocence and righteousness. Job 4:7-8 illustrates Eliphaz's viewpoint: "Consider now: Who, being innocent, has ever perished? Where were the upright ever destroyed? As I have observed, those who plow evil and those who sow trouble reap it."

2. Job's Defense: Job defended his integrity and expressed his confusion about his suffering. He sought an explanation from God, yearning for a direct encounter to plead his case. Job 13:3-4 shows his plea: "But I desire to speak to the Almighty and to argue my case with God. You,

however, smear me with lies; you are worthless physicians, all of you!"

3. God's Response: God eventually responded to Job out of a whirlwind, challenging Job's understanding of divine wisdom and sovereignty. God's speeches in Job 38-41 reveal His power and the limitations of human knowledge. Job 38:4-7 begins God's response: "Where were you when I laid the earth's foundation? Tell me, if you understand. Who marked off its dimensions? Surely you know! Who stretched a measuring line across it? On what were its footings set, or who laid its cornerstone—while the morning stars sang together and all the angels shouted for joy?"

After Job's encounters with God, he humbly repented for questioning God's wisdom. God then restored Job's fortunes, blessing him abundantly.

1. Job's Repentance: Job acknowledged God's greatness and his own limitations. Job 42:1-6 captures his repentance: "Then Job replied to the Lord: 'I know that you can do all things; no purpose of yours can be thwarted. You asked, "Who is this that obscures my plans without knowledge?" Surely I spoke of things I did not understand, things too wonderful for me to know. "You said, 'Listen now, and I will speak; I will question you, and you shall answer me.' My ears had heard of you but now my eyes have seen you. Therefore I despise myself and repent in dust and ashes.'"

2. Restoration and Prosperity: God restored Job's fortunes, giving him twice as much as he had before. Job 42:10-12 details this restoration: "After Job had prayed for his friends, the Lord restored his fortunes and gave him twice as much as he had before. All his brothers and sisters and everyone who had known him before came and ate with him in his house. They comforted and consoled him over all the trouble the Lord had brought on him, and each one gave him a piece of silver and a gold ring. The Lord blessed the latter part of Job's life more than the former part. He had fourteen thousand sheep, six thousand camels, a thousand yoke of oxen and a thousand donkeys."

3. Family and Longevity: Job was blessed with new children and lived a long, full life. Job 42:13-17 describes his latter years: "And he also had seven sons and three daughters. The first daughter he named Jemimah, the second Keziah and the third Keren-Happuch. Nowhere in all the land were there found women as beautiful as Job's daughters, and their father granted them an inheritance along with their brothers. After this, Job lived a hundred and forty years; he saw his children and their children to the fourth generation. And so Job died, an old man and full of years."

Job's story offers profound lessons about faith, suffering, and divine restoration.

1. Faithfulness in Adversity: Job's unwavering faith amidst severe trials teaches the importance of maintaining faith in God regardless of circumstances. His story exemplifies steadfastness and trust in God's sovereignty.

2. God's Sovereignty and Wisdom: Job's encounters with God highlight the limitations of human understanding and the necessity of trusting in God's greater wisdom and plan. God's speeches remind believers of His unparalleled power and knowledge.

3. Restoration and Blessing: Job's restoration underscores the concept that God can bring about renewal and blessing after periods of suffering. It affirms that faith and righteousness can lead to divine favor and prosperity.

4. Compassion and Support: The comfort Job received from his friends and family after his restoration emphasizes the importance of community and support during times of hardship. Believers are encouraged to show compassion and provide support to those who are suffering.

Practical Applications for Modern Believers

Job's story provides practical insights for modern believers navigating their own trials and seeking restoration.

1. Maintain Faith and Integrity: Believers are encouraged to maintain their faith and integrity, even in difficult times. Trusting in God's plan and remaining steadfast in faith are crucial.

2. Seek Understanding and Wisdom: While questioning and seeking understanding is natural, believers should ultimately trust in God's wisdom and sovereignty. Prayer and studying Scripture can provide comfort and guidance.

3. Support Others in Suffering: Job's friends initially came to comfort him, highlighting the importance of being present and supportive of those in distress. Offering compassionate support and avoiding judgment is vital.

4. Hope in Restoration: Job's restoration provides hope that God can bring renewal and blessing after periods of suffering. Believers are encouraged to hold onto this hope and trust in God's restorative power.

The story of Job is a profound testament to enduring faith, divine sovereignty, and ultimate restoration. Despite immense suffering and loss, Job remained faithful to God, and his story culminates in a powerful example of God's ability to restore and bless abundantly. Job's life teaches valuable lessons about maintaining faith in adversity, trusting in God's wisdom, and the potential for divine restoration. By applying these lessons, modern believers can navigate their own trials with hope and trust in God's unfailing love and power. Job's narrative remains a timeless reminder of the transformative power of faith and divine favor.

THE PROVERBS: WISDOM LITERATURE ON WEALTH

The Book of Proverbs is a treasure trove of practical wisdom, offering insights into the relationship between diligence, righteousness, and prosperity. This ancient wisdom literature provides timeless principles for managing wealth and emphasizes that true prosperity comes from God's blessing rather than mere human effort. Proverbs also underscores the importance of honoring God with one's wealth and using it responsibly. This chapter explores key teachings from Proverbs on wealth, highlighting their relevance for modern believers.

The Proverbs consistently present wealth as a blessing from God, emphasizing that prosperity is a result of divine favor rather than solely human endeavor.

1. Divine Blessing: Proverbs 10:22 declares, "The blessing of the Lord brings wealth, without painful toil for it." This verse underscores the idea that true prosperity comes

from God's blessing. While hard work and diligence are important, it is ultimately God's favor that brings lasting wealth and fulfillment.

2. Contentment and Trust: The Proverbs also teach that trusting in God and being content with His provisions are crucial for experiencing true wealth. Proverbs 15:16-17 advises, "Better a little with the fear of the Lord than great wealth with turmoil. Better a small serving of vegetables with love than a fattened calf with hatred." These verses highlight the value of contentment and a righteous life over the pursuit of wealth at the expense of peace and relationships.

The Proverbs emphasize the importance of diligence and righteousness as pathways to prosperity, contrasting them with the consequences of laziness and wickedness.

1. Diligence: Proverbs 10:4 states, "Lazy hands make for poverty, but diligent hands bring wealth." This proverb teaches that hard work and diligence are essential for achieving prosperity. It encourages a strong work ethic and perseverance in one's endeavors.

2. Righteousness: Righteousness is repeatedly linked to prosperity in the Proverbs. Proverbs 11:18-19 asserts, "A wicked person earns deceptive wages, but the one who sows righteousness reaps a sure reward. Truly the righteous attain life, but whoever pursues evil finds death." These verses

highlight that living righteously leads to lasting rewards, both materially and spiritually.

3. Avoiding Wickedness: Proverbs 13:11 warns, "Dishonest money dwindles away, but whoever gathers money little by little makes it grow." This verse emphasizes the importance of integrity in financial matters. Wealth obtained through dishonest means is not only unsustainable but also displeasing to God.

Proverbs teaches that wealth should be used to honor God and serve others, reflecting a heart of gratitude and stewardship.

1. Firstfruits and Tithing: Proverbs 3:9-10 instructs, "Honor the Lord with your wealth, with the firstfruits of all your crops; then your barns will be filled to overflowing, and your vats will brim over with new wine." These verses highlight the principle of giving the first and best portion of one's income to God as an act of worship and acknowledgment of His provision.

2. Generosity: Generosity is a recurring theme in Proverbs, emphasizing that wealth should be shared with those in need. Proverbs 11:24-25 teaches, "One person gives freely, yet gains even more; another withholds unduly, but comes to poverty. A generous person will prosper; whoever refreshes others will be refreshed." These verses underscore

the paradoxical truth that generosity leads to greater prosperity and blessing.

3. Social Justice: Proverbs also calls for the use of wealth to promote justice and support the marginalized. Proverbs 31:8-9 urges, "Speak up for those who cannot speak for themselves, for the rights of all who are destitute. Speak up and judge fairly; defend the rights of the poor and needy." This wisdom literature encourages believers to use their resources to advocate for and assist those who are less fortunate.

While Proverbs acknowledges the blessings of wealth, it also warns against the dangers and temptations that can accompany prosperity.

1. Pride and Arrogance: Proverbs 16:18 cautions, "Pride goes before destruction, a haughty spirit before a fall." Wealth can lead to pride and self-reliance, tempting individuals to forget their dependence on God. Believers are reminded to remain humble and grateful, recognizing that all blessings come from God.

2. Greed and Materialism: Proverbs 28:22 warns, "The stingy are eager to get rich and are unaware that poverty awaits them." The pursuit of wealth for its own sake can lead to greed and materialism, which ultimately result in spiritual and relational poverty. Proverbs 11:4 reinforces this idea: "Wealth

is worthless in the day of wrath, but righteousness delivers from death."

3. Security in Wealth: Proverbs 18:11 highlights the false security wealth can bring: "The wealth of the rich is their fortified city; they imagine it a wall too high to scale." This verse reminds believers that true security is found in God, not in material possessions.

The wisdom from Proverbs offers practical guidance for modern believers on how to manage wealth in a way that honors God.

1. Seek Divine Wisdom: Believers should regularly seek God's wisdom in financial matters through prayer and study of Scripture. James 1:5 encourages, "If any of you lacks wisdom, you should ask God, who gives generously to all without finding fault, and it will be given to you."

2. Practice Diligence and Integrity: A strong work ethic and integrity are essential for achieving and maintaining prosperity. Believers are called to work diligently and honestly, trusting that God will bless their efforts.

3. Honor God with Firstfruits: Practicing the principle of firstfruits by giving the first portion of income to God helps prioritize Him in financial matters. Regular tithing and generous giving reflect a heart of gratitude and stewardship.

4. Be Generous and Just: Using wealth to support those in need and promote justice aligns with biblical

principles. Believers are encouraged to be generous and advocate for the marginalized, reflecting God's love and compassion.

5. Guard Against Temptations: Believers should be aware of the dangers of pride, greed, and false security that wealth can bring. Regular self-reflection and accountability can help maintain a balanced perspective on wealth.

The Book of Proverbs provides profound wisdom on the relationship between diligence, righteousness, and prosperity. It emphasizes that true wealth is a blessing from God and comes with the responsibility to honor Him and serve others. By practicing diligence, integrity, and generosity, believers can manage their wealth in a way that aligns with biblical principles and reflects God's character. The teachings from Proverbs remain relevant and applicable, offering timeless guidance for navigating the complexities of wealth in a manner that honors God and blesses others.

CHAPTER 10

THE NEW TESTAMENT PERSPECTIVE ON PROSPERITY

The New Testament offers a nuanced perspective on prosperity, emphasizing spiritual wealth over material wealth while acknowledging that God cares for His people's needs. Jesus' teachings, along with those of the apostles, provide guidance on how believers should view and handle prosperity. This chapter explores the New Testament's insights into prosperity, focusing on Jesus' teachings, parables, and apostolic instructions that highlight the principles of prioritizing God's kingdom, using wealth wisely, and living generously.

Jesus frequently addressed issues related to wealth, cautioning against its potential pitfalls while also recognizing God's provision for His followers.

1. Prioritizing God's Kingdom: In the Sermon on the Mount, Jesus emphasized the importance of seeking God's kingdom above all else. Matthew 6:33 captures this principle:

"But seek first his kingdom and his righteousness, and all these things will be given to you as well." Jesus taught that prioritizing God's kingdom and righteousness would lead to the provision of material needs, underscoring the importance of spiritual priorities over material concerns.

2. The Danger of Loving Wealth: Jesus often warned about the dangers of loving wealth more than God. In Matthew 6:24, He stated, "No one can serve two masters. Either you will hate the one and love the other, or you will be devoted to the one and despise the other. You cannot serve both God and money." This teaching highlights the incompatibility of serving God and being enslaved by the pursuit of wealth, urging believers to keep their focus on God.

3. Trusting in God's Provision: Jesus reassured His followers of God's care and provision. In Matthew 6:25-27, He encouraged them not to worry about their material needs: "Therefore I tell you, do not worry about your life, what you will eat or drink; or about your body, what you will wear. Is not life more than food, and the body more than clothes? Look at the birds of the air; they do not sow or reap or store away in barns, and yet your heavenly Father feeds them. Are you not much more valuable than they?" This passage emphasizes that trusting in God's provision is central to the Christian faith.

Jesus used parables to teach important lessons about wealth, stewardship, and generosity.

1. The Parable of the Talents: In Matthew 25:14-30, Jesus told the Parable of the Talents, illustrating the principles of stewardship and accountability. The parable describes a master who entrusts his servants with talents (a form of money) before going on a journey. Upon his return, he rewards the servants who invested and multiplied their talents and punishes the one who buried his talent out of fear. This parable underscores the importance of using God-given resources wisely and productively, highlighting that faithful stewardship is rewarded.

2. The Parable of the Rich Fool: In Luke 12:16-21, Jesus told the Parable of the Rich Fool, warning against greed and the accumulation of wealth for its own sake. The rich fool built larger barns to store his surplus grain, thinking he could then relax and enjoy life. However, God called him a fool, saying his life would be demanded that very night. Jesus concluded with a powerful lesson: "This is how it will be with whoever stores up things for themselves but is not rich toward God." This parable emphasizes the futility of hoarding wealth and the importance of being rich in spiritual matters.

3. The Parable of the Unjust Steward: In Luke 16:1-13, Jesus told the Parable of the Unjust Steward, which highlights the shrewdness in handling worldly wealth to

secure eternal rewards. The steward, knowing he was about to be dismissed, reduced the debts of his master's debtors to gain their favor. Jesus used this story to teach that believers should use their worldly resources to make friends and advance God's kingdom, concluding with the admonition, "You cannot serve both God and money." This parable encourages using wealth strategically for eternal purposes.

The apostles continued to build on Jesus' teachings, offering additional insights into the relationship between faith, wealth, and generosity.

1. Contentment and Godliness: The Apostle Paul emphasized contentment and godliness over the pursuit of wealth. In 1 Timothy 6:6-10, he wrote, "But godliness with contentment is great gain. For we brought nothing into the world, and we can take nothing out of it. But if we have food and clothing, we will be content with that. Those who want to get rich fall into temptation and a trap and into many foolish and harmful desires that plunge people into ruin and destruction. For the love of money is a root of all kinds of evil. Some people, eager for money, have wandered from the faith and pierced themselves with many griefs." Paul warned that the love of money leads to spiritual ruin, urging believers to find contentment in godliness.

2. Generosity and Sharing: Paul also taught the importance of generosity and sharing with those in need. In 2 Corinthians 9:6-8, he encouraged the Corinthian church to give generously: "Remember this: Whoever sows sparingly will also reap sparingly, and whoever sows generously will also reap generously. Each of you should give what you have decided in your heart to give, not reluctantly or under compulsion, for God loves a cheerful giver. And God is able to bless you abundantly, so that in all things at all times, having all that you need, you will abound in every good work." This passage highlights the principle that generosity leads to God's blessings and sufficiency for every good work.

3. Wealth and Good Deeds: In 1 Timothy 6:17-19, Paul instructed the wealthy to use their resources for good deeds and to store up treasures in heaven: "Command those who are rich in this present world not to be arrogant nor to put their hope in wealth, which is so uncertain, but to put their hope in God, who richly provides us with everything for our enjoyment. Command them to do good, to be rich in good deeds, and to be generous and willing to share. In this way, they will lay up treasure for themselves as a firm foundation for the coming age, so that they may take hold of the life that is truly life." Paul emphasized that wealth should be used to do good, be generous, and invest in eternal rewards.

The New Testament's teachings on prosperity offer practical guidance for modern believers on managing wealth in a way that honors God and benefits others.

1. Seek God's Kingdom First: Believers are encouraged to prioritize their relationship with God and His kingdom above material pursuits. This involves focusing on spiritual growth, serving others, and trusting in God's provision. By seeking God's kingdom first, believers can ensure that their material needs will be met.

2. Practice Generosity: Generosity is a key principle in the New Testament. Believers are called to share their resources with those in need and support the work of the church. Regular giving, tithing, and acts of kindness reflect a heart of generosity and obedience to God's commands.

3. Be Content and Trust in God: Contentment with God's provision and trust in His care are essential attitudes for believers. Avoiding the pursuit of wealth for its own sake and finding satisfaction in God's blessings help maintain a balanced perspective on prosperity.

4. Use Wealth Wisely: Believers are encouraged to use their resources strategically to further God's kingdom and help others. This includes wise financial management, avoiding debt, and investing in activities that have eternal significance.

5. Avoid Greed and Materialism: The New Testament warns against the dangers of greed and materialism. Believers should guard their hearts against the love of money and the temptation to accumulate wealth at the expense of their spiritual well-being.

The New Testament provides a comprehensive perspective on prosperity, emphasizing spiritual wealth and the responsible use of material resources. Jesus' teachings and parables highlight the importance of prioritizing God's kingdom, trusting in His provision, and using wealth wisely. The apostles further expound on these principles, encouraging contentment, generosity, and good deeds. By applying these teachings, modern believers can manage their wealth in a way that honors God, serves others, and reflects the true essence of prosperity as envisioned in the New Testament.

The Bible presents a multifaceted perspective on prosperity, where material wealth is often portrayed as a sign of divine favor and blessing. Through the stories of Abraham, Joseph, Solomon, and Job, and the wisdom literature in Proverbs, we see a consistent theme that prosperity can be a manifestation of God's grace and favor. However, these blessings come with the responsibility to honor God, act righteously, and use wealth for the greater good. As we continue exploring biblical perspectives on prosperity, it becomes clear that God's love and favor can manifest in material abundance, underscoring the importance of faith, righteousness, and stewardship.

PART III

WEALTH AS A BLESSING

CHAPTER 11

WEALTH IN THE OLD TESTAMENT

The Old Testament is replete with accounts of God blessing individuals and nations with wealth. These stories illustrate that material prosperity is often seen as a sign of God's favor and a means to glorify Him and serve His people. This chapter explores notable examples of wealth in the Old Testament, examining the lives of figures such as King Solomon and Job, and the broader implications of wealth as a divine blessing.

King Solomon is one of the most prominent examples of divine wisdom and wealth in the Old Testament. His riches were not only a personal blessing but also a testament to God's glory and the wisdom granted to him.

1. Solomon's Request for Wisdom: As discussed in the previous chapter, Solomon's wealth was a direct result of his request for wisdom. When Solomon asked God for the wisdom to govern his people, God was pleased and granted him not only unparalleled wisdom but also immense wealth and honor. 1 Kings 3:12-13 captures this divine response: "I

will do what you have asked. I will give you a wise and discerning heart so that there will never have been anyone like you, nor will there ever be. Moreover, I will give you what you have not asked for—both wealth and honor—so that in your lifetime you will have no equal among kings."

2. Solomon's Wealth and Its Purpose: Solomon's wealth was legendary, encompassing vast amounts of gold, silver, and precious stones. His riches were not just a personal luxury but a means to glorify God and serve His people. 1 Kings 10:23-24 emphasizes Solomon's unparalleled status: "King Solomon was greater in riches and wisdom than all the other kings of the earth. The whole world sought an audience with Solomon to hear the wisdom God had put in his heart." Solomon used his wealth to build the Temple in Jerusalem, a magnificent structure that became the center of Israelite worship and a symbol of God's presence among His people.

Job's story provides a profound narrative of suffering, faith, and ultimate restoration. Despite experiencing profound loss, Job remained faithful to God, which led to his eventual restoration and increased prosperity.

1. Job's Initial Wealth: Job was initially a man of considerable wealth and influence, known for his righteousness and piety. Job 1:1-3 describes his prosperity: "In the land of Uz, there lived a man whose name was Job. This man was blameless and upright; he feared God and shunned

evil. He had seven sons and three daughters, and he owned seven thousand sheep, three thousand camels, five hundred yoke of oxen and five hundred donkeys, and had a large number of servants. He was the greatest man among all the people of the East."

2. Job's Trials and Faithfulness: Job faced immense suffering, losing his wealth, health, and children. Despite these trials, Job remained steadfast in his faith. Job 1:20-22 highlights his response to his losses: "At this, Job got up and tore his robe and shaved his head. Then he fell to the ground in worship and said: 'Naked I came from my mother's womb, and naked I will depart. The Lord gave and the Lord has taken away; may the name of the Lord be praised.' In all this, Job did not sin by charging God with wrongdoing."

3. Restoration and Increased Prosperity: Job's faithfulness was ultimately rewarded. God restored Job's fortunes, giving him twice as much as he had before. Job 42:12-13 details this restoration: "The Lord blessed the latter part of Job's life more than the former part. He had fourteen thousand sheep, six thousand camels, a thousand yoke of oxen, and a thousand donkeys. And he also had seven sons and three daughters." Job's story highlights that wealth, when seen as a blessing from God, can be restored and multiplied through faithfulness.

The Old Testament contains many other examples of God blessing individuals and nations with wealth, each providing unique insights into the nature and purpose of prosperity.

1. Abraham: Abraham, the patriarch of the Israelite nation, was blessed with significant wealth. His prosperity was a sign of God's covenant and favor. Genesis 13:2 states, "Abram had become very wealthy in livestock and in silver and gold." Abraham's wealth enabled him to fulfill God's purposes, including providing for his household and being a blessing to others.

2. Isaac and Jacob: Abraham's son Isaac and grandson Jacob also experienced God's blessings of wealth. Genesis 26:12-14 recounts Isaac's prosperity: "Isaac planted crops in that land and the same year reaped a hundredfold because the Lord blessed him. The man became rich, and his wealth continued to grow until he became very wealthy. He had so many flocks and herds and servants that the Philistines envied him." Similarly, Jacob's wealth increased through his industriousness and God's favor, as described in Genesis 30:43: "In this way the man grew exceedingly prosperous and came to own large flocks, and female and male servants, and camels and donkeys."

3. Joseph: Joseph's rise to power in Egypt, as detailed in Genesis 41, showcases how God can elevate and bless His

faithful servants. Despite being sold into slavery and imprisoned unjustly, Joseph's faithfulness led to his appointment as the second most powerful man in Egypt, managing vast resources and ensuring the survival of many during a severe famine.

The Old Testament provides several theological insights into the nature of wealth and its role in the lives of God's people.

1. Wealth as a Sign of God's Favor: Wealth is often depicted as a sign of God's favor and blessing. The prosperity of individuals like Solomon, Job, and Abraham reflects God's provision and His desire to bless His people. However, these blessings come with the expectation of faithfulness, righteousness, and stewardship.

2. Stewardship and Responsibility: Wealth is given not only for personal enjoyment but also for the purpose of fulfilling God's plans and serving others. The stories of Solomon and Job illustrate that wealth should be used to honor God, support His work, and help those in need.

3. Faithfulness in Adversity: Job's story, in particular, highlights the importance of maintaining faith in God even in the face of severe trials. His eventual restoration underscores that God can bring renewal and increased blessings to those who remain faithful.

4. The Dangers of Wealth: While wealth is often seen as a blessing, the Old Testament also warns of its potential dangers. Deuteronomy 8:17-18 cautions, "You may say to yourself, 'My power and the strength of my hands have produced this wealth for me.' But remember the Lord your God, for it is he who gives you the ability to produce wealth, and so confirms his covenant, which he swore to your ancestors, as it is today." This passage reminds believers to acknowledge God as the source of their prosperity and avoid the pitfalls of pride and self-reliance.

The Old Testament's teachings on wealth offer practical guidance for modern believers on how to view and manage prosperity in a way that honors God.

1. Recognize Wealth as a Blessing from God: Believers should view their material blessings as gifts from God, given out of His abundant grace. This perspective fosters gratitude and humility, recognizing that all prosperity ultimately comes from Him.

2. Practice Stewardship: Wealth should be managed responsibly and used to further God's purposes. This includes supporting the church, helping those in need, and using resources to promote justice and righteousness.

3. Maintain Faithfulness in All Circumstances: Like Job, believers are called to maintain their faith and trust in

God, regardless of their material circumstances. Faithfulness in adversity can lead to restoration and increased blessings.

4. Avoid the Dangers of Wealth: Believers should be aware of the potential dangers associated with wealth, such as pride, greed, and self-reliance. Regular self-reflection and a commitment to living according to God's principles can help mitigate these risks.

The Old Testament provides a rich tapestry of stories and teachings that illustrate the nature of wealth as a divine blessing. From Solomon's unparalleled riches and wisdom to Job's profound journey of suffering and restoration, these accounts offer valuable insights into how wealth can be both a sign of God's favor and a means to serve His purposes. By recognizing wealth as a blessing from God, practicing responsible stewardship, maintaining faithfulness in all circumstances, and avoiding the dangers associated with prosperity, modern believers can honor God and use their material resources to further His kingdom. The Old Testament's teachings on wealth remain relevant and applicable, offering timeless wisdom for navigating the complexities of prosperity in a manner that glorifies God.

CHAPTER 12

WEALTH IN THE NEW TESTAMENT

The New Testament provides a comprehensive perspective on wealth, acknowledging it as a blessing from God while emphasizing its proper use. The teachings of Jesus and the apostles offer valuable insights into how believers should view and manage their material resources. This chapter explores key passages and parables that illustrate the principles of generosity, stewardship, and the spiritual dangers associated with wealth, highlighting the New Testament's nuanced approach to prosperity.

One of the central themes in the New Testament concerning wealth is the principle of generosity leading to blessing. Jesus emphasized the importance of giving and the reciprocal nature of generosity.

1. The Principle of Generosity: In Luke 6:38, Jesus teaches, "Give, and it will be given to you. A good measure, pressed down, shaken together and running over, will be poured into your lap. For with the measure you use, it will be measured to you." This verse underscores that generosity

brings about blessings in abundance. Jesus highlights that the act of giving is not only beneficial to the recipient but also brings spiritual and material blessings to the giver.

2. The Widow's Offering: Another powerful example of generosity is the story of the widow's offering. In Mark 12:41-44, Jesus observes a poor widow putting two small coins into the temple treasury. He tells His disciples, "Truly I tell you, this poor widow has put more into the treasury than all the others. They all gave out of their wealth; but she, out of her poverty, put in everything—all she had to live on." This story illustrates that the value of a gift is not in its amount but in the sacrifice and faith behind it. The widow's act of giving everything she had demonstrates profound trust in God's provision.

The New Testament also emphasizes the importance of wise stewardship and accountability in managing wealth. Jesus' parables often highlight the responsibilities that come with material blessings.

1. The Parable of the Talents: In Matthew 25:14-30, Jesus tells the Parable of the Talents, which illustrates the principles of stewardship and accountability. The master entrusts his servants with different amounts of money (talents) before going on a journey. Upon his return, he rewards the servants who invested and multiplied their talents

and punishes the one who buried his talent out of fear. This parable teaches that God expects believers to use their resources wisely and productively. Faithful stewardship is rewarded, while neglect and misuse lead to judgment.

2. The Parable of the Shrewd Manager: In Luke 16:1-13, Jesus tells the Parable of the Shrewd Manager, which highlights the importance of using worldly wealth to secure eternal rewards. The manager, knowing he was about to be dismissed, reduces the debts of his master's debtors to gain their favor. Jesus uses this story to teach that believers should use their resources strategically for eternal purposes, concluding with the admonition, "No one can serve two masters. Either you will hate the one and love the other, or you will be devoted to the one and despise the other. You cannot serve both God and money." This parable encourages believers to use their wealth to build relationships and further God's kingdom.

While acknowledging the blessings of wealth, the New Testament also warns of its potential spiritual dangers. Jesus' teachings and parables often caution against the misuse of wealth and the attitudes that can lead to spiritual peril.

1. The Parable of the Rich Fool: In Luke 12:16-21, Jesus tells the Parable of the Rich Fool, a cautionary tale about the misuse of wealth. The rich man in the parable hoards his wealth, thinking it will secure his future. However, God calls

him a fool and demands his life that very night. Jesus concludes the parable with the warning, "This is how it will be with whoever stores up things for themselves but is not rich toward God." This parable illustrates that hoarding wealth and relying on material possessions for security can lead to spiritual ruin. It underscores the importance of using wealth according to God's purposes and being rich in spiritual matters.

2. The Rich Young Ruler: Another illustrative encounter is the story of the rich young ruler in Matthew 19:16-22. The young man asks Jesus what he must do to inherit eternal life. Jesus tells him to keep the commandments, which he claims to have done. Then Jesus adds, "If you want to be perfect, go, sell your possessions and give to the poor, and you will have treasure in heaven. Then come, follow me." The young man goes away sad because he has great wealth. This story highlights the challenge of letting go of material possessions and the difficulty of prioritizing spiritual wealth over material wealth.

3. Warnings from the Apostles: The apostles also provide warnings about the spiritual dangers of wealth. In 1 Timothy 6:9-10, Paul writes, "Those who want to get rich fall into temptation and a trap and into many foolish and harmful desires that plunge people into ruin and destruction. For the

love of money is the root of all kinds of evil. Some people, eager for money, have wandered from the faith and pierced themselves with many griefs." Paul emphasizes that the love of money can lead to spiritual destruction and urges believers to pursue godliness and contentment.

The New Testament teaches that wealth should be used to glorify God, support the needy, and advance God's kingdom. Generosity and good stewardship are central to this proper use of wealth.

1. Supporting the Needy: Generosity towards the poor and needy is a recurring theme in the New Testament. In Acts 2:44-45, the early church set an example of communal generosity: "All the believers were together and had everything in common. They sold property and possessions to give to anyone who had need." This spirit of generosity reflects the teachings of Jesus and the importance of supporting those in need.

2. Advancing God's Kingdom: Wealth can be a powerful tool for advancing God's kingdom. In Philippians 4:15-18, Paul thanks the Philippians for their financial support, describing their gifts as "a fragrant offering, an acceptable sacrifice, pleasing to God." Financial resources can support ministry efforts, spread the gospel, and build up the church.

3. Investing in Eternal Treasures: Jesus encouraged His followers to invest in eternal treasures rather than earthly wealth. In Matthew 6:19-21, He teaches, "Do not store up for yourselves treasures on earth, where moths and vermin destroy, and where thieves break in and steal. But store up for yourselves treasures in heaven, where moths and vermin do not destroy, and where thieves do not break in and steal. For where your treasure is, there your heart will be also." This teaching emphasizes that true wealth is found in spiritual treasures and eternal rewards.

The New Testament's teachings on wealth provide practical guidance for modern believers on how to manage their resources in a way that honors God and benefits others.

1. Practice Generosity: Believers are encouraged to give generously, reflecting God's generosity towards them. Regular tithing, supporting charitable causes, and helping those in need are practical ways to practice generosity.

2. Be Good Stewards: Managing resources wisely and responsibly is crucial. This includes budgeting, avoiding debt, investing prudently, and using wealth to support God's work and help others.

3. Guard Against Greed: Believers should be vigilant against the dangers of greed and the love of money. Regular

self-reflection, accountability, and a focus on spiritual growth can help maintain a healthy perspective on wealth.

4. Trust in God's Provision: Trusting in God's provision and prioritizing His kingdom over material pursuits is essential. Believers are called to seek first the kingdom of God, trusting that their needs will be met.

5. Use Wealth to Advance God's Kingdom: Using wealth to support ministry efforts, spread the gospel, and build up the church aligns with the New Testament's teachings. Believers can contribute to their local church, support missionaries, and fund projects that further God's purposes.

The New Testament offers a balanced and comprehensive perspective on wealth, acknowledging it as a blessing while emphasizing its proper use. Jesus' teachings and parables, along with the apostolic instructions, highlight the principles of generosity, stewardship, and the spiritual dangers associated with wealth. By practicing generosity, managing resources wisely, guarding against greed, trusting in God's provision, and using wealth to advance God's kingdom, modern believers can honor God and use their material resources in a way that reflects the true essence of prosperity as envisioned in the New Testament.

CHAPTER 13

WEALTH AS A RESPONSIBILITY

Wealth is not merely a blessing from God; it comes with significant responsibilities. Those who are blessed with material abundance are called to be stewards of God's resources, using their wealth to honor God, help others, and advance His kingdom. The New Testament provides clear instructions on how the wealthy should manage their resources, emphasizing generosity, good deeds, and the importance of placing hope in God rather than riches. This chapter explores the biblical perspective on wealth as a responsibility, drawing from key passages and practical applications for modern believers.

The Bible, particularly the New Testament, offers detailed guidance on the responsibilities that come with wealth. These teachings underscore the importance of stewardship, generosity, and humility.

1. Stewardship and Accountability: Wealth is entrusted to individuals by God, and they are called to manage it wisely.

The Parable of the Talents (Matthew 25:14-30) illustrates the principle of stewardship. The servants who invest their master's money and generate returns are commended and rewarded, while the servant who buries his talent is rebuked. This parable highlights that God expects His followers to use their resources productively and responsibly.

2. Generosity and Good Deeds: In 1 Timothy 6:17-19, Paul provides explicit instructions to those who are wealthy: "Command those who are rich in this present world not to be arrogant nor to put their hope in wealth, which is so uncertain, but to put their hope in God, who richly provides us with everything for our enjoyment. Command them to do good, to be rich in good deeds, and to be generous and willing to share. In this way, they will lay up treasure for themselves as a firm foundation for the coming age, so that they may take hold of the life that is truly life." Paul emphasizes that wealth should be used to perform good deeds, support others, and invest in eternal treasures.

3. Humility and Dependence on God: Wealth can lead to pride and a false sense of security. The Bible warns against placing trust in riches instead of God. Proverbs 18:11 states, "The wealth of the rich is their fortified city; they imagine it a wall too high to scale." Believers are reminded to remain humble and dependent on God, acknowledging that He is the source of all blessings.

Understanding wealth as a responsibility involves practical actions and attitudes that reflect biblical principles. Here are several key areas where believers can apply these teachings:

1. Generosity and Giving: One of the primary responsibilities of wealth is to share it generously with others. This includes regular tithing, supporting charitable causes, and helping those in need. Luke 6:38 encourages generosity: "Give, and it will be given to you. A good measure, pressed down, shaken together and running over, will be poured into your lap. For with the measure you use, it will be measured to you." Generosity not only benefits the recipient but also brings blessings to the giver.

2. Support for Ministry and Missions: Wealth can be used to support the work of the church, missionaries, and Christian organizations. Philippians 4:15-18 highlights the importance of financial support for ministry: "Moreover, as you Philippians know, in the early days of your acquaintance with the gospel, when I set out from Macedonia, not one church shared with me in the matter of giving and receiving, except you only; for even when I was in Thessalonica, you sent me aid more than once when I was in need. Not that I desire your gifts; what I desire is that more be credited to your account. I have received full payment and have more than

enough. I am amply supplied, now that I have received from Epaphroditus the gifts you sent. They are a fragrant offering, an acceptable sacrifice, pleasing to God."

3. Ethical Financial Practices: Believers are called to manage their resources ethically and responsibly. This includes avoiding dishonest gain, paying fair wages, and conducting business with integrity. Proverbs 11:1 teaches, "The Lord detests dishonest scales, but accurate weights find favor with him." Ethical financial practices reflect a commitment to God's standards and build trust in relationships.

4. Investment in Eternal Treasures: Wealth should be used to invest in what has eternal value. This includes supporting evangelism, discipleship, and other activities that advance God's kingdom. Matthew 6:19-21 advises, "Do not store up for yourselves treasures on earth, where moths and vermin destroy, and where thieves break in and steal. But store up for yourselves treasures in heaven, where moths and vermin do not destroy, and where thieves do not break in and steal. For where your treasure is, there your heart will be also." Investing in eternal treasures ensures that one's wealth has a lasting impact.

5. Helping the Poor and Marginalized: The Bible repeatedly emphasizes the importance of caring for the poor and marginalized. Proverbs 19:17 states, "Whoever is kind to

the poor lends to the Lord, and he will reward them for what they have done." Supporting those in need is a tangible expression of God's love and compassion.

The Bible provides several examples of individuals who managed their wealth responsibly, using it to honor God and serve others.

1. Joseph of Arimathea: Joseph of Arimathea was a wealthy man who used his resources to honor Jesus. He provided a tomb for Jesus' burial, demonstrating his faith and commitment. Matthew 27:57-60 recounts his act of generosity: "As evening approached, there came a rich man from Arimathea, named Joseph, who had himself become a disciple of Jesus. Going to Pilate, he asked for Jesus' body, and Pilate ordered that it be given to him. Joseph took the body, wrapped it in a clean linen cloth, and placed it in his own new tomb that he had cut out of the rock."

2. The Early Church: The early Christian community practiced communal sharing, ensuring that everyone's needs were met. Acts 2:44-45 describes their generosity: "All the believers were together and had everything in common. They sold property and possessions to give to anyone who had need." This practice of sharing reflects their commitment to caring for one another and using their resources for the common good.

Modern believers can apply the biblical principles of wealth as a responsibility in various practical ways.

1. Budgeting and Financial Planning: Developing a budget and financial plan helps manage resources effectively, ensuring that one can give generously, save responsibly, and spend wisely. This practice aligns with the principle of stewardship.

2. Charitable Giving and Volunteering: Regularly supporting charitable organizations and volunteering time and skills are practical ways to demonstrate generosity and care for others. These actions reflect the biblical call to help those in need.

3. Investing in Christian Education and Discipleship: Supporting Christian education, discipleship programs, and other initiatives that promote spiritual growth helps advance God's kingdom. This investment in spiritual development has lasting value.

4. Advocating for Social Justice: Using wealth and influence to advocate for social justice and support marginalized communities aligns with biblical teachings. Believers can support initiatives that address systemic issues and promote equality and fairness.

5. Personal Reflection and Accountability: Regularly reflecting on one's financial practices and seeking accountability from trusted mentors or advisors helps ensure

that wealth is managed responsibly. This practice fosters humility and alignment with God's principles.

Wealth, while a blessing from God, comes with significant responsibilities. The New Testament provides clear guidance on how believers should manage their material resources, emphasizing stewardship, generosity, and humility. By recognizing wealth as a responsibility, practicing generosity, supporting ministry and missions, managing resources ethically, investing in eternal treasures, and helping the poor and marginalized, modern believers can honor God and use their wealth to further His kingdom. The principles outlined in the Bible remain relevant and applicable, offering timeless wisdom for managing prosperity in a way that reflects God's love and purposes.

CHAPTER 14

BIBLICAL EXAMPLES OF WEALTH USED FOR GOOD

The Bible provides numerous examples of individuals who used their wealth to further God's purposes and support His work. These stories illustrate the principles of generosity, stewardship, and the responsible use of resources. This chapter explores several notable examples, including Barnabas, the wealthy women who supported Jesus' ministry, and others, highlighting how their financial contributions and actions significantly impacted their communities and advanced God's kingdom.

Barnabas, a prominent figure in the early church, exemplifies the use of wealth to support and strengthen the Christian community.

1. Barnabas' Generosity: Barnabas, whose name means "son of encouragement," sold a field he owned and brought the money to the apostles to support the early church. Acts 4:36-37 records this act of generosity: "Joseph, a

Levite from Cyprus, whom the apostles called Barnabas (which means 'son of encouragement'), sold a field he owned and brought the money and put it at the apostles' feet." Barnabas' contribution helped meet the needs of the growing Christian community, demonstrating his commitment to supporting the church.

2. Impact on the Community: Barnabas' generosity encouraged others to give and supported the unity and growth of the early church. His actions set an example of sacrificial giving and highlighted the importance of using personal resources for the common good. This spirit of generosity helped foster a sense of community and mutual support among believers.

The New Testament also highlights the significant contributions of wealthy women who supported Jesus' ministry financially.

1. Mary Magdalene, Joanna, and Susanna: Luke 8:1-3 mentions several women who provided for Jesus and His disciples out of their own means: "After this, Jesus traveled about from one town and village to another, proclaiming the good news of the kingdom of God. The Twelve were with him, and also some women who had been cured of evil spirits and diseases: Mary (called Magdalene) from whom seven demons had come out; Joanna the wife of Chuza, the manager

of Herod's household; Susanna; and many others. These women were helping to support them out of their own means." Their financial support enabled Jesus' ministry to continue and expand, illustrating the critical role of women in the early church.

2. Significance of Their Support: The contributions of these women provided essential resources for Jesus and His disciples, ensuring they could focus on their ministry work. Their support underscores the importance of financial backing in sustaining ministry efforts and highlights how individuals can use their resources to support God's work.

Joseph of Arimathea is another example of a wealthy individual who used his resources to honor Jesus and fulfill God's purposes.

1. Provision of the Tomb: Joseph of Arimathea, a wealthy man and a member of the Sanhedrin, provided his own new tomb for Jesus' burial. Matthew 27:57-60 recounts this act of devotion: "As evening approached, there came a rich man from Arimathea, named Joseph, who had himself become a disciple of Jesus. Going to Pilate, he asked for Jesus' body, and Pilate ordered that it be given to him. Joseph took the body, wrapped it in a clean linen cloth, and placed it in his own new tomb that he had cut out of the rock." Joseph's generosity ensured that Jesus received a proper burial, fulfilling prophetic scriptures.

2. Impact of His Action: Joseph's provision of the tomb was a significant act of faith and courage, as it publicly identified him with Jesus at a time when doing so could have brought repercussions. His generosity not only honored Jesus but also played a crucial role in the events following the crucifixion, including the resurrection.

Lydia, a successful businesswoman, is another example of someone who used her wealth to support the early Christian movement.

1. Conversion and Hospitality: Lydia was a dealer in purple cloth from the city of Thyatira, and she is described as a worshiper of God. Acts 16:14-15 details her conversion and subsequent hospitality: "One of those listening was a woman from the city of Thyatira named Lydia, a dealer in purple cloth. She was a worshiper of God. The Lord opened her heart to respond to Paul's message. When she and the members of her household were baptized, she invited us to her home. 'If you consider me a believer in the Lord,' she said, 'come and stay at my house.' And she persuaded us." Lydia's home became a center for Paul's ministry in Philippi.

2. Impact on Paul's Ministry: Lydia's hospitality and support provided a base of operations for Paul and his companions, facilitating their missionary work in the region.

Her generosity and willingness to open her home played a crucial role in the spread of the Gospel in Philippi.

Cornelius, a Roman centurion, is noted for his generosity and his pivotal role in the early church.

1. Generosity and Devotion: Cornelius is described as a devout man who feared God, gave generously to those in need, and prayed regularly. Acts 10:1-2 introduces him: "At Caesarea there was a man named Cornelius, a centurion in what was known as the Italian Regiment. He and all his family were devout and God-fearing; he gave generously to those in need and prayed to God regularly."

2. Divine Encounter and Impact: Cornelius' generosity and faithfulness led to a significant divine encounter. An angel appeared to him, instructing him to send for Peter. This event led to Peter's visit and the outpouring of the Holy Spirit on Cornelius and his household, marking a pivotal moment in the early church as the Gospel began to spread to the Gentiles. Cornelius' generosity and faith played a key role in this important transition.

The examples of Barnabas, the wealthy women supporting Jesus, Joseph of Arimathea, Lydia, and Cornelius provide valuable lessons for modern believers on how to use wealth for good.

1. Generosity and Support: Believers are encouraged to support their church, ministries, and those in need through

financial contributions and acts of service. Regular giving, tithing, and charitable donations are practical ways to practice generosity.

2. Hospitality and Service: Opening one's home and resources to support ministry efforts, as Lydia did, can have a significant impact. Believers can offer hospitality to missionaries, church leaders, and those in need.

3. Courage and Public Identification: Like Joseph of Arimathea, believers may be called to publicly identify with their faith through acts of generosity and support, even when it involves personal risk or sacrifice.

4. Faith and Obedience: The examples of Cornelius and Lydia highlight the importance of faith and obedience to God's leading. Believers are encouraged to be attentive to God's guidance and willing to use their resources to further His purposes.

5. Community and Fellowship: Supporting the needs of the Christian community, as Barnabas did, helps build unity and strength within the church. Believers can contribute to the well-being of their community through financial support and active participation in church life.

Conclusion

The Bible provides numerous examples of individuals who used their wealth to further God's purposes and support

His work. These stories of Barnabas, the wealthy woman who supported Jesus' ministry, Joseph of Arimathea, Lydia, and Cornelius illustrate the principles of generosity, stewardship, and the responsible use of resources. By following these examples, modern believers can use their wealth to honor God, support the church, and help those in need. The teachings and examples from the Bible offer timeless guidance for managing prosperity in a way that reflects God's love and advances His kingdom.

CHAPTER 15

MODERN APPLICATIONS OF WEALTH AS A BLESSING

In contemporary society, wealth remains a powerful tool for doing good. Philanthropy, charitable giving, and social entrepreneurship are modern expressions of using wealth to bless others. Christian organizations and individuals often leverage their resources to support missions, provide humanitarian aid, and address social injustices. This chapter explores the modern applications of wealth as a blessing, emphasizing the principle that wealth, as a blessing from God, is meant to be shared and used to reflect God's love and grace in the world.

Philanthropy is one of the most prominent ways that modern individuals and organizations use their wealth to bless others. Through substantial financial donations, philanthropists address various social, educational, and health-related issues.

1. Foundations and Trusts: Many wealthy individuals establish foundations or trusts to manage their philanthropic

activities. These entities focus on a wide range of causes, including education, healthcare, poverty alleviation, and environmental conservation. For example, the Bill and Melinda Gates Foundation focuses on global health, development, and education, leveraging significant financial resources to address some of the world's most pressing issues.

2. Scholarships and Grants: Philanthropy often includes funding scholarships and grants to support education and research. These contributions enable individuals to access educational opportunities and pursue innovative projects that can lead to significant societal benefits. By investing in education, philanthropists help build a knowledgeable and skilled workforce, fostering long-term social and economic development.

3. Humanitarian Aid: Philanthropic efforts also extend to providing humanitarian aid during crises. Organizations and individuals contribute to relief efforts during natural disasters, conflicts, and pandemics. These contributions provide immediate support and resources to those affected, reflecting a commitment to global compassion and solidarity.

Charitable giving is another vital way to use wealth as a blessing. Through regular donations to charities, individuals support various initiatives that improve community well-being and address social needs.

1. Church and Religious Organizations: Many Christians prioritize giving to their local church or religious organizations. These contributions support the church's mission, including worship services, community outreach, and missionary work. Regular tithing and offerings reflect obedience to biblical principles and a commitment to supporting God's work.

2. Nonprofit Organizations: Donations to nonprofit organizations enable them to carry out their missions effectively. Nonprofits work in diverse areas, including health, education, social services, and environmental protection. By supporting these organizations, individuals contribute to meaningful causes and help address societal challenges.

3. Community Initiatives: Charitable giving also includes supporting local community initiatives, such as food banks, shelters, and youth programs. These contributions directly impact the lives of community members, providing essential services and support to those in need.

Social entrepreneurship combines business principles with a commitment to social impact. Social entrepreneurs use their wealth and business acumen to address social, environmental, and economic issues.

1. Mission-Driven Businesses: Social enterprises prioritize social or environmental goals alongside profit.

These businesses address issues such as poverty, access to education, and environmental sustainability. For example, TOMS Shoes follows a one-for-one model, donating a pair of shoes for every pair sold, thereby addressing footwear needs in impoverished communities.

2. Impact Investing: Impact investing involves investing in businesses and projects that generate positive social or environmental outcomes. Investors seek financial returns while supporting ventures that address critical issues. This approach aligns financial goals with a commitment to creating a better world.

3. Corporate Social Responsibility (CSR): Many corporations adopt CSR strategies, integrating social and environmental considerations into their business operations. CSR initiatives can include sustainable practices, community engagement, and philanthropy. By prioritizing CSR, companies use their resources and influence to make a positive impact.

Christian organizations play a crucial role in leveraging wealth to support missions, humanitarian aid, and social justice efforts. These organizations embody the principles of generosity and stewardship, reflecting God's love in their work.

1. Mission Support: Christian organizations often focus on supporting missionary work, spreading the Gospel,

and meeting spiritual and physical needs. Organizations like the International Mission Board and World Vision provide resources and support to missionaries and local communities, facilitating evangelism and community development.

2. Humanitarian Aid: Christian humanitarian organizations provide aid and relief during crises, offering food, shelter, medical care, and other essential services. Samaritan's Purse, for example, responds to emergencies worldwide, providing practical assistance and sharing the love of Christ with those in need.

3. Social Justice and Advocacy: Christian organizations also engage in social justice and advocacy, addressing issues such as human trafficking, poverty, and racial inequality. Organizations like the International Justice Mission work to protect the vulnerable and promote justice, using their resources and influence to effect change.

Several guiding principles can help modern believers use their wealth effectively to bless others and honor God.

1. Generosity: Generosity is a core principle of using wealth as a blessing. Believers are called to give freely and cheerfully, supporting causes that reflect God's love and compassion. 2 Corinthians 9:7 encourages this attitude: "Each of you should give what you have decided in your heart to

give, not reluctantly or under compulsion, for God loves a cheerful giver."

2. Stewardship: Responsible stewardship involves managing wealth wisely and using it to further God's purposes. This includes budgeting, saving, and investing in ways that align with biblical principles. Luke 16:10 highlights the importance of faithfulness in stewardship: "Whoever can be trusted with very little can also be trusted with much, and whoever is dishonest with very little will also be dishonest with much."

3. Purposeful Giving: Purposeful giving means intentionally supporting causes and organizations that align with one's values and beliefs. Believers should seek to understand the impact of their contributions and prioritize efforts that make a meaningful difference.

4. Humility and Gratitude: Recognizing that wealth is a blessing from God fosters humility and gratitude. Believers should acknowledge God's provision and remain humble in their use of resources. Proverbs 22:4 emphasizes this mindset: "Humility is the fear of the Lord; its wages are riches and honor and life."

5. Impact and Legacy: Considering the long-term impact and legacy of one's wealth is essential. Believers should aim to create lasting positive change and invest in initiatives that have enduring benefits. Matthew 6:19-21 advises

focusing on eternal treasures: "Do not store up for yourselves treasures on earth, where moths and vermin destroy, and where thieves break in and steal. But store up for yourselves treasures in heaven, where moths and vermin do not destroy, and where thieves do not break in and steal. For where your treasure is, there your heart will be also."

In contemporary society, wealth remains a powerful tool for doing good. Through philanthropy, charitable giving, social entrepreneurship, and the efforts of Christian organizations, individuals and groups can use their resources to bless others and reflect God's love and grace. By following biblical principles of generosity, stewardship, purposeful giving, humility, and focusing on impact and legacy, modern believers can manage their wealth in ways that honor God and make a meaningful difference in the world. The timeless guidance of Scripture continues to offer valuable insights for using wealth as a blessing, ensuring that it serves to further God's kingdom and benefit humanity.

PART IV

FAITH AND FINANCIAL SUCCESS

CHAPTER 16

BIBLICAL TEACHINGS ON FAITH AND PROSPERITY

The Bible frequently links faith to prosperity, illustrating that God rewards those who are faithful and obedient to His commands. This principle is evident throughout both the Old and New Testaments, where numerous examples highlight how unwavering faith and integrity can lead to material blessings and financial success. This chapter explores key biblical teachings on the relationship between faith and prosperity, drawing from notable examples such as the Israelites' covenantal blessings and the story of Joseph.

One of the clearest biblical teachings linking faith to prosperity is found in the covenantal blessings promised to the Israelites in Deuteronomy 28:1-6.

1. Obedience and Blessing: In Deuteronomy 28, God promises blessings to the Israelites if they fully obey His commands. Verses 1-6 state: "If you fully obey the Lord your

God and carefully follow all his commands I give you today, the Lord your God will set you high above all the nations on earth. All these blessings will come on you and accompany you if you obey the Lord your God: You will be blessed in the city and blessed in the country. The fruit of your womb will be blessed, and the crops of your land and the young of your livestock—the calves of your herds and the lambs of your flocks. Your basket and your kneading trough will be blessed. You will be blessed when you come in and blessed when you go out." This passage emphasizes that obedience to God leads to comprehensive blessings, including financial and material prosperity.

2. Holistic Prosperity: The blessings promised in Deuteronomy 28 encompass all areas of life—agriculture, family, and daily activities. This holistic view of prosperity indicates that God's blessings are not limited to financial success but include overall well-being and flourishing.

Joseph's story, detailed in Genesis, is a powerful example of how faith and integrity can lead to prosperity even in the face of adversity.

1. Joseph's Trials and Faith: Joseph faced numerous challenges, including being sold into slavery by his brothers and being unjustly imprisoned in Egypt. Despite these hardships, Joseph remained faithful to God. His unwavering faith and commitment to integrity are evident throughout his

story. For example, when tempted by Potiphar's wife, Joseph refused to sin against God (Genesis 39:9).

2. God's Favor and Prosperity: Joseph's faithfulness was rewarded with God's favor. Even as a slave and prisoner, God was with Joseph, and he prospered in everything he did. Genesis 39:2-3 notes, "The Lord was with Joseph so that he prospered, and he lived in the house of his Egyptian master. When his master saw that the Lord was with him and that the Lord gave him success in everything he did, Joseph found favor in his eyes and became his attendant."

3. Rise to Power: Joseph's faith and integrity eventually led to his rise to power as the second most powerful man in Egypt. His ability to interpret Pharaoh's dreams and his wise management during the years of abundance and famine brought immense wealth and power. Genesis 41:41-43 records, "So Pharaoh said to Joseph, 'I hereby put you in charge of the whole land of Egypt.' Then Pharaoh took his signet ring from his finger and put it on Joseph's finger. He dressed him in robes of fine linen and put a gold chain around his neck. He had him ride in a chariot as his second-in-command, and people shouted before him, 'Make way!' Thus he put him in charge of the whole land of Egypt."

The New Testament also emphasizes the relationship between faith and prosperity, focusing on spiritual well-being alongside material blessings.

1. Seek First the Kingdom of God: In the Sermon on the Mount, Jesus teaches about the priorities of life. In Matthew 6:33, He says, "But seek first his kingdom and his righteousness, and all these things will be given to you as well." This verse underscores the principle that prioritizing God's kingdom and righteousness leads to the provision of material needs. Jesus encourages His followers to trust in God's provision and focus on spiritual pursuits.

2. The Parable of the Talents: Jesus' Parable of the Talents (Matthew 25:14-30) illustrates the importance of faithful stewardship. The servants who invested their talents and generated returns were rewarded, while the servant who buried his talent was rebuked. This parable highlights that faithfulness and wise management of resources lead to increased blessings and prosperity.

3. Generosity and Blessing: The New Testament also links generosity to prosperity. In Luke 6:38, Jesus teaches, "Give, and it will be given to you. A good measure, pressed down, shaken together and running over, will be poured into your lap. For with the measure you use, it will be measured to you." This principle suggests that generous giving, rooted in faith, results in abundant blessings.

Understanding the biblical teachings on faith and prosperity offers practical guidance for modern believers on how to align their financial practices with their faith.

1. Prioritize God's Kingdom: Believers are encouraged to seek God's kingdom first, trusting that their material needs will be met. This involves focusing on spiritual growth, serving others, and living in accordance with God's will.

2. Practice Integrity and Faithfulness: Like Joseph, believers should maintain their integrity and faithfulness to God, even in challenging circumstances. Trusting in God and adhering to His principles can lead to His favor and blessings.

3. Generosity and Stewardship: Practicing generosity and wise stewardship is essential. Believers are called to manage their resources responsibly, give generously to support others, and invest in God's work. This includes regular tithing, charitable donations, and supporting ministries.

4. Trust in God's Provision: Trusting in God's provision involves letting go of anxiety about material needs and relying on His faithfulness. Matthew 6:25-27 encourages believers not to worry about their needs but to trust that God will provide.

5. Faith-Fueled Actions: Believers should take faith-fueled actions in their financial decisions, such as making ethical investments, supporting fair trade, and engaging in business practices that reflect Christian values.

The Bible clearly links faith to prosperity, illustrating that God rewards those who are faithful and obedient to His commands. From the covenantal blessings promised to the Israelites to the story of Joseph, the scriptures highlight how unwavering faith and integrity can lead to material blessings and financial success. The New Testament continues this theme, emphasizing the importance of seeking God's kingdom, practicing generosity, and trusting in God's provision. By aligning their financial practices with these biblical principles, modern believers can experience God's blessings and use their resources to further His kingdom. The teachings on faith and prosperity remain relevant and offer timeless guidance for navigating the complexities of wealth in a manner that honors God and reflects His love.

CHAPTER 17

THE PROSPERITY GOSPEL

The Prosperity Gospel is a modern Christian teaching that emphasizes faith as a pathway to financial and physical well-being. Proponents argue that God's will is for His followers to be prosperous and that faith, positive confession, and donations to religious causes will lead to material wealth. Key scriptures often cited by proponents include Malachi 3:10, which speaks of God opening the "windows of heaven" and pouring out blessings on those who bring tithes into the storehouse. While the Prosperity Gospel has garnered a significant following, it has also faced considerable criticism for promoting materialism and neglecting the broader aspects of faith. This chapter explores the teachings, popularity, and controversies surrounding the Prosperity Gospel, offering a balanced perspective on this influential but contentious movement.

The Prosperity Gospel, also known as the "Health and Wealth Gospel" or "Word of Faith," focuses on the belief that God wants His people to be healthy, wealthy, and successful in all areas of life. Key teachings include:

1. Faith as a Pathway to Prosperity: Proponents of the Prosperity Gospel emphasize that faith is the key to unlocking God's blessings. They teach that by believing in God's promises and confessing them positively, believers can experience financial and physical well-being.

2. Positive Confession: Positive confession, also known as "naming and claiming," is the practice of declaring God's promises over one's life. According to this teaching, speaking words of faith can bring about the desired outcomes, such as health, wealth, and success.

3. Tithing and Giving: The Prosperity Gospel strongly encourages tithing and generous giving, often promising that God will return these gifts with abundant blessings. Malachi 3:10 is frequently cited: "Bring the whole tithe into the storehouse, that there may be food in my house. Test me in this," says the Lord Almighty, "and see if I will not throw open the floodgates of heaven and pour out so much blessing that there will not be room enough to store it."

4. God's Will for Prosperity: Proponents argue that it is God's will for His followers to prosper financially and physically. They cite scriptures such as 3 John 1:2, which

states, "Dear friend, I pray that you may enjoy good health and that all may go well with you, even as your soul is getting along well."

The Prosperity Gospel has gained substantial popularity, particularly in the United States, Africa, and Latin America. Several factors contribute to its widespread appeal:

1. Prominent Leaders and Ministries: High-profile preachers and televangelists, such as Joel Osteen, Kenneth Copeland, and Creflo Dollar, have significantly promoted the Prosperity Gospel. Their charismatic preaching, books, and television programs have reached millions of people worldwide.

2. Appeal to Human Desires: The promise of health, wealth, and success resonates with many people, especially those facing financial difficulties or health issues. The Prosperity Gospel offers hope and a sense of control over one's circumstances through faith and positive actions.

3. Cultural Context: In societies where economic disparity and poverty are prevalent, the Prosperity Gospel's message of financial breakthrough and divine favor can be particularly attractive. It provides a sense of empowerment and the possibility of upward mobility.

4. Media and Technology: The rise of media and technology has played a significant role in spreading the

Prosperity Gospel. Television, radio, and the internet have enabled prosperity preachers to reach a global audience, amplifying their influence.

Despite its popularity, the Prosperity Gospel has faced substantial criticism from various quarters, including theologians, pastors, and laypeople. Key criticisms include:

1. Promoting Materialism: Critics argue that the Prosperity Gospel promotes materialism by equating faith with financial success. This focus on wealth can overshadow the spiritual and relational aspects of Christianity, reducing faith to a means of acquiring material goods.

2. Theological Concerns: Many theologians contend that the Prosperity Gospel distorts biblical teachings. They argue that it selectively uses scripture, ignoring passages that emphasize suffering, sacrifice, and the transient nature of earthly wealth. The teachings of Jesus and the apostles often highlight the spiritual dangers of wealth and the importance of serving others.

3. Exploitation and False Promises: Critics assert that the Prosperity Gospel can exploit vulnerable individuals by promising guaranteed financial returns in exchange for donations. This can lead to disillusionment and financial hardship when the promised blessings do not materialize.

4. Neglect of Broader Aspects of Faith: The Prosperity Gospel is often criticized for neglecting the broader aspects

of Christian faith, such as humility, self-sacrifice, and social justice. It can lead to a self-centered spirituality focused on personal gain rather than a holistic approach to faith that includes serving others and addressing societal issues.

While the Prosperity Gospel has significant shortcomings, it is essential to recognize that the desire for God's blessings and well-being is not inherently wrong. The Bible contains numerous promises of God's provision and care for His people. However, a balanced perspective on faith and prosperity includes the following principles:

1. God's Sovereignty and Will: Believers should recognize that God's will and timing are paramount. While it is appropriate to pray for blessings and prosperity, it is crucial to submit to God's sovereign will, trusting that He knows what is best.

2. Holistic Understanding of Prosperity: True prosperity encompasses more than financial wealth. It includes spiritual growth, healthy relationships, and a sense of purpose and fulfillment. Believers should seek a holistic understanding of prosperity that aligns with biblical teachings.

3. Generosity and Stewardship: The Bible teaches that wealth is a responsibility and a tool for serving others. Generosity and stewardship are essential aspects of managing resources in a way that honors God and supports His work.

4. Contentment and Trust: Contentment is a vital aspect of Christian faith. Philippians 4:11-13 emphasizes the importance of being content in all circumstances, trusting in God's provision and care.

5. Social Justice and Compassion: A balanced view of prosperity includes a commitment to social justice and compassion. Believers are called to address the needs of the poor and marginalized, reflecting God's love and justice in their actions.

The Prosperity Gospel is a modern Christian teaching that emphasizes faith as a pathway to financial and physical well-being. While it has garnered a significant following and offers hope to many, it also faces substantial criticism for promoting materialism and neglecting the broader aspects of faith. A balanced perspective on faith and prosperity recognizes that while God's blessings are real, they encompass more than financial wealth. True prosperity involves spiritual growth, healthy relationships, and a commitment to serving others. By aligning their understanding of prosperity with biblical teachings, believers can experience the fullness of God's blessings while honoring Him and supporting His work in the world.

CHAPTER 18

ETHICAL CONSIDERATIONS

While faith can be associated with financial success, it is essential to approach this relationship with ethical considerations. The Bible provides numerous warnings against the dangers of loving money more than God and emphasizes the importance of spiritual wealth over material riches. This chapter explores the ethical considerations that should guide the pursuit and management of wealth, drawing on key biblical teachings to highlight the principles of integrity, generosity, and prioritizing spiritual growth.

The Bible clearly warns against the dangers of loving money more than God. This misplaced priority can lead to spiritual peril and ethical compromises.

1. The Love of Money: In 1 Timothy 6:10, Paul writes, "For the love of money is a root of all kinds of evil. Some people, eager for money, have wandered from the faith and pierced themselves with many griefs." This verse highlights the potential spiritual dangers associated with prioritizing

wealth over faith. The love of money can lead to unethical behavior, such as dishonesty, greed, and exploitation, which ultimately harms one's spiritual well-being.

2. Idolatry and Distraction: Jesus also warned about the dangers of wealth becoming an idol. In Matthew 6:24, He teaches, "No one can serve two masters. Either you will hate the one and love the other, or you will be devoted to the one and despise the other. You cannot serve both God and money." This teaching underscores that wealth can easily become a competing priority, distracting believers from their devotion to God.

Ethical considerations in the management of wealth involve integrity, fairness, and a commitment to using resources in ways that honor God and benefit others.

1. Integrity in Financial Practices: Believers are called to practice integrity in all their financial dealings. This includes honesty in business transactions, fair treatment of employees, and transparency in financial reporting. Proverbs 11:1 states, "The Lord detests dishonest scales, but accurate weights find favor with him." Ethical financial practices build trust and reflect a commitment to God's standards.

2. Fair Treatment of Workers: The Bible emphasizes the importance of fair treatment and just compensation for workers. James 5:4 warns against exploiting laborers: "Look! The wages you failed to pay the workers who mowed your

fields are crying out against you. The cries of the harvesters have reached the ears of the Lord Almighty." Ensuring fair wages and humane working conditions is an ethical imperative for Christian employers.

3. Avoiding Exploitation: Ethical wealth management also involves avoiding exploitation of vulnerable individuals or communities. This includes predatory lending practices, unfair business tactics, and any form of economic injustice. Micah 6:8 calls believers to act justly, love mercy, and walk humbly with God, which includes advocating for and practicing economic fairness.

Ethical considerations extend to how wealth is used, emphasizing generosity and responsible stewardship.

1. Generosity as a Moral Duty: The Bible teaches that wealth should be used to support those in need. Proverbs 19:17 states, "Whoever is kind to the poor lends to the Lord, and he will reward them for what they have done." Generosity is not only a moral duty but also a reflection of God's character. Believers are called to be generous, using their resources to support the church, charitable causes, and those who are less fortunate.

2. Responsible Stewardship: Wealth should be managed responsibly, with an awareness that it ultimately belongs to God. In the Parable of the Talents (Matthew 25:14-

30), Jesus teaches about the importance of wise stewardship. The servants who invested their master's money were rewarded, while the one who hid his talent was rebuked. This parable emphasizes that responsible management of resources is an ethical obligation.

3. Prioritizing Eternal Investments: Jesus' teachings often highlighted the importance of investing in eternal treasures rather than earthly wealth. In Matthew 6:19-21, He advises, "Do not store up for yourselves treasures on earth, where moths and vermin destroy, and where thieves break in and steal. But store up for yourselves treasures in heaven, where moths and vermin do not destroy, and where thieves do not break in and steal. For where your treasure is, there your heart will be also." This teaching underscores that true wealth is found in spiritual growth and a relationship with God.

The Bible places a higher value on spiritual wealth than material riches, teaching that a relationship with God and spiritual growth are paramount.

1. Contentment and Trust in God: Believers are encouraged to find contentment and trust in God's provision rather than in material wealth. Philippians 4:11-13 reflects this attitude: "I am not saying this because I am in need, for I have learned to be content whatever the circumstances. I know what it is to be in need, and I know what it is to have plenty.

I have learned the secret of being content in any and every situation, whether well fed or hungry, whether living in plenty or in want. I can do all this through him who gives me strength." Contentment is a crucial aspect of ethical wealth management, focusing on gratitude and trust in God's care.

2. Spiritual Priorities: Ethical considerations also involve prioritizing spiritual growth and well-being over material accumulation. In Mark 8:36, Jesus asks, "What good is it for someone to gain the whole world, yet forfeit their soul?" This rhetorical question highlights the futility of pursuing material wealth at the expense of one's spiritual health. Believers are called to seek first the kingdom of God and His righteousness (Matthew 6:33).

3. Compassion and Social Justice: The pursuit of wealth should not overshadow the call to compassion and social justice. The Prophet Amos denounced those who amassed wealth while neglecting the poor and marginalized. Amos 5:24 calls for justice and righteousness to flow like a river. Believers are encouraged to advocate for social justice, addressing systemic inequalities and supporting those who are oppressed.

Modern believers can apply these ethical considerations in various practical ways to ensure their financial practices align with biblical principles.

1. Ethical Investing: Investing in companies and projects that align with Christian values and avoid supporting unethical practices is a practical way to manage wealth responsibly. Ethical investing includes considering the social and environmental impact of investments.

2. Budgeting and Financial Planning: Creating and adhering to a budget helps ensure responsible management of resources. Financial planning should include provisions for generous giving, saving, and prudent spending, reflecting a balanced approach to wealth.

3. Support for Charitable Causes: Regularly supporting charitable organizations and initiatives that address social, economic, and environmental issues is an important aspect of ethical wealth management. This support can include financial donations, volunteering, and advocacy.

4. Transparency and Accountability: Practicing transparency and accountability in financial matters helps maintain integrity and build trust. This includes keeping accurate records, being open about financial practices, and seeking accountability from trusted advisors or financial professionals.

5. Advocating for Fair Practices: Believers can use their influence to advocate for fair and just economic practices, supporting policies and initiatives that promote economic justice and protect vulnerable populations.

While faith can be associated with financial success, it is essential to approach this relationship with ethical considerations. The Bible provides clear warnings against the dangers of loving money more than God and emphasizes the importance of spiritual wealth over material riches. Ethical wealth management involves integrity, generosity, responsible stewardship, and prioritizing spiritual growth. By adhering to these principles, modern believers can ensure that their financial practices honor God, reflect His love and justice, and contribute to the well-being of others. The teachings on ethical considerations offer timeless guidance for navigating the complexities of wealth in a manner that aligns with Christian values and promotes holistic well-being.

FAITH, WORK ETHIC, AND FINANCIAL SUCCESS

A strong work ethic, grounded in faith, is often seen as a pathway to financial success. The Bible emphasizes the importance of diligence, honesty, and ethical behavior in one's work, teaching that these qualities can lead to prosperity. This chapter explores the biblical principles linking faith and work ethic to financial success, examining key scriptures and parables that highlight the value of hard work, wise stewardship, and the effective use of one's abilities and resources.

The Bible contains numerous teachings that emphasize the importance of a strong work ethic. These principles encourage believers to approach their work with diligence, integrity, and a sense of purpose.

1. Diligence and Prosperity: Proverbs 10:4 states, "Lazy hands make for poverty, but diligent hands bring wealth." This verse highlights the biblical principle that hard work can lead to prosperity. Diligence in one's work is a key

factor in achieving financial success, and the Bible consistently commends those who are industrious and committed to their tasks.

2. Integrity and Honesty: Honesty and integrity are crucial components of a strong work ethic. Proverbs 11:1 teaches, "The Lord detests dishonest scales, but accurate weights find favor with him." Ethical behavior in business and work is essential for building trust and achieving long-term success. Faith encourages individuals to uphold these values, knowing that their work reflects their commitment to God's principles.

3. Purpose and Calling: Colossians 3:23-24 reminds believers to work with a sense of purpose and dedication: "Whatever you do, work at it with all your heart, as working for the Lord, not for human masters, since you know that you will receive an inheritance from the Lord as a reward. It is the Lord Christ you are serving." Viewing work as a calling from God provides motivation and a sense of fulfillment, encouraging believers to give their best effort in all they do.

The Parable of the Talents (Matthew 25:14-30) is a powerful illustration of the importance of using one's abilities and resources wisely. This parable teaches that God expects His followers to be good stewards of what they have been given, which can lead to financial growth and success.

1. Faithful Stewardship: In the parable, a master entrusts his servants with varying amounts of money (talents) before going on a journey. Upon his return, he rewards the servants who have invested and multiplied their talents and chastises the one who buried his talent out of fear. This parable highlights the importance of faithful stewardship, demonstrating that using one's skills and resources effectively is pleasing to God and leads to rewards.

2. Risk and Reward: The servants who invested their talents took risks, but their efforts were rewarded. This aspect of the parable teaches that financial success often involves taking calculated risks and being willing to invest time, effort, and resources. It encourages believers to step out in faith and make wise decisions that can lead to growth and prosperity.

3. Consequences of Inaction: The servant who did nothing with his talent faced negative consequences. This part of the parable emphasizes that inaction and fear can lead to missed opportunities and stagnation. God expects His followers to be proactive and diligent, using their abilities to produce positive outcomes.

The New Testament continues to emphasize the connection between a strong work ethic and financial success, reinforcing the importance of diligence and responsibility.

1. Paul's Example: The Apostle Paul often highlighted the importance of hard work. In 2 Thessalonians 3:10, he

writes, "For even when we were with you, we gave you this rule: 'The one who is unwilling to work shall not eat.'" Paul's own life was an example of diligent work, as he supported himself through tentmaking while spreading the Gospel. His teachings encourage believers to work hard and be self-sufficient.

2. Responsibility and Provision: In 1 Timothy 5:8, Paul stresses the responsibility of providing for one's family: "Anyone who does not provide for their relatives, and especially for their own household, has denied the faith and is worse than an unbeliever." This verse underscores the ethical responsibility to work diligently and ensure the well-being of one's family, linking faith with the practical aspect of financial provision.

3. Contentment and Ambition: While promoting hard work, the New Testament also encourages contentment. Philippians 4:11-13 teaches, "I have learned to be content whatever the circumstances. I know what it is to be in need, and I know what it is to have plenty. I have learned the secret of being content in any and every situation, whether well fed or hungry, whether living in plenty or in want. I can do all this through him who gives me strength." Balancing ambition with contentment is crucial, ensuring that the pursuit of

financial success does not overshadow one's relationship with God.

Applying the biblical principles of faith and work ethic in contemporary settings can lead to financial success and a fulfilling life. Here are practical steps for modern believers:

1. Embrace Diligence and Hard Work: Approach all tasks with diligence and a strong work ethic, recognizing that hard work is a key factor in achieving financial success. Whether in professional careers, personal projects, or community service, putting in consistent effort can lead to growth and prosperity.

2. Maintain Integrity and Ethics: Uphold integrity and honesty in all business and work-related activities. Ethical behavior builds trust and reputation, essential components for long-term success. Ensure that all dealings are transparent and fair, reflecting Christian values.

3. Develop Skills and Talents: Invest in personal and professional development to enhance skills and abilities. Continuous learning and improvement can open up new opportunities and lead to financial growth. Seek to use God-given talents effectively, as illustrated in the Parable of the Talents.

4. Balance Ambition with Contentment: Pursue financial goals with ambition, but maintain a sense of contentment and trust in God's provision. Avoid the trap of

materialism by prioritizing spiritual growth and relationships over financial gain. Balance work with rest and spiritual practices to ensure holistic well-being.

5. Practice Stewardship and Generosity: Manage financial resources wisely, practicing good stewardship. Budgeting, saving, and investing responsibly are important aspects of financial management. Additionally, be generous with wealth, supporting charitable causes and helping those in need. Generosity reflects God's love and aligns with biblical teachings.

A strong work ethic, grounded in faith, is a pathway to financial success. The Bible emphasizes the importance of diligence, integrity, and ethical behavior in one's work, teaching that these qualities can lead to prosperity. The Parable of the Talents and other biblical teachings illustrate the value of using one's abilities and resources wisely. By embracing these principles, modern believers can achieve financial success while maintaining a focus on spiritual growth and ethical behavior. The connection between faith, work ethic, and financial success remains relevant, offering timeless guidance for navigating the complexities of the modern world in a manner that honors God and reflects His love.

CHAPTER 20

FAITH AS A SOURCE OF WISDOM

Faith provides believers with wisdom and discernment, which are crucial for financial success and overall well-being. The Bible teaches that seeking God's guidance through prayer and faith can lead to wise decision-making and prosperity. This chapter explores the biblical principles linking faith and wisdom, with a focus on key scriptures and the example of King Solomon. By understanding and applying these principles, believers can navigate life's challenges and opportunities with divine wisdom.

The Bible emphasizes the importance of seeking wisdom and promises that God will generously provide it to those who ask in faith.

1. Asking for Wisdom: James 1:5 advises, "If any of you lacks wisdom, you should ask God, who gives generously to all without finding fault, and it will be given to you." This

verse underscores that wisdom is available to all believers who seek it sincerely. Prayer and faith are the means through which believers can access divine guidance for their decisions.

2. The Value of Wisdom: Proverbs 3:13-18 extols the virtues of wisdom, highlighting its value: "Blessed are those who find wisdom, those who gain understanding, for she is more profitable than silver and yields better returns than gold. She is more precious than rubies; nothing you desire can compare with her. Long life is in her right hand; in her left hand are riches and honor. Her ways are pleasant ways, and all her paths are peace. She is a tree of life to those who take hold of her; those who hold her fast will be blessed." This passage emphasizes that wisdom leads to prosperity and blessings, far exceeding material wealth alone.

3. The Fear of the Lord: Proverbs 9:10 teaches, "The fear of the Lord is the beginning of wisdom, and knowledge of the Holy One is understanding." Reverence for God and a deep relationship with Him are foundational to acquiring true wisdom. This wisdom, rooted in faith, guides believers in making decisions that honor God and lead to successful outcomes.

King Solomon is a prime example of how faith and wisdom can lead to financial success and honor. His story provides valuable insights into the benefits of seeking God's wisdom.

1. Solomon's Request for Wisdom: When Solomon became king, he prayed for wisdom to govern his people effectively. 1 Kings 3:7-9 records his prayer: "Now, Lord my God, you have made your servant king in place of my father David. But I am only a little child and do not know how to carry out my duties. Your servant is here among the people you have chosen, a great people, too numerous to count or number. So give your servant a discerning heart to govern your people and to distinguish between right and wrong. For who is able to govern this great people of yours?" Solomon's humble request for wisdom, rather than wealth or power, pleased God.

2. God's Response: God was pleased with Solomon's request and granted him unparalleled wisdom, along with wealth and honor. 1 Kings 3:10-13 states, "The Lord was pleased that Solomon had asked for this. So God said to him, 'Since you have asked for this and not for long life or wealth for yourself, nor have asked for the death of your enemies but for discernment in administering justice, I will do what you have asked. I will give you a wise and discerning heart so that there will never have been anyone like you, nor will there ever be. Moreover, I will give you what you have not asked for—both wealth and honor—so that in your lifetime you will have

no equal among kings.'" Solomon's example demonstrates that seeking God's wisdom can lead to comprehensive blessings, including financial success.

3. The Impact of Solomon's Wisdom: Solomon's wisdom became renowned throughout the world, attracting visitors from far and wide, including the Queen of Sheba. His ability to make just decisions, manage resources effectively, and lead his people contributed to Israel's prosperity during his reign. Solomon's story illustrates that divine wisdom can lead to both spiritual and material prosperity, benefiting not only the individual but also the broader community.

Faith-based wisdom is not only a biblical principle but also a practical tool for navigating modern life's complexities, particularly in financial matters.

1. Prayer and Seeking Guidance: Believers are encouraged to seek God's guidance in all decisions, particularly financial ones. Regular prayer and seeking wisdom from the Holy Spirit can provide clarity and direction. Philippians 4:6-7 advises, "Do not be anxious about anything, but in every situation, by prayer and petition, with thanksgiving, present your requests to God. And the peace of God, which transcends all understanding, will guard your hearts and your minds in Christ Jesus."

2. Studying Scripture: Immersing oneself in the Bible is essential for gaining wisdom. Scripture offers timeless principles and practical advice on managing resources, making ethical decisions, and living a life that honors God. Psalm 119:105 says, "Your word is a lamp for my feet, a light on my path." Regular Bible study helps believers align their decisions with God's will.

3. Seeking Counsel: Proverbs 15:22 teaches, "Plans fail for lack of counsel, but with many advisers they succeed." Seeking advice from trusted, godly mentors and financial advisors can provide valuable perspectives and prevent costly mistakes. Faith-based counsel combines practical expertise with spiritual insight, ensuring well-rounded decision-making.

4. Discernment and Ethical Decisions: Faith-based wisdom helps believers discern right from wrong and make ethical decisions. This discernment is crucial in financial matters, where ethical considerations can significantly impact outcomes. Proverbs 2:6-9 highlights that wisdom and understanding come from the Lord and guide one in the path of righteousness and justice.

5. Long-Term Perspective: Wisdom from faith encourages a long-term perspective, focusing on sustainable and ethical financial practices rather than short-term gains. Proverbs 13:11 advises, "Dishonest money dwindles away, but whoever gathers money little by little makes it grow." This

perspective helps believers build lasting wealth while maintaining integrity.

Wisdom derived from faith can significantly enhance financial success by guiding believers in making prudent and ethical decisions.

1. Risk Management: Wisdom helps in assessing risks and making informed decisions that balance potential rewards with possible drawbacks. This discernment is crucial in investments, business ventures, and personal finance. By seeking God's guidance, believers can navigate risks with confidence and peace.

2. Stewardship and Resource Management: Faith-based wisdom emphasizes responsible stewardship of resources. This includes budgeting, saving, and investing wisely. Luke 16:10-11 teaches, "Whoever can be trusted with very little can also be trusted with much, and whoever is dishonest with very little will also be dishonest with much. So if you have not been trustworthy in handling worldly wealth, who will trust you with true riches?" Effective resource management honors God and leads to financial stability.

3. Generosity and Blessings: Wisdom encourages generosity, recognizing that giving leads to blessings. Proverbs 11:25 states, "A generous person will prosper; whoever refreshes others will be refreshed." Faith-based

generosity aligns with God's principles and creates a cycle of blessing, benefiting both the giver and the recipient.

Faith provides believers with wisdom and discernment, which are crucial for financial success and overall well-being. The Bible teaches that seeking God's guidance through prayer and faith can lead to wise decision-making and prosperity. The example of King Solomon demonstrates that divine wisdom can result in both spiritual and material blessings. By embracing biblical principles of wisdom, prayer, study, and counsel, modern believers can navigate financial challenges and opportunities with confidence, integrity, and a long-term perspective. Faith-based wisdom remains a timeless and invaluable resource for achieving success in all areas of life while honoring God and reflecting His love.

CHAPTER 21

THE ROLE OF GENEROSITY

Generosity is a key component of the relationship between faith and financial success. The Bible teaches that giving to others opens believers to receiving God's blessings in return. Generosity reflects God's character and promotes a spirit of community and mutual support. This chapter explores the biblical principles of generosity, its impact on early Christian communities, and its practical applications for modern believers. By understanding and practicing generosity, believers can experience God's blessings and contribute to the well-being of others.

The Bible consistently emphasizes the importance of generosity, highlighting the blessings that come from giving to others.

1. Generosity and Blessings: Luke 6:38 teaches, "Give, and it will be given to you. A good measure, pressed down, shaken together and running over, will be poured into your lap. For with the measure you use, it will be measured to you."

This verse underscores the principle that generosity leads to blessings. By giving to others, believers open themselves up to receiving God's abundant blessings in return.

2. Cheerful Giving: 2 Corinthians 9:6-7 emphasizes the importance of a willing and cheerful heart in giving: "Remember this: Whoever sows sparingly will also reap sparingly, and whoever sows generously will also reap generously. Each of you should give what you have decided in your heart to give, not reluctantly or under compulsion, for God loves a cheerful giver." Generosity should come from a sincere desire to help others, reflecting joy and gratitude.

3. Generosity as Worship: Proverbs 3:9-10 teaches that honoring God with one's wealth is a form of worship: "Honor the Lord with your wealth, with the firstfruits of all your crops; then your barns will be filled to overflowing, and your vats will brim over with new wine." Giving to God and to others acknowledges that all blessings come from Him and expresses gratitude and reverence.

The early Christian community exemplified the principle of generosity through their communal sharing and mutual support.

1. Sharing Possessions: Acts 2:44-45 describes the generosity of the early believers: "All the believers were together and had everything in common. They sold property and possessions to give to anyone who had need." This

communal approach ensured that no one in the community lacked necessities, fostering a sense of unity and collective responsibility.

2. Mutual Support and Unity: The early Christians' generosity created a strong sense of community and mutual support. Acts 4:32-35 further illustrates this: "All the believers were one in heart and mind. No one claimed that any of their possessions was their own, but they shared everything they had. With great power the apostles continued to testify to the resurrection of the Lord Jesus. And God's grace was so powerfully at work in them all that there were no needy persons among them. For from time to time those who owned land or houses sold them, brought the money from the sales and put it at the apostles' feet, and it was distributed to anyone who had need." This passage highlights the power of generosity to create a supportive and unified community.

Generosity has profound impacts on both the giver and the recipient, fostering spiritual growth, community well-being, and social justice.

1. Spiritual Growth: Generosity fosters spiritual growth by aligning believers' hearts with God's purposes. Acts 20:35 quotes Jesus, saying, "It is more blessed to give than to receive." Giving cultivates a heart of compassion, gratitude,

and humility, drawing believers closer to God and His desires for their lives.

2. Community Well-Being: Generosity enhances the well-being of the community by meeting the needs of its members. Proverbs 11:25 states, "A generous person will prosper; whoever refreshes others will be refreshed." Helping others creates a cycle of blessing that strengthens the entire community.

3. Social Justice: Generosity addresses social injustices by providing resources and support to those who are marginalized or in need. Isaiah 58:10-11 promises blessings for those who help the oppressed: "If you spend yourselves in behalf of the hungry and satisfy the needs of the oppressed, then your light will rise in the darkness, and your night will become like the noonday. The Lord will guide you always; he will satisfy your needs in a sun-scorched land and will strengthen your frame. You will be like a well-watered garden, like a spring whose waters never fail." Generosity promotes justice and equality, reflecting God's heart for the vulnerable.

Modern believers can practice generosity in various ways, enhancing their spiritual growth and contributing to the well-being of others.

1. Tithing and Offerings: Regular tithing and offerings are foundational practices of generosity. Malachi 3:10 encourages believers to bring their tithes into the storehouse:

"Bring the whole tithe into the storehouse, that there may be food in my house. Test me in this," says the Lord Almighty, "and see if I will not throw open the floodgates of heaven and pour out so much blessing that there will not be room enough to store it." Consistent giving supports the work of the church and honors God.

2. Charitable Donations: Supporting charitable organizations and causes is another way to practice generosity. These donations can address various needs, such as poverty alleviation, education, healthcare, and disaster relief. Proverbs 19:17 says, "Whoever is kind to the poor lends to the Lord, and he will reward them for what they have done."

3. Volunteering Time and Skills: Generosity is not limited to financial giving. Volunteering time and skills to help others is a valuable way to contribute. Whether through mentoring, community service, or providing professional expertise, these acts of service reflect God's love and compassion.

4. Practicing Hospitality: Opening one's home and resources to others is a practical expression of generosity. Romans 12:13 instructs, "Share with the Lord's people who are in need. Practice hospitality." Hospitality creates opportunities for fellowship, support, and encouragement.

5. Encouraging a Generous Mindset: Cultivating a mindset of generosity involves recognizing opportunities to give and being willing to share resources. This mindset is characterized by an awareness of others' needs and a readiness to act. Philippians 2:4 encourages, "Not looking to your own interests but each of you to the interests of the others."

The Bible promises various rewards for those who practice generosity, both in this life and in eternity.

1. Divine Blessings: Generosity invites God's blessings into the giver's life. Proverbs 22:9 says, "The generous will themselves be blessed, for they share their food with the poor." God's blessings can manifest in various ways, including financial provision, spiritual growth, and personal fulfillment.

2. Heavenly Rewards: Generosity also stores up treasures in heaven. Matthew 6:19-21 teaches, "Do not store up for yourselves treasures on earth, where moths and vermin destroy, and where thieves break in and steal. But store up for yourselves treasures in heaven, where moths and vermin do not destroy, and where thieves do not break in and steal. For where your treasure is, there your heart will be also." Eternal rewards are the ultimate benefit of living a generous life.

3. Joy and Fulfillment: Generosity brings joy and fulfillment to the giver. Acts 20:35 highlights this truth: "In everything I did, I showed you that by this kind of hard work, we must help the weak, remembering the words the Lord

Jesus himself said: 'It is more blessed to give than to receive.'" Giving enriches the giver's life, providing a sense of purpose and satisfaction.

Generosity is a key component of the relationship between faith and financial success. The Bible teaches that giving to others opens believers to receiving God's blessings in return. The early Christian community exemplified this principle through their communal sharing and mutual support, demonstrating the power of faith in action. By practicing generosity in various forms—tithing, charitable donations, volunteering, hospitality, and cultivating a generous mindset—modern believers can experience God's blessings and contribute to the well-being of others. The rewards of generosity, both in this life and in eternity, affirm its importance as a central tenet of Christian faith and practice.

PART V

CHARITABLE GIVING

CHAPTER 22

BIBLICAL FOUNDATIONS OF CHARITABLE GIVING

The Bible is rich with teachings that emphasize the importance of charity and generosity. Both the Old and New Testaments contain numerous exhortations for the faithful to support the less fortunate. This chapter explores the biblical foundations of charitable giving, examining key scriptures that highlight the expectation for believers to assist those in need. By understanding and applying these principles, modern believers can fulfill their calling to reflect God's love and compassion through acts of charity.

The Old Testament lays a strong foundation for the principle of charitable giving, emphasizing that those with resources should willingly support those in need.

1. The Law of Moses: Deuteronomy 15:7-8 provides a clear directive for generosity: "If anyone is poor among your fellow Israelites in any of the towns of the land the Lord your

God is giving you, do not be hardhearted or tightfisted toward them. Rather, be openhanded and freely lend them whatever they need." This passage underscores the expectation that individuals should be compassionate and generous, providing for the poor among them.

2. The Principle of Jubilee: Leviticus 25 outlines the Year of Jubilee, a time every 50 years when debts were forgiven, slaves were freed, and land was returned to its original owners. This system was designed to prevent the permanent impoverishment of individuals and families, ensuring a reset and a fresh start. Leviticus 25:35-37 also emphasizes the need to support the poor: "If any of your fellow Israelites become poor and are unable to support themselves among you, help them as you would a foreigner and stranger, so they can continue to live among you. Do not take interest or any profit from them, but fear your God, so that they may continue to live among you."

3. The Example of Boaz: In the Book of Ruth, Boaz exemplifies charitable giving through his treatment of Ruth, a poor Moabite widow. He allows her to glean in his fields and provides her with extra grain, ensuring her and Naomi's survival. Ruth 2:16 records his generosity: "Even pull out some stalks for her from the bundles and leave them for her to pick up, and don't rebuke her." Boaz's actions demonstrate

a practical application of the law and a personal commitment to helping those in need.

The New Testament builds on the principles established in the Old Testament, with Jesus and the apostles reinforcing the importance of charity.

1. Jesus' Teachings on Charity: Jesus often taught about the importance of helping the less fortunate. In Matthew 25:35-36, He speaks of the final judgment, saying, "For I was hungry and you gave me something to eat, I was thirsty and you gave me something to drink, I was a stranger and you invited me in, I needed clothes and you clothed me, I was sick and you looked after me, I was in prison and you came to visit me." This teaching highlights that acts of charity are seen as direct service to God Himself, emphasizing the spiritual significance of helping others.

2. The Parable of the Good Samaritan: In Luke 10:25-37, Jesus tells the Parable of the Good Samaritan to illustrate the concept of loving one's neighbor. The Samaritan's compassion and generosity towards the injured man, whom others had ignored, serve as a powerful example of selfless charity. Jesus concludes by instructing, "Go and do likewise," urging believers to show mercy and kindness to those in need.

3. The Early Church's Example: The early Christian community exemplified charitable giving through their

communal sharing. Acts 2:44-45 describes their generosity: "All the believers were together and had everything in common. They sold property and possessions to give to anyone who had need." This practice ensured that the needs of all members were met, fostering a sense of unity and mutual support.

Charitable giving is deeply rooted in theological principles that reflect God's character and His expectations for His people.

1. Reflecting God's Love: God's love and compassion for humanity are foundational to the call for charitable giving. 1 John 3:17-18 emphasizes this: "If anyone has material possessions and sees a brother or sister in need but has no pity on them, how can the love of God be in that person? Dear children, let us not love with words or speech but with actions and in truth." Believers are called to reflect God's love through tangible acts of charity.

2. Stewardship and Responsibility: The Bible teaches that all resources ultimately belong to God and that individuals are stewards of these blessings. 1 Peter 4:10 instructs, "Each of you should use whatever gift you have received to serve others, as faithful stewards of God's grace in its various forms." Charitable giving is an expression of responsible stewardship, using God's blessings to support and uplift others.

3. Justice and Righteousness: Charitable giving is also an aspect of biblical justice and righteousness. Isaiah 58:6-7 connects charity with true worship: "Is not this the kind of fasting I have chosen: to loose the chains of injustice and untie the cords of the yoke, to set the oppressed free and break every yoke? Is it not to share your food with the hungry and to provide the poor wanderer with shelter—when you see the naked, to clothe them, and not to turn away from your own flesh and blood?" Acts of charity are integral to living out God's justice and righteousness.

Understanding the biblical foundations of charitable giving encourages modern believers to incorporate these principles into their lives through various practical actions.

1. Regular Giving: Establishing a habit of regular giving, such as tithing to the church and supporting charitable organizations, helps maintain a consistent commitment to generosity. Malachi 3:10 encourages bringing tithes into the storehouse to support God's work and the needs of the community.

2. Volunteering: In addition to financial contributions, believers can give their time and skills to support charitable causes. Volunteering at local shelters, food banks, or community centers allows individuals to directly engage in acts of service and compassion.

3. Supporting Social Justice Initiatives: Engaging in and supporting initiatives that address systemic issues such as poverty, inequality, and injustice aligns with the biblical call for justice. This can include advocacy, education, and partnering with organizations that work towards societal transformation.

4. Practicing Hospitality: Opening one's home and resources to those in need, as instructed in Romans 12:13, is a practical way to demonstrate charity. Offering meals, temporary shelter, or a listening ear can make a significant difference in someone's life.

5. Mentorship and Empowerment: Providing mentorship and opportunities for empowerment, such as job training, educational support, and financial literacy programs, helps individuals achieve long-term stability and independence. This approach aligns with the biblical principle of helping others to become self-sufficient.

The Bible promises various rewards for those who practice charitable giving, both in this life and in eternity.

1. Divine Blessings: Proverbs 11:25 states, "A generous person will prosper; whoever refreshes others will be refreshed." God's blessings often follow acts of generosity, providing for the giver's needs and enriching their lives.

2. Eternal Rewards: Jesus teaches that charitable giving stores up treasures in heaven. Matthew 6:19-21 advises,

"Do not store up for yourselves treasures on earth, where moths and vermin destroy, and where thieves break in and steal. But store up for yourselves treasures in heaven, where moths and vermin do not destroy, and where thieves do not break in and steal. For where your treasure is, there your heart will be also." Generosity has eternal significance, reflecting the believer's heart and priorities.

3. Joy and Fulfillment: Acts of charity bring joy and fulfillment to the giver. Acts 20:35 quotes Jesus, saying, "It is more blessed to give than to receive." Giving enriches the giver's life, providing a sense of purpose and satisfaction.

The Bible provides a rich foundation for the practice of charitable giving, emphasizing its importance in both the Old and New Testaments. The teachings of Moses, the prophets, Jesus, and the apostles all highlight the expectation for believers to support those in need, reflecting God's love, justice, and compassion. By understanding and applying these principles, modern believers can fulfill their calling to practice generosity, contribute to the well-being of others, and experience the blessings that come from living out God's commands. The biblical foundations of charitable giving offer timeless guidance for living a life that honors God and serves humanity.

CHAPTER 23

THE ROLE OF WEALTHY INDIVIDUALS IN SOCIETY

Wealthy individuals possess a unique capacity to make significant contributions to the well-being of society. Their resources can address critical needs, support important causes, and create lasting positive change. The Bible provides several examples of wealthy individuals who used their resources for good, demonstrating how their generosity and influence can have profound impacts on their communities and beyond. This chapter explores the biblical examples of Cornelius and Joseph of Arimathea, as well as the broader role of wealthy individuals in society.

The Bible highlights several wealthy individuals whose acts of generosity and faith had lasting impacts on their communities and the spread of the Gospel.

1. Cornelius: A Model of Devotion and Generosity: Cornelius, a Roman centurion, is described in Acts 10:1-4 as a devout man who feared God, gave generously to those in

need, and prayed regularly. His charitable acts were recognized by God, leading to a divine vision and the spread of the Gospel to the Gentiles. Acts 10:4 records the angel's message to Cornelius: "Your prayers and gifts to the poor have come up as a memorial offering before God." Cornelius' generosity and faithfulness opened the door for Peter's visit and the outpouring of the Holy Spirit on the Gentiles, marking a pivotal moment in the early church.

2. Joseph of Arimathea: Generosity and Reverence: Joseph of Arimathea is another example of a wealthy individual who used his resources for a significant purpose. According to Matthew 27:57-60, Joseph provided his own tomb for the burial of Jesus: "As evening approached, there came a rich man from Arimathea, named Joseph, who had himself become a disciple of Jesus. Going to Pilate, he asked for Jesus' body, and Pilate ordered that it be given to him. Joseph took the body, wrapped it in a clean linen cloth, and placed it in his own new tomb that he had cut out of the rock." This act of generosity ensured that Jesus had a dignified burial, fulfilling prophetic scriptures and highlighting the impact of Joseph's charitable act.

Wealthy individuals have the potential to create substantial positive change in society through their resources, influence, and leadership.

1. Addressing Critical Needs: Wealthy individuals can address critical societal needs by funding healthcare, education, and social services. Their contributions can provide immediate relief in times of crisis, support long-term development projects, and improve the quality of life for many people. For example, funding medical research can lead to breakthroughs in treatment and disease prevention, while supporting educational initiatives can provide opportunities for future generations.

2. Supporting Important Causes: Wealthy individuals often champion important causes, using their resources to raise awareness and drive change. This can include environmental conservation, human rights, poverty alleviation, and more. Their financial support and public advocacy can bring attention to issues that might otherwise be overlooked, mobilizing resources and inspiring others to take action.

3. Creating Lasting Change: By investing in sustainable projects and initiatives, wealthy individuals can create lasting positive change. This can involve establishing foundations, endowing scholarships, or supporting social enterprises that address systemic issues. Their long-term investments can help build resilient communities and promote social justice.

The Bible provides principles for wealthy individuals on how to use their resources ethically and effectively to benefit society.

1. Generosity and Stewardship: Wealth should be used to benefit others, reflecting God's generosity. 1 Timothy 6:17-19 instructs, "Command those who are rich in this present world not to be arrogant nor to put their hope in wealth, which is so uncertain, but to put their hope in God, who richly provides us with everything for our enjoyment. Command them to do good, to be rich in good deeds, and to be generous and willing to share. In this way, they will lay up treasure for themselves as a firm foundation for the coming age, so that they may take hold of the life that is truly life." Generosity and stewardship are key principles for managing wealth in a way that honors God and benefits society.

2. Humility and Service: Wealthy individuals are called to serve others with humility, recognizing that their resources are a blessing from God. Philippians 2:3-4 advises, "Do nothing out of selfish ambition or vain conceit. Rather, in humility value others above yourselves, not looking to your own interests but each of you to the interests of the others." Humility and a servant's heart are essential for using wealth to uplift others and promote the common good.

3. Justice and Righteousness: Using wealth to promote justice and righteousness aligns with biblical teachings. Isaiah 1:17 calls for active engagement in social justice: "Learn to do right; seek justice. Defend the oppressed. Take up the cause of the fatherless; plead the case of the widow." Wealthy individuals can use their influence and resources to advocate for and support marginalized and vulnerable populations, promoting fairness and equity.

Wealthy individuals can apply biblical principles to their lives through various practical actions, contributing to the well-being of society.

1. Philanthropy and Charitable Giving: Regular philanthropic efforts and charitable giving are foundational ways for wealthy individuals to support important causes. Establishing foundations, making significant donations to nonprofit organizations, and funding community projects are practical expressions of generosity and stewardship.

2. Supporting Education and Healthcare: Investing in education and healthcare can have long-term positive impacts. Funding scholarships, building schools, and supporting medical research and healthcare facilities can provide opportunities and improve the quality of life for many people.

3. Social Entrepreneurship and Impact Investing: Wealthy individuals can engage in social entrepreneurship and

impact investing, supporting businesses and projects that generate positive social and environmental outcomes. This approach aligns financial goals with ethical considerations, promoting sustainable and inclusive growth.

4. Advocacy and Leadership: Using their influence and platforms, wealthy individuals can advocate for social justice and policy changes that benefit society. By raising awareness and mobilizing resources, they can drive significant societal improvements and inspire others to join their efforts.

5. Mentorship and Empowerment: Providing mentorship and empowerment opportunities, such as leadership training, job creation, and entrepreneurship support, helps individuals and communities achieve self-sufficiency and long-term success. Empowering others to succeed creates a ripple effect, fostering economic and social development.

The Bible promises rewards for those who use their wealth to serve others, both in this life and in eternity.

1. Divine Blessings: Proverbs 11:25 states, "A generous person will prosper; whoever refreshes others will be refreshed." God's blessings often follow acts of generosity, providing for the giver's needs and enriching their lives.

2. Eternal Rewards: Jesus teaches that using wealth to serve others stores up treasures in heaven. Matthew 6:19-21

advises, "Do not store up for yourselves treasures on earth, where moths and vermin destroy, and where thieves break in and steal. But store up for yourselves treasures in heaven, where moths and vermin do not destroy, and where thieves do not break in and steal. For where your treasure is, there your heart will be also." Generosity has eternal significance, reflecting the believer's heart and priorities.

3. Joy and Fulfillment: Acts of charity and service bring joy and fulfillment to the giver. Acts 20:35 quotes Jesus, saying, "It is more blessed to give than to receive." Giving enriches the giver's life, providing a sense of purpose and satisfaction.

Wealthy individuals have a unique capacity to make significant contributions to the well-being of society. The Bible provides several examples of wealthy individuals who used their resources for good, such as Cornelius and Joseph of Arimathea, demonstrating the impact of generosity and faithfulness. By adhering to biblical principles of generosity, stewardship, humility, and justice, wealthy individuals can use their resources to address critical needs, support important causes, and create lasting positive change. The role of wealthy individuals in society is essential for promoting the common good, reflecting God's love, and contributing to the flourishing of all.

CHAPTER 24

MODERN EXAMPLES OF CHARITABLE GIVING

In contemporary society, many wealthy individuals and philanthropists continue to embody the principles of charitable giving. By establishing foundations and supporting various causes, these modern philanthropists follow in the biblical tradition of using their resources to address societal issues and improve the lives of others. This chapter explores modern examples of charitable giving, examining the impact of notable philanthropists and the ongoing practice of tithing. Through these examples, we can see how the principles of generosity and stewardship continue to make a significant difference in the world today.

Several wealthy individuals and families have made significant contributions to global health, education, poverty alleviation, and other critical areas through their philanthropic efforts. These modern examples highlight the power of charitable giving to effect positive change.

1. The Bill and Melinda Gates Foundation: The Bill and Melinda Gates Foundation is one of the most prominent examples of modern philanthropy. Established by Bill and Melinda Gates, the foundation focuses on global health, education, and poverty alleviation. It has invested billions of dollars in initiatives to eradicate diseases like malaria and polio, improve educational outcomes, and provide resources to impoverished communities. The foundation's work reflects the biblical principle of using wealth to serve and uplift others, making a tangible impact on millions of lives worldwide.

2. Warren Buffett and The Giving Pledge: Warren Buffett, one of the wealthiest individuals in the world, has pledged to give away the majority of his fortune to charitable causes. In 2010, he, along with Bill and Melinda Gates, launched The Giving Pledge, an initiative encouraging billionaires to commit to giving away at least half of their wealth during their lifetimes or in their wills. This movement has inspired numerous wealthy individuals to engage in significant philanthropic efforts, addressing a wide range of societal issues.

3. Oprah Winfrey: Oprah Winfrey is another notable philanthropist who has used her wealth and influence to support various causes. Through her foundation, she has contributed to education, women's empowerment, and disaster relief. Winfrey's commitment to improving the lives

of others through charitable giving exemplifies the impact that individual generosity can have on society.

4. The Chan Zuckerberg Initiative: Founded by Facebook CEO Mark Zuckerberg and his wife, Priscilla Chan, the Chan Zuckerberg Initiative aims to advance human potential and promote equal opportunity. The initiative focuses on areas such as education, science, and criminal justice reform. By leveraging their resources and expertise, the Chan Zuckerberg Initiative seeks to create lasting positive change and address some of the world's most pressing challenges.

The concept of tithing, giving a portion of one's income to charitable causes, remains a common practice among many religious individuals. This practice is rooted in the biblical injunction to give back to God a portion of what He has provided.

1. Biblical Foundation of Tithing: The practice of tithing is based on several biblical passages that instruct believers to give a tenth of their income to support the work of God and help those in need. Malachi 3:10 states, "Bring the whole tithe into the storehouse, that there may be food in my house. Test me in this," says the Lord Almighty, "and see if I will not throw open the floodgates of heaven and pour out so much blessing that there will not be room enough to store it."

Tithing is seen as an act of obedience, gratitude, and trust in God's provision.

2. Modern Applications of Tithing: Many religious individuals and families continue to practice tithing, supporting their local churches, religious organizations, and various charitable causes. This consistent financial support enables these organizations to carry out their missions, provide essential services, and address the needs of their communities. Tithing remains a vital source of funding for many faith-based and charitable initiatives.

3. Tithing and Financial Stewardship: Tithing also encourages responsible financial stewardship. By setting aside a portion of their income for charitable giving, individuals develop disciplined financial habits and prioritize generosity. This practice fosters a mindset of abundance and gratitude, recognizing that all resources ultimately come from God.

Modern charitable giving has a profound impact on society, addressing critical needs, promoting social justice, and enhancing the well-being of communities.

1. Global Health and Disease Eradication: Philanthropic efforts in global health have led to significant advancements in disease prevention and treatment. Initiatives funded by organizations like the Bill and Melinda Gates Foundation have contributed to the reduction of malaria and

polio cases, improved access to vaccines, and strengthened healthcare systems in developing countries.

2. Education and Empowerment: Charitable giving in education has expanded access to quality education, provided scholarships, and supported educational innovations. Programs funded by philanthropists like Oprah Winfrey and the Chan Zuckerberg Initiative have empowered students, improved educational outcomes, and created opportunities for disadvantaged communities.

3. Poverty Alleviation and Economic Development: Philanthropic initiatives aimed at poverty alleviation and economic development have provided resources, training, and support to vulnerable populations. Efforts such as microfinance, vocational training, and community development projects have helped individuals and families achieve financial independence and improve their living conditions.

4. Social Justice and Equality: Modern philanthropy has also played a crucial role in promoting social justice and equality. Charitable organizations and initiatives addressing issues such as criminal justice reform, racial equality, and women's rights have worked to create a more just and equitable society.

Modern believers can engage in charitable giving in various ways, drawing inspiration from both biblical teachings and contemporary examples.

1. Regular Giving and Tithing: Practicing regular giving and tithing helps support the work of religious organizations and charitable causes. Setting aside a portion of income for donation fosters a habit of generosity and ensures consistent support for important initiatives.

2. Volunteering and Service: In addition to financial contributions, believers can give their time and skills to support charitable efforts. Volunteering at local shelters, participating in community service projects, and offering professional expertise are valuable ways to contribute.

3. Supporting Social Enterprises and Impact Investing: Engaging in social entrepreneurship and impact investing allows individuals to support businesses and projects that generate positive social and environmental outcomes. This approach aligns financial goals with ethical considerations and promotes sustainable development.

4. Advocacy and Awareness: Raising awareness and advocating for important causes can amplify the impact of charitable giving. By using their influence and platforms, individuals can mobilize resources, inspire others to take action, and drive significant societal improvements.

5. Mentorship and Empowerment: Providing mentorship and support for individuals and communities helps empower them to achieve long-term success. Programs that offer leadership training, educational support, and job creation opportunities can create lasting positive change.

In contemporary society, many wealthy individuals and philanthropists continue to embody the principles of charitable giving. By establishing foundations and supporting various causes, they follow in the biblical tradition of using their resources to address societal issues and improve the lives of others. The practice of tithing remains a common and impactful way for religious individuals to support charitable causes and reflect their faith. Modern charitable giving has a profound impact on global health, education, poverty alleviation, and social justice, demonstrating the enduring power of generosity and stewardship. By drawing inspiration from both biblical teachings and contemporary examples, modern believers can engage in charitable giving that honors God and contributes to the well-being of society.

CHAPTER 25

THE SPIRITUAL AND MORAL IMPERATIVE

Charitable giving is not just a societal expectation but a spiritual and moral imperative. The Bible teaches that generosity is a reflection of God's character and a demonstration of His love. Through acts of charity, believers can directly serve God and receive His blessings. This chapter explores the biblical foundations of the spiritual and moral imperative of charitable giving, highlighting key scriptures and teachings of Jesus that emphasize the significance of generosity.

The Bible presents charitable giving as a core aspect of faithful living, rooted in the nature of God and His expectations for His people.

1. Reflection of God's Character: Generosity is a reflection of God's character. Proverbs 19:17 states, "Whoever is kind to the poor lends to the Lord, and he will reward them for what they have done." This verse highlights

that acts of charity are seen as direct service to God, who promises to reward such kindness. God's generous nature is evident throughout the Bible, and His followers are called to emulate this attribute.

2. Commandment to Love: The greatest commandments, as stated by Jesus in Matthew 22:37-39, are to love God and love one's neighbor: "Jesus replied: 'Love the Lord your God with all your heart and with all your soul and with all your mind.' This is the first and greatest commandment. And the second is like it: 'Love your neighbor as yourself.'" Charitable giving is a practical expression of this love, fulfilling the moral imperative to care for others.

3. Obedience and Sacrifice: The Bible emphasizes that true obedience to God includes acts of generosity and sacrifice. Hebrews 13:16 urges, "And do not forget to do good and to share with others, for with such sacrifices God is pleased." Charitable giving is seen as a form of worship and a tangible way to please God.

Jesus' teachings in the New Testament highlight the spiritual significance of giving and the blessings that accompany generosity.

1. The Principle of Reciprocity: In Luke 6:38, Jesus teaches, "Give, and it will be given to you. A good measure, pressed down, shaken together and running over, will be

poured into your lap. For with the measure you use, it will be measured to you." This teaching underscores the principle that generosity leads to blessings, both spiritual and material. By giving generously, believers open themselves to receiving God's abundant blessings.

2. The Parable of the Good Samaritan: The Parable of the Good Samaritan (Luke 10:25-37) illustrates the moral imperative to help those in need. The Samaritan's compassionate actions towards a stranger highlight the importance of selfless giving and caring for others, regardless of their background or circumstances. Jesus concludes the parable with the command, "Go and do likewise," urging believers to act with compassion and generosity.

3. The Rich Young Ruler: In Matthew 19:21, Jesus challenges a wealthy young man to sell his possessions and give to the poor: "Jesus answered, 'If you want to be perfect, go, sell your possessions and give to the poor, and you will have treasure in heaven. Then come, follow me.'" This encounter emphasizes that spiritual completeness involves a willingness to give up material wealth for the sake of helping others and following Christ.

The Impact of Charitable Giving on Spiritual Growth

Charitable giving not only benefits the recipients but also significantly impacts the spiritual growth and development of the giver.

1. Cultivating a Generous Heart: Regular acts of giving help cultivate a generous heart and a spirit of compassion. Proverbs 11:24-25 explains, "One person gives freely, yet gains even more; another withholds unduly, but comes to poverty. A generous person will prosper; whoever refreshes others will be refreshed." Generosity transforms the giver, fostering a heart that mirrors God's love and generosity.

2. Trusting in God's Provision: Charitable giving requires trust in God's provision. By giving away resources, believers demonstrate their reliance on God to meet their needs. Malachi 3:10 encourages this trust: "Bring the whole tithe into the storehouse, that there may be food in my house. Test me in this," says the Lord Almighty, "and see if I will not throw open the floodgates of heaven and pour out so much blessing that there will not be room enough to store it." Trusting God with one's resources deepens faith and reliance on His promises.

3. Storing Up Treasures in Heaven: Jesus teaches that acts of charity store up eternal rewards. Matthew 6:19-21 advises, "Do not store up for yourselves treasures on earth, where moths and vermin destroy, and where thieves break in and steal. But store up for yourselves treasures in heaven, where moths and vermin do not destroy, and where thieves do not break in and steal. For where your treasure is, there

your heart will be also." By focusing on heavenly treasures, believers align their priorities with eternal values.

The spiritual and moral imperative of charitable giving calls believers to take practical steps to live out their faith through acts of generosity.

1. Supporting the Church and Ministry: Giving to the church supports its mission and ministry, enabling it to reach out to the community and beyond. Regular tithes and offerings are a foundational way to practice generosity and support the work of God.

2. Helping the Needy: Charitable giving should prioritize helping the needy and marginalized. James 1:27 states, "Religion that God our Father accepts as pure and faultless is this: to look after orphans and widows in their distress and to keep oneself from being polluted by the world." Supporting those who are vulnerable and in need is a direct reflection of God's love.

3. Engaging in Acts of Kindness: Everyday acts of kindness and generosity, such as helping a neighbor, volunteering, or providing support during difficult times, demonstrate the moral imperative to care for others. These actions contribute to a culture of compassion and community.

4. Advocating for Justice: Charitable giving can also involve advocating for justice and supporting initiatives that address systemic issues. Micah 6:8 calls believers to "act justly

and to love mercy and to walk humbly with your God." Working towards social justice and equality is a powerful expression of faith in action.

The Bible promises various rewards for those who live generously, both in this life and in eternity.

1. Spiritual Fulfillment: Acts of generosity bring spiritual fulfillment and joy. Acts 20:35 quotes Jesus, saying, "It is more blessed to give than to receive." Giving enriches the giver's life, providing a sense of purpose and satisfaction.

2. Divine Blessings: God promises blessings to those who are generous. Proverbs 22:9 states, "The generous will themselves be blessed, for they share their food with the poor." These blessings can manifest in various forms, including spiritual growth, financial provision, and personal well-being.

3. Eternal Rewards: Generosity stores up treasures in heaven. Matthew 19:21 emphasizes the eternal significance of charitable acts: "Jesus answered, 'If you want to be perfect, go, sell your possessions and give to the poor, and you will have treasure in heaven. Then come, follow me.'" The rewards of living generously extend beyond this life, reflecting the eternal values of God's kingdom.

Charitable giving is a spiritual and moral imperative deeply rooted in biblical teachings. Generosity reflects God's character and demonstrates His love, fulfilling the command to love one's neighbor and serve others. Jesus' teachings and the biblical principles of generosity highlight the spiritual significance of giving and the blessings that accompany it. By embracing the spiritual and moral imperative of charitable giving, modern believers can live out their faith, support the needy, and contribute to a more compassionate and just society. The rewards of living generously, both in this life and in eternity, affirm its importance as a central tenet of Christian faith and practice.

CHAPTER 26

PRACTICAL WAYS TO GIVE

Wealthy individuals have numerous opportunities to engage in charitable giving and make a significant impact on society. While financial donations to charitable organizations, foundations, and religious institutions are the most common forms of giving, there are various other ways to contribute to the well-being of communities. This chapter explores practical ways that wealthy individuals can engage in charitable giving, including creating scholarships, funding medical research, supporting disaster relief efforts, and investing in social enterprises. These acts of generosity reflect the principles of stewardship and responsibility, and they can have a profound and lasting impact on individuals and communities.

1. Charitable Organizations and Foundations: One of the most straightforward ways for wealthy individuals to give is through financial donations to established charitable

organizations and foundations. These entities focus on various causes such as poverty alleviation, education, healthcare, and environmental conservation. By providing financial support, donors can help these organizations carry out their missions effectively.

2. Religious Institutions: Donations to churches, synagogues, mosques, and other religious institutions support their spiritual and community-based activities. These contributions often fund worship services, community outreach programs, and mission work. Religious institutions also play a crucial role in providing social services and support to those in need.

3. Direct Giving: Wealthy individuals can also practice direct giving by providing financial assistance to individuals and families facing financial hardship. This approach allows donors to see the immediate impact of their generosity and develop personal connections with the beneficiaries.

1. Community Projects: Volunteering time and expertise to support community projects is a valuable way to give back. This can include participating in local clean-up efforts, building homes for the homeless, or organizing community events. By engaging directly with the community, wealthy individuals can make a tangible difference and inspire others to get involved.

2. Mentorship and Coaching: Offering mentorship and coaching to aspiring entrepreneurs, students, and young professionals is another impactful way to give. Sharing knowledge and experience can help individuals achieve their goals and build successful careers. Mentorship programs can be particularly beneficial in underserved communities, providing guidance and support to those who need it most.

3. Pro Bono Services: Professionals such as lawyers, doctors, and consultants can offer pro bono services to individuals and organizations that cannot afford to pay for them. Providing free legal advice, medical care, or business consulting can have a significant impact on the lives of those in need and help nonprofit organizations operate more effectively.

1. Educational Scholarships: Establishing educational scholarships is a powerful way to support the next generation of leaders and professionals. Scholarships can provide financial assistance to students who may not have the means to pursue higher education. By funding scholarships, wealthy individuals can help reduce financial barriers and promote access to quality education.

2. Targeted Scholarships: Scholarships can also be targeted to support specific groups, such as women in STEM fields, students from low-income families, or individuals

pursuing careers in public service. Targeted scholarships can address specific needs and promote diversity and inclusion in various fields.

3. Endowed Scholarships: Endowing scholarships through universities and colleges ensures that the funds will support students for generations to come. Endowed scholarships create a lasting legacy and provide ongoing support to educational institutions.

1. Supporting Medical Research Institutions: Funding medical research institutions and initiatives can lead to significant advancements in healthcare. Donations can support research on diseases such as cancer, diabetes, and Alzheimer's, leading to new treatments and cures. By investing in medical research, wealthy individuals can contribute to improving public health and saving lives.

2. Grant Programs: Establishing grant programs to fund innovative research projects can encourage scientific discoveries and breakthroughs. Grants can be awarded to researchers and institutions working on cutting-edge projects with the potential to transform healthcare.

3. Collaborative Research: Supporting collaborative research efforts that bring together scientists, healthcare providers, and institutions can accelerate progress and foster innovation. Collaborative research initiatives can address

complex health challenges and promote interdisciplinary approaches to solving them.

1. Emergency Relief Funds: Contributing to emergency relief funds helps provide immediate assistance to communities affected by natural disasters, such as hurricanes, earthquakes, and floods. These funds support rescue operations, medical care, shelter, and food distribution, helping affected individuals and communities recover and rebuild.

2. Rebuilding and Recovery: In addition to immediate relief, funding long-term rebuilding and recovery efforts is crucial for helping communities recover from disasters. This can include rebuilding homes, schools, and infrastructure, as well as providing ongoing support for affected families.

3. Disaster Preparedness: Investing in disaster preparedness initiatives can help communities mitigate the impact of future disasters. This can include funding early warning systems, emergency response training, and community education programs on disaster preparedness.

1. Social Entrepreneurship: Investing in social enterprises that address social and environmental challenges can create a sustainable impact. Social enterprises combine business principles with a commitment to social good, generating revenue while addressing issues such as poverty,

education, and environmental sustainability. By supporting social entrepreneurs, wealthy individuals can help drive innovative solutions to pressing problems.

2. Impact Investing: Impact investing involves making investments in companies, organizations, and funds with the intention of generating positive social and environmental impact alongside financial returns. Impact investments can support a wide range of initiatives, from renewable energy projects to affordable housing developments.

3. Supporting Small Businesses: Providing financial support and mentorship to small businesses, especially those in underserved communities, can promote economic development and job creation. By helping small businesses thrive, wealthy individuals can contribute to local economies and empower entrepreneurs.

1. Develop a Giving Strategy: Creating a clear giving strategy helps ensure that charitable efforts are focused and effective. This involves identifying priority areas, setting goals, and determining the most impactful ways to contribute. A well-defined strategy can guide decision-making and maximize the impact of charitable efforts.

2. Partner with Reputable Organizations: Collaborating with reputable charitable organizations and foundations can enhance the effectiveness of giving. These organizations often have the expertise, infrastructure, and

networks to implement programs efficiently and achieve meaningful results.

3. Measure Impact: Evaluating the impact of charitable contributions is essential for ensuring that resources are used effectively. Wealthy individuals can work with charitable organizations to track progress, assess outcomes, and make data-driven decisions to improve future efforts.

4. Engage in Ongoing Learning: Staying informed about social issues, best practices in philanthropy, and innovative solutions can enhance the effectiveness of charitable giving. Engaging in ongoing learning and seeking input from experts can help wealthy individuals make informed decisions and adapt their strategies as needed.

5. Involve Family and Community: Encouraging family members and community members to participate in charitable giving can amplify its impact. Involving others in philanthropic efforts fosters a culture of generosity and collective action, multiplying the positive effects of giving.

Wealthy individuals have numerous opportunities to engage in charitable giving and make a significant impact on society. Financial donations, volunteering time and expertise, creating scholarships, funding medical research, supporting disaster relief efforts, and investing in social enterprises are all practical ways to contribute to societal well-being. These acts of generosity reflect the principles of stewardship and responsibility, and they can have a profound and lasting impact on individuals and communities. By developing a clear giving strategy, partnering with reputable organizations, measuring impact, engaging in ongoing learning, and involving others, wealthy individuals can ensure that their charitable efforts are effective and transformative. The principles of generosity and stewardship continue to be essential for creating a more just, compassionate, and prosperous world.

CHAPTER 27

THE IMPACT OF CHARITABLE GIVING

The impact of charitable giving extends far beyond the immediate benefits to recipients. It fosters a culture of generosity, encourages others to give, and strengthens social bonds. Charitable acts inspire hope, provide opportunities, and improve the overall quality of life for many. Moreover, charitable giving aligns with the biblical principle of sowing and reaping. As individuals give generously, they often experience a sense of fulfillment and purpose, knowing that their resources are making a difference. This chapter explores the multifaceted impact of charitable giving, emphasizing both its practical benefits and its alignment with biblical teachings.

1. Meeting Basic Needs: Charitable giving often provides immediate relief by meeting basic needs such as food, shelter, clothing, and medical care. For those facing

financial hardship, these contributions can be life-saving and offer a sense of security and stability.

2. Access to Education: Scholarships and educational funding open doors for individuals who might not otherwise afford education. This access not only transforms individual lives but also has a ripple effect on families and communities, promoting long-term economic and social development.

3. Healthcare and Wellness: Funding for medical research, healthcare facilities, and treatment programs improves the overall health and wellness of communities. Charitable contributions can lead to advancements in medical science, better healthcare infrastructure, and improved patient outcomes.

1. Encouraging Others to Give: Acts of charity often inspire others to follow suit. When individuals see the positive impact of generosity, they are more likely to contribute themselves. This ripple effect can lead to a community-wide culture of giving, where helping others becomes a shared value and practice.

2. Strengthening Social Bonds: Charitable giving can strengthen social bonds by fostering a sense of solidarity and mutual support. Communities that engage in collective acts of charity develop stronger connections and a greater sense of unity, as individuals work together to address common challenges and support one another.

3. Building Trust and Cooperation: Generosity helps build trust and cooperation within communities. When people see that resources are shared fairly and transparently, it enhances trust in institutions and fosters a collaborative spirit. This cooperation can lead to more effective problem-solving and community resilience.

1. Creating Opportunities: Charitable giving creates opportunities for individuals to improve their circumstances and achieve their potential. Whether through education, job training, or entrepreneurship support, these opportunities empower individuals to build better futures for themselves and their families.

2. Inspiring Hope: Acts of charity can inspire hope in those who are struggling. Knowing that others care and are willing to help can provide emotional and psychological support, motivating individuals to persevere and overcome challenges. This hope can be a powerful catalyst for personal and community transformation.

3. Enhancing Quality of Life: Charitable contributions improve the overall quality of life by addressing social determinants of health and well-being. Access to education, healthcare, safe housing, and nutritious food all contribute to healthier, more vibrant communities where individuals can thrive.

The Biblical Principle of Sowing and Reaping

1. Sowing Generously: The biblical principle of sowing and reaping underscores the spiritual and practical benefits of generosity. 2 Corinthians 9:6-7 teaches, "Remember this: Whoever sows sparingly will also reap sparingly, and whoever sows generously will also reap generously. Each of you should give not reluctantly or under compulsion, for God loves a cheerful giver." This passage highlights that generous giving leads to abundant blessings, both for the giver and the recipient.

2. Experiencing Fulfillment and Purpose: Generosity aligns with the biblical teaching that giving leads to a deeper sense of fulfillment and purpose. By contributing to the well-being of others, individuals experience the joy and satisfaction of making a positive difference in the world. This sense of purpose enhances overall well-being and spiritual growth.

3. God's Blessings: The Bible promises that those who give generously will be blessed. Proverbs 11:24-25 states, "One person gives freely, yet gains even more; another withholds unduly but comes to poverty. A generous person will prosper; whoever refreshes others will be refreshed." This principle reflects God's promise that acts of generosity will be rewarded, often in unexpected and abundant ways.

1. Promoting Social Justice: Charitable giving plays a crucial role in promoting social justice by addressing

inequalities and supporting marginalized populations. By funding initiatives that tackle systemic issues such as poverty, discrimination, and access to education and healthcare, philanthropy contributes to a more just and equitable society.

2. Economic Development: Philanthropic efforts can stimulate economic development by supporting entrepreneurship, job creation, and infrastructure projects. These initiatives help build stronger economies, reduce unemployment, and improve living standards for communities.

3. Sustainable Development: Investing in sustainable development projects, such as renewable energy, clean water access, and environmental conservation, ensures that resources are used responsibly and future generations are considered. Charitable giving that focuses on sustainability helps create a balanced and healthy environment, promoting long-term prosperity.

1. Global Health Initiatives: The Bill and Melinda Gates Foundation's efforts in global health, particularly in eradicating diseases like polio and malaria, have had transformative impacts on public health. These initiatives have saved millions of lives and improved the health and well-being of entire populations.

2. Educational Scholarships: Programs like the Gates Millennium Scholars Program provide financial support to outstanding minority students, enabling them to pursue higher education. These scholarships have empowered thousands of students to achieve academic and professional success, breaking the cycle of poverty and contributing to their communities.

3. Disaster Relief and Recovery: Charitable organizations such as the Red Cross and various disaster relief funds provide critical support during natural disasters. Their efforts in immediate response and long-term recovery help communities rebuild and recover from crises, restoring hope and stability.

1. Strategic Giving: Wealthy individuals can maximize the impact of their charitable efforts by developing a strategic giving plan. This involves identifying priority areas, setting clear goals, and selecting effective organizations and initiatives to support. Strategic giving ensures that resources are used efficiently and achieve meaningful results.

2. Collaborative Efforts: Collaborating with other philanthropists, organizations, and community leaders can amplify the impact of charitable giving. By pooling resources and expertise, collaborative efforts can tackle complex challenges more effectively and achieve greater scale.

3. Ongoing Evaluation: Regularly evaluating the impact of charitable contributions helps ensure that resources are used effectively and goals are met. Wealthy individuals can work with charitable organizations to track progress, measure outcomes, and make data-driven decisions to improve future efforts.

4. Engaging Stakeholders: Engaging stakeholders, including beneficiaries, community members, and other donors, can provide valuable insights and foster a sense of shared ownership. Involving stakeholders in the planning and implementation of charitable initiatives helps ensure that efforts are responsive to community needs and have a lasting impact.

The impact of charitable giving extends far beyond the immediate benefits to recipients. It fosters a culture of generosity, encourages others to give, and strengthens social bonds. Charitable acts inspire hope, provide opportunities, and improve the overall quality of life for many. Moreover, charitable giving aligns with the biblical principle of sowing and reaping, leading to a sense of fulfillment and purpose for the giver. By practicing strategic, collaborative, and impactful giving, wealthy individuals can create lasting positive change and contribute to a more just, compassionate, and prosperous world. The principles of generosity and stewardship continue to be essential for transforming lives and communities, reflecting the enduring power of charitable giving.

PART VI

THE RESPONSIBILITY OF ABUNDANCE

CHAPTER 28

BIBLICAL FOUNDATIONS OF STEWARDSHIP

The Bible provides clear guidance on the responsibilities that come with wealth. Central to this guidance is the concept of stewardship—the idea that wealth is not solely for personal use but is entrusted to individuals by God to manage wisely and for His purposes. This chapter explores the biblical foundations of stewardship, examining key scriptures and teachings that emphasize the responsible and productive use of resources. Through understanding and practicing stewardship, believers can honor God and contribute to the well-being of others.

One of the most powerful teachings on stewardship comes from the Parable of the Talents, found in Matthew 25:14-30. This parable illustrates the expectations God has for His followers in managing the resources He has entrusted to them.

1. The Master's Entrustment: In the parable, a master entrusts his servants with varying amounts of money (talents) before going on a journey. He gives five talents to one servant,

two talents to another, and one talent to the third, each according to their ability. This distribution highlights that God entrusts individuals with resources based on their capabilities and expects them to manage these resources responsibly.

2. The Servants' Actions: The servants who received five and two talents immediately put their money to work and doubled their master's investment. In contrast, the servant who received one talent hid it in the ground, failing to use it productively. Upon the master's return, he rewards the two diligent servants, saying, "Well done, good and faithful servant! You have been faithful with a few things; I will put you in charge of many things. Come and share your master's happiness!" However, the servant who hid his talent is reprimanded and his talent is taken away.

3. The Principle of Stewardship: This parable emphasizes that God expects His followers to use their resources productively and responsibly. It underscores the principle that wealth is not merely for personal enjoyment but for purposeful management that aligns with God's intentions. The diligent servants are rewarded for their faithfulness, while the unproductive servant faces consequences for his inaction.

Stewardship extends beyond financial management to include using all gifts and resources to serve others. This principle is reinforced in 1 Peter 4:10.

1. Using Gifts to Serve Others: 1 Peter 4:10 states, "Each of you should use whatever gift you have received to serve others, as faithful stewards of God's grace in its various forms." This verse highlights that wealth and other blessings are to be used in service to others. Stewardship involves recognizing that all resources are gifts from God and should be managed in ways that benefit others and advance His kingdom.

2. Faithful Stewardship of God's Grace: The concept of being "faithful stewards of God's grace" encompasses a broad range of responsibilities, including time, talents, and treasures. Believers are called to use their skills, opportunities, and resources to serve others, reflecting God's generosity and love.

The Bible provides numerous teachings that emphasize the responsibilities that come with wealth, reinforcing the principles of stewardship.

1. The Responsibility of the Rich: 1 Timothy 6:17-19 instructs wealthy believers on how to handle their resources: "Command those who are rich in this present world not to be arrogant nor to put their hope in wealth, which is so uncertain, but to put their hope in God, who richly provides us with

everything for our enjoyment. Command them to do good, to be rich in good deeds, and to be generous and willing to share. In this way, they will lay up treasure for themselves as a firm foundation for the coming age, so that they may take hold of the life that is truly life." This passage underscores the importance of humility, generosity, and good deeds as key aspects of stewardship.

2. Accountability and Judgment: The Bible teaches that everyone will be held accountable for how they manage their resources. Romans 14:12 states, "So then, each of us will give an account of ourselves to God." This accountability motivates believers to handle their resources responsibly, knowing that they will answer to God for their stewardship.

3. Wisdom in Financial Management: Proverbs 21:20 offers practical advice on financial stewardship: "The wise store up choice food and olive oil, but fools gulp theirs down." This verse emphasizes the importance of wise financial management, including saving and prudent use of resources, as part of faithful stewardship.

Understanding the biblical principles of stewardship calls for practical applications in various aspects of life. Here are some ways believers can practice stewardship effectively.

1. Budgeting and Financial Planning: Developing and adhering to a budget helps manage resources wisely. Financial

planning includes setting aside money for savings, investments, and charitable giving. This disciplined approach ensures that resources are used effectively and aligned with God's purposes.

2. Generosity and Giving: Practicing generosity is a key aspect of stewardship. Regular tithing, supporting charitable causes, and helping those in need reflect God's love and fulfill the biblical call to serve others. Proverbs 11:24-25 highlights the blessings of generosity: "One person gives freely, yet gains even more; another withholds unduly but comes to poverty. A generous person will prosper; whoever refreshes others will be refreshed."

3. Investing in God's Kingdom: Investing resources in ways that advance God's kingdom includes supporting ministries, missions, and church projects. By prioritizing spiritual investments, believers contribute to the spread of the Gospel and the growth of the Christian community.

4. Environmental Stewardship: Caring for God's creation is also an aspect of stewardship. Genesis 2:15 instructs, "The Lord God took the man and put him in the Garden of Eden to work it and take care of it." Believers are called to responsibly manage natural resources, promoting sustainability and environmental conservation.

5. Time Management: Stewardship extends to how believers use their time. Ephesians 5:15-16 advises, "Be very

careful, then, how you live—not as unwise but as wise, making the most of every opportunity, because the days are evil." Effective time management involves prioritizing activities that align with God's will and contribute to personal and spiritual growth.

The Bible promises various rewards for those who practice faithful stewardship, both in this life and in eternity.

1. Divine Blessings: Faithful stewardship invites God's blessings. Proverbs 3:9-10 teaches, "Honor the Lord with your wealth, with the firstfruits of all your crops; then your barns will be filled to overflowing, and your vats will brim over with new wine." Honoring God with resources leads to His provision and abundance.

2. Spiritual Growth: Practicing stewardship fosters spiritual growth and a deeper relationship with God. By managing resources according to biblical principles, believers develop qualities such as discipline, generosity, and trust in God's provision.

3. Eternal Rewards: Jesus teaches that faithful stewardship stores up treasures in heaven. Matthew 6:19-21 advises, "Do not store up for yourselves treasures on earth, where moths and vermin destroy, and where thieves break in and steal. But store up for yourselves treasures in heaven, where moths and vermin do not destroy, and where thieves

do not break in and steal. For where your treasure is, there your heart will be also." The eternal rewards of stewardship reflect the lasting impact of using resources for God's purposes.

The Bible provides clear guidance on the responsibilities that come with wealth, emphasizing the concept of stewardship. Through teachings such as the Parable of the Talents and verses like 1 Peter 4:10, believers are called to manage their resources wisely and for God's purposes. Stewardship involves using wealth and other blessings to serve others, reflecting God's generosity and love. By practicing principles of budgeting, generosity, investment in God's kingdom, environmental care, and time management, believers can fulfill their call to stewardship and experience the blessings and rewards that come from faithful management of God's gifts. The biblical foundations of stewardship offer timeless guidance for living a life that honors God and benefits humanity.

CHAPTER 29

THE ETHICAL IMPERATIVE OF STEWARDSHIP

Stewardship involves more than just managing resources; it encompasses ethical responsibility and moral integrity. Wealthy individuals are called to use their resources in ways that align with God's values and contribute to the common good. This chapter explores the ethical imperative of stewardship, drawing on biblical teachings that emphasize the importance of honoring God with wealth, remaining humble, doing good deeds, and being generous. By adhering to these principles, wealthy individuals can ensure their resources are used ethically and for the benefit of society.

1. Prioritizing God in Financial Matters: Proverbs 3:9-10 advises, "Honor the Lord with your wealth, with the firstfruits of all your crops; then your barns will be filled to overflowing, and your vats will brim over with new wine." This passage underscores the importance of prioritizing God

in financial matters. Honoring God with wealth involves recognizing that all resources come from Him and using them in ways that reflect His values and purposes.

2. Ethical Financial Practices: Honoring God with wealth also means engaging in ethical financial practices. This includes honesty in business dealings, fair treatment of employees, and transparency in financial reporting. Proverbs 11:1 states, "The Lord detests dishonest scales, but accurate weights find favor with him." Ethical financial practices build trust and demonstrate a commitment to integrity.

1. Humility and Wealth: The Apostle Paul, in 1 Timothy 6:17-19, provides specific instructions for the wealthy: "Command those who are rich in this present world not to be arrogant nor to put their hope in wealth, which is so uncertain, but to put their hope in God, who richly provides us with everything for our enjoyment." This passage highlights the importance of humility for the wealthy. Recognizing that wealth is a gift from God, not a personal achievement, helps prevent arrogance and fosters a spirit of gratitude and dependence on God.

2. Trusting in God's Provision: Trusting in God's provision rather than relying on wealth is a key aspect of ethical stewardship. Wealth can be uncertain and fleeting, but God's provision is constant and reliable. By putting their hope

in God, wealthy individuals can find security and peace, knowing that He will provide for their needs.

1. The Call to Good Deeds: Paul continues in 1 Timothy 6:18, "Command them to do good, to be rich in good deeds, and to be generous and willing to share." This passage emphasizes that wealth comes with a responsibility to do good deeds. Wealthy individuals are called to use their resources to support charitable causes, help those in need, and contribute to the common good.

2. Generosity as a Virtue: Generosity is a central virtue in the ethical imperative of stewardship. Proverbs 11:25 states, "A generous person will prosper; whoever refreshes others will be refreshed." Generosity not only benefits the recipients but also brings blessings to the giver. By being generous and willing to share, wealthy individuals can create positive ripple effects in their communities and beyond.

1. Philanthropy and Charitable Giving: One of the most effective ways to practice ethical stewardship is through philanthropy and charitable giving. Establishing foundations, supporting nonprofit organizations, and funding community projects are practical ways to use wealth for the common good. Philanthropy addresses various societal issues, from poverty and education to healthcare and environmental conservation.

2. Sustainable and Responsible Investing: Ethical stewardship also involves making investment decisions that align with God's values. This includes avoiding investments in industries or companies that engage in unethical practices and instead supporting those that promote sustainability, social justice, and positive environmental impact. Responsible investing ensures that wealth is used in ways that contribute to a better world.

3. Fair Wages and Employee Welfare: Treating employees fairly and ensuring their welfare is an essential aspect of ethical stewardship. This includes paying fair wages, providing safe working conditions, and offering benefits that support employees' well-being. Colossians 4:1 instructs, "Masters, provide your slaves with what is right and fair, because you know that you also have a Master in heaven." Ethical treatment of employees reflects God's justice and compassion.

4. Advocacy and Social Justice: Wealthy individuals can use their influence to advocate for social justice and policy changes that benefit the marginalized and oppressed. This involves supporting initiatives that address systemic issues such as income inequality, discrimination, and access to education and healthcare. Advocacy for social justice aligns with the biblical call to act justly and love mercy (Micah 6:8).

1. Divine Blessings and Prosperity: Honoring God with wealth and practicing ethical stewardship invite divine blessings. Proverbs 3:9-10 promises that those who honor God with their wealth will experience abundance: "then your barns will be filled to overflowing, and your vats will brim over with new wine." God's blessings manifest in various ways, including financial prosperity, personal fulfillment, and spiritual growth.

2. Eternal Rewards: Ethical stewardship also stores up treasures in heaven. Matthew 6:19-21 teaches, "Do not store up for yourselves treasures on earth, where moths and vermin destroy, and where thieves break in and steal. But store up for yourselves treasures in heaven, where moths and vermin do not destroy, and where thieves do not break in and steal. For where your treasure is, there your heart will be also." The eternal rewards of stewardship reflect the lasting impact of using resources for God's purposes.

3. Positive Impact on Society: Ethical stewardship creates a positive impact on society by addressing critical needs, promoting justice, and improving quality of life. Wealthy individuals who use their resources ethically contribute to the common good, creating stronger, healthier, and more equitable communities.

Stewardship involves more than just managing resources; it encompasses ethical responsibility and moral integrity. Wealthy individuals are called to use their resources in ways that align with God's values and contribute to the common good. By honoring God with wealth, remaining humble, doing good deeds, and being generous, they can practice ethical stewardship effectively. The rewards of ethical stewardship, both in this life and in eternity, affirm its importance as a central tenet of Christian faith and practice. Through philanthropy, responsible investing, fair treatment of employees, and advocacy for social justice, wealthy individuals can ensure their resources are used ethically and for the benefit of society, reflecting the enduring principles of biblical stewardship.

CHAPTER 30

MODERN APPLICATIONS OF STEWARDSHIP

In contemporary society, the principles of stewardship can be applied in various ways. Wealthy individuals have the opportunity to make significant contributions to societal well-being through philanthropy, ethical business practices, and responsible investment. This chapter explores how these modern applications of stewardship align with biblical principles and can lead to positive and lasting impacts on society.

Philanthropy, or the practice of giving to charitable causes, is a powerful way for the wealthy to fulfill their stewardship responsibilities. By supporting initiatives in education, healthcare, poverty alleviation, and other areas, philanthropists can address critical needs and create positive change.

1. Supporting Education: Investing in education can transform lives and communities. Philanthropists can fund scholarships, build schools, and support educational

programs that provide opportunities for disadvantaged students. Programs like the Gates Millennium Scholars Program, funded by the Bill and Melinda Gates Foundation, have enabled thousands of students to pursue higher education and achieve their potential.

2. Improving Healthcare: Philanthropic efforts in healthcare can lead to significant advancements and improve public health. Funding medical research, building hospitals, and supporting healthcare initiatives can save lives and enhance the quality of life for many. The Bill and Melinda Gates Foundation's work in eradicating diseases like malaria and polio exemplifies the impact of strategic philanthropy in healthcare.

3. Poverty Alleviation: Addressing poverty through philanthropy involves supporting initiatives that provide food, shelter, and economic opportunities to those in need. By funding programs that offer job training, microloans, and community development projects, philanthropists can help individuals achieve financial independence and improve their living conditions.

4. Environmental Conservation: Philanthropic efforts in environmental conservation can protect natural resources and promote sustainability. Supporting projects that focus on renewable energy, wildlife preservation, and climate change

mitigation helps ensure a healthier planet for future generations.

Ethical Business Practices: Operating with Integrity and Responsibility

Ethical business practices are another important aspect of modern stewardship. Wealthy individuals who own or lead businesses have the responsibility to ensure their companies operate with integrity, fairness, and a commitment to social responsibility.

1. Fair Treatment of Employees: Ensuring fair wages, safe working conditions, and opportunities for professional growth are essential aspects of ethical business practices. Companies that prioritize employee welfare not only comply with ethical standards but also benefit from increased productivity and employee loyalty.

2. Minimizing Environmental Impact: Businesses have a significant impact on the environment, and it is crucial for companies to adopt sustainable practices. This includes reducing carbon emissions, minimizing waste, and using resources efficiently. Companies like Patagonia and Tesla have set examples by integrating sustainability into their business models.

3. Community Engagement: Businesses can contribute to the communities in which they operate by

supporting local initiatives, providing jobs, and engaging in community service. Corporate social responsibility (CSR) programs enable companies to give back to their communities and foster positive relationships.

4. Transparency and Accountability: Ethical business practices also involve maintaining transparency and accountability in operations. This includes honest communication with stakeholders, ethical marketing practices, and responsible financial reporting. Companies that prioritize transparency build trust and credibility with customers, investors, and the public.

Responsible investment, or investing in companies and projects that align with ethical values and contribute to social good, is another way to practice stewardship. Socially responsible investing (SRI) and environmental, social, and governance (ESG) criteria are frameworks that guide investors in making choices that reflect their values and promote sustainability.

1. Socially Responsible Investing (SRI): SRI involves selecting investments based on ethical criteria, such as avoiding companies involved in harmful industries (e.g., tobacco, firearms) and supporting those that make positive contributions to society. SRI allows investors to align their portfolios with their values while seeking financial returns.

2. Environmental, Social, and Governance (ESG) Criteria: ESG criteria provide a comprehensive framework for evaluating investments based on their environmental impact, social responsibility, and governance practices. Investors use ESG criteria to assess how companies address issues like climate change, human rights, and corporate ethics. ESG investing promotes long-term sustainability and ethical business practices.

3. Impact Investing: Impact investing involves investing in projects and companies that generate measurable social and environmental benefits alongside financial returns. This approach focuses on creating positive change through investments in areas such as renewable energy, affordable housing, and education. Impact investors seek to make a difference while achieving financial goals.

4. Engaging with Companies: Investors can also engage with companies to encourage better ESG practices. Shareholder advocacy and proxy voting allow investors to influence corporate policies and promote ethical practices. By engaging with companies, investors can drive positive change from within.

1. The Bill and Melinda Gates Foundation: The foundation's strategic philanthropy in global health, education, and poverty alleviation has made a significant

impact worldwide. By focusing on high-impact areas and leveraging partnerships, the foundation exemplifies how modern stewardship can address critical global challenges.

2. Patagonia: As an outdoor clothing company, Patagonia has integrated environmental stewardship into its business model. The company donates a portion of its profits to environmental causes, uses sustainable materials, and advocates for climate action. Patagonia's commitment to sustainability demonstrates ethical business practices in action.

3. Generation Investment Management: Co-founded by former Vice President Al Gore, Generation Investment Management focuses on sustainable investing. The firm integrates ESG criteria into its investment decisions and promotes long-term value creation. This approach reflects responsible investment practices that align with ethical values.

4. The Chan Zuckerberg Initiative: Founded by Mark Zuckerberg and Priscilla Chan, the initiative focuses on advancing human potential and promoting equal opportunity. By funding education, healthcare, and social justice projects, the initiative demonstrates how modern philanthropy can drive positive change and address systemic issues.

1. Develop a Stewardship Plan: Creating a comprehensive stewardship plan helps ensure that resources are used effectively and ethically. This involves setting clear

goals, identifying priority areas, and developing strategies for philanthropy, ethical business practices, and responsible investing.

2. Partner with Reputable Organizations: Collaborating with reputable organizations and experts enhances the effectiveness of stewardship efforts. By partnering with established nonprofits, research institutions, and sustainability experts, wealthy individuals can leverage expertise and resources to achieve greater impact.

3. Evaluate Impact and Adjust Strategies: Regularly evaluating the impact of stewardship efforts helps ensure that goals are being met and resources are used efficiently. Continuous assessment and feedback allow for adjustments to strategies and the adoption of best practices.

4. Engage Stakeholders and Communities: Involving stakeholders and communities in stewardship initiatives fosters a sense of ownership and collaboration. Engaging with employees, customers, community members, and other stakeholders helps ensure that efforts are aligned with the needs and values of those affected.

5. Promote a Culture of Stewardship: Encouraging a culture of stewardship within organizations and communities amplifies the impact of individual efforts. By promoting values of generosity, sustainability, and ethical responsibility,

wealthy individuals can inspire others to adopt similar practices.

In contemporary society, the principles of stewardship can be applied in various ways, including philanthropy, ethical business practices, and responsible investment. Wealthy individuals have the opportunity to make significant contributions to societal well-being by supporting initiatives in education, healthcare, poverty alleviation, and environmental conservation. Ethical business practices ensure that companies operate with integrity, fairness, and social responsibility, while responsible investment aligns financial decisions with ethical values and promotes sustainability. By developing a comprehensive stewardship plan, partnering with reputable organizations, evaluating impact, engaging stakeholders, and promoting a culture of stewardship, wealthy individuals can ensure their resources are used effectively and ethically. The modern applications of stewardship reflect enduring biblical principles and contribute to a more just, compassionate, and sustainable world.

CHAPTER 31

THE SPIRITUAL DIMENSIONS OF STEWARDSHIP

Stewardship is not just an ethical duty but a spiritual calling. It involves recognizing that all resources ultimately belong to God and that individuals are caretakers of these blessings. This perspective fosters humility, gratitude, and a sense of purpose. This chapter explores the spiritual dimensions of stewardship, emphasizing the biblical principles that guide believers in managing their resources with a heart aligned with God's will.

1. God as the Ultimate Owner: Psalm 24:1 states, "The earth is the Lord's, and everything in it, the world, and all who live in it." This verse serves as a fundamental reminder that everything we possess is part of God's creation. Recognizing God's ownership of all things helps believers understand that their role is that of a steward, not an owner. This perspective is crucial for fostering a heart of humility and gratitude.

2. Stewardship as Caretaking: As caretakers of God's creation, believers are called to manage resources responsibly and with reverence. This involves using wealth, time, and talents in ways that honor God and reflect His purposes. Luke 12:42-43 illustrates this, where Jesus says, "Who then is the faithful and wise manager, whom the master puts in charge of his servants to give them their food allowance at the proper time? It will be good for that servant whom the master finds doing so when he returns."

1. Fostering Humility: Recognizing that all resources come from God helps foster humility. James 1:17 reminds believers, "Every good and perfect gift is from above, coming down from the Father of the heavenly lights, who does not change like shifting shadows." Acknowledging that our abilities and resources are gifts from God prevents pride and encourages a humble attitude towards wealth and possessions.

2. Cultivating Gratitude: Gratitude is a natural response to recognizing God's provision. Psalm 100:4 encourages believers to "Enter his gates with thanksgiving and his courts with praise; give thanks to him and praise his name." Gratitude for God's blessings motivates believers to use their resources generously and joyfully, reflecting God's generosity to others.

1. Dependence on God: Stewardship involves trusting in God's provision and timing. In Matthew 6:31-33, Jesus

encourages His followers not to worry about material needs but to seek God's kingdom first: "So do not worry, saying, 'What shall we eat?' or 'What shall we drink?' or 'What shall we wear?' For the pagans run after all these things, and your heavenly Father knows that you need them. But seek first his kingdom and his righteousness, and all these things will be given to you as well." This teaching emphasizes that putting God first leads to His provision for our needs.

2. Living by Faith: Trusting in God's provision requires living by faith, especially in managing resources. Hebrews 11:1 defines faith as "confidence in what we hope for and assurance about what we do not see." By placing trust in God's promises, believers can approach stewardship with confidence, knowing that God will provide for their needs as they prioritize His kingdom.

1. Aligning with God's Will: Purposeful stewardship involves aligning one's use of resources with God's will. This means seeking to understand God's purposes and allowing them to guide decisions about wealth, time, and talents. Romans 12:2 advises, "Do not conform to the pattern of this world, but be transformed by the renewing of your mind. Then you will be able to test and approve what God's will is— his good, pleasing and perfect will."

2. Serving Others: One of the primary purposes of stewardship is to serve others. 1 Peter 4:10 instructs, "Each of you should use whatever gift you have received to serve others, as faithful stewards of God's grace in its various forms." This verse highlights that stewardship is not solely for personal benefit but for the well-being of others. Using resources to support charitable causes, help those in need, and contribute to community welfare reflects the heart of true stewardship.

1. Blessings of Giving: Generosity is a key aspect of stewardship that brings joy and blessings. Acts 20:35 quotes Jesus, saying, "It is more blessed to give than to receive." This principle teaches that giving leads to greater fulfillment and joy than hoarding resources. Generosity also opens the door to experiencing God's blessings in various forms.

2. Cheerful Giving: 2 Corinthians 9:6-7 emphasizes the attitude of giving: "Remember this: Whoever sows sparingly will also reap sparingly, and whoever sows generously will also reap generously. Each of you should give what you have decided in your heart to give, not reluctantly or under compulsion, for God loves a cheerful giver." Cheerful giving reflects a heart that is aligned with God's generosity and experiences the joy of participating in His work.

1. Storing Treasures in Heaven: Jesus teaches that true wealth is found in eternal treasures. Matthew 6:19-21 advises, "Do not store up for yourselves treasures on earth, where moths and vermin destroy, and where thieves break in and steal. But store up for yourselves treasures in heaven, where moths and vermin do not destroy, and where thieves do not break in and steal. For where your treasure is, there your heart will be also." This teaching encourages believers to focus on eternal investments that have lasting value.

2. Rewards in Eternity: Faithful stewardship is rewarded in eternity. Matthew 25:21, in the Parable of the Talents, illustrates this reward: "His master replied, 'Well done, good and faithful servant! You have been faithful with a few things; I will put you in charge of many things. Come and share your master's happiness!'" The promise of eternal rewards motivates believers to manage resources with an eternal perspective, prioritizing God's kingdom over temporary earthly gains.

1. Prayer and Discernment: Seeking God's guidance through prayer is essential for spiritual stewardship. Philippians 4:6 encourages believers, "Do not be anxious about anything, but in every situation, by prayer and petition, with thanksgiving, present your requests to God." Prayer

helps discern God's will for managing resources and making decisions that align with His purposes.

2. Scripture Study: Regularly studying the Bible provides wisdom and direction for stewardship. Psalm 119:105 declares, "Your word is a lamp for my feet, a light on my path." Scripture offers principles and examples that guide ethical and purposeful management of resources.

3. Accountability and Community: Engaging in accountability and community support helps maintain faithful stewardship. Proverbs 27:17 states, "As iron sharpens iron, so one person sharpens another." Being part of a community of believers provides encouragement, accountability, and shared wisdom for managing resources effectively.

4. Generosity and Service: Actively seeking opportunities to give and serve reflects the heart of stewardship. Whether through financial donations, volunteering time, or offering talents, practical acts of generosity and service demonstrate commitment to God's kingdom and the well-being of others.

Stewardship is not just an ethical duty but a spiritual calling. Recognizing that all resources ultimately belong to God and viewing oneself as a caretaker fosters humility, gratitude, and a sense of purpose. By trusting in God's provision, aligning with His will, and practicing generosity, believers can fulfill the spiritual dimensions of stewardship.

The joy of giving, the focus on eternal investments, and the promise of rewards in eternity provide motivation and direction for managing resources in ways that honor God and contribute to the common good. Through prayer, Scripture study, accountability, and active service, believers can cultivate a heart of stewardship that reflects God's love and generosity.

CHAPTER 32

CHALLENGES AND REWARDS OF STEWARDSHIP

Practicing stewardship can present challenges, especially in a culture that often equates success with accumulating wealth. The temptation to prioritize personal gain over ethical responsibility can be strong. However, the rewards of faithful stewardship are both temporal and eternal. This chapter explores the challenges and rewards of stewardship, providing biblical insights and practical guidance to help believers navigate these aspects of their spiritual journey.

1. Cultural Pressures: In contemporary society, there is a strong emphasis on material success and personal wealth. This cultural pressure can make it difficult for individuals to prioritize ethical responsibility and generosity over personal gain. The desire for status, luxury, and financial security often conflicts with the principles of stewardship.

2. Temptation to Hoard: The temptation to hoard resources rather than use them for the common good is a

significant challenge. Jesus addresses this in Luke 12:15, saying, "Watch out! Be on your guard against all kinds of greed; life does not consist in an abundance of possessions." The tendency to accumulate wealth for personal comfort can hinder the practice of generous stewardship.

3. Fear of Scarcity: Fear of not having enough can prevent individuals from giving generously. Worries about future financial security, unexpected expenses, and economic downturns can lead to a reluctance to share resources. This fear often stems from a lack of trust in God's provision.

4. Balancing Priorities: Balancing personal financial needs, family responsibilities, and the call to stewardship can be challenging. Determining how much to give, save, and invest requires wisdom and discernment. This balancing act can be difficult, especially when faced with competing demands and limited resources.

5. Complexity of Ethical Choices: Making ethical decisions about how to use wealth can be complex. Issues such as fair wages, ethical investments, and corporate social responsibility involve navigating nuanced and often conflicting values. Determining the most responsible and impactful way to manage resources requires careful consideration and ongoing learning.

1. Sense of Fulfillment: Faithful stewardship leads to a sense of fulfillment and alignment with God's purposes. Knowing that resources are being used to advance God's kingdom and help others provides deep satisfaction and joy. Acts 20:35 quotes Jesus, saying, "It is more blessed to give than to receive."

2. Positive Impact on Society: Stewardship allows individuals to contribute to the well-being of others and make a positive impact on society. Generosity can address critical needs, support important causes, and foster community development. The tangible results of stewardship reflect God's love and justice in practical ways.

3. Joy of Giving: The joy of giving is a significant reward of stewardship. 2 Corinthians 9:7 states, "Each of you should give what you have decided in your heart to give, not reluctantly or under compulsion, for God loves a cheerful giver." Cheerful giving brings joy to both the giver and the recipient, creating a cycle of blessing.

4. Spiritual Growth: Practicing stewardship fosters spiritual growth by developing qualities such as generosity, humility, and trust in God. Stewardship challenges individuals to deepen their faith, rely on God's provision, and prioritize eternal values over temporary gains. This spiritual growth strengthens one's relationship with God.

5. Eternal Rewards: Jesus teaches that faithful stewardship lays up treasures in heaven. In Matthew 6:20-21, He says, "But store up for yourselves treasures in heaven, where moths and vermin do not destroy, and where thieves do not break in and steal. For where your treasure is, there your heart will be also." The eternal rewards of stewardship reflect the lasting impact of using resources for God's purposes.

6. Increased Trust in God: Trusting God with resources and seeing His provision in response to generosity increases faith and reliance on Him. Malachi 3:10 invites believers to test God's faithfulness: "Bring the whole tithe into the storehouse, that there may be food in my house. Test me in this," says the Lord Almighty, "and see if I will not throw open the floodgates of heaven and pour out so much blessing that there will not be room enough to store it."

1. Cultivating a Generous Heart: Developing a generous heart requires intentional effort and practice. Regularly reflecting on God's generosity, practicing gratitude, and seeking opportunities to give can help cultivate a spirit of generosity. Luke 6:38 encourages, "Give, and it will be given to you. A good measure, pressed down, shaken together and running over, will be poured into your lap. For with the measure you use, it will be measured to you."

2. Trusting God's Provision: Overcoming the fear of scarcity involves trusting in God's provision. Matthew 6:31-33 reassures believers that God knows their needs and will provide: "So do not worry, saying, 'What shall we eat?' or 'What shall we drink?' or 'What shall we wear?' For the pagans run after all these things, and your heavenly Father knows that you need them. But seek first his kingdom and his righteousness, and all these things will be given to you as well." Trusting God's faithfulness helps alleviate fears and encourages generous giving.

3. Seeking Wisdom and Counsel: Balancing priorities and making ethical decisions about wealth management requires wisdom and discernment. Seeking guidance from Scripture, prayer, and wise counsel from trusted advisors can help navigate these complexities. Proverbs 15:22 states, "Plans fail for lack of counsel, but with many advisers they succeed."

4. Setting Clear Goals: Establishing clear goals for giving, saving, and investing helps ensure that resources are used effectively and responsibly. Creating a stewardship plan that aligns with God's purposes and reflects personal values can provide direction and accountability.

5. Embracing Community Support: Engaging with a community of believers provides encouragement and support for practicing stewardship. Sharing experiences, learning from

others, and participating in collective acts of generosity can strengthen commitment and provide a sense of shared purpose.

Practicing stewardship can present challenges, especially in a culture that often equates success with accumulating wealth. The temptation to prioritize personal gain over ethical responsibility can be strong. However, the rewards of faithful stewardship are both temporal and eternal. By cultivating a generous heart, trusting in God's provision, seeking wisdom, setting clear goals, and embracing community support, believers can overcome challenges and experience the profound rewards of stewardship.

Faithful stewardship leads to a sense of fulfillment and alignment with God's purposes. It allows individuals to contribute to the well-being of others, make a positive impact on society, and experience the joy of giving. Moreover, stewardship lays up treasures in heaven, as Jesus taught in Matthew 6:20-21: "But store up for yourselves treasures in heaven, where moths and vermin do not destroy, and where thieves do not break in and steal. For where your treasure is, there your heart will be also." Embracing the challenges and rewards of stewardship enables believers to live out their calling and reflect God's love and generosity in the world.

PART VII

OVERCOMING MISCONCEPTIONS

CHAPTER 33

MISCONCEPTION 1: WEALTH IS INHERENTLY EVIL

One of the most pervasive misconceptions is that wealth is inherently evil. This idea is often derived from a misinterpretation of 1 Timothy 6:10, which states, "For the love of money is a root of all kinds of evil." It is crucial to note that the verse does not say money itself is evil but that the love of money—the prioritization of wealth over God and ethical values—can lead to harmful outcomes. This chapter aims to clarify this misconception by examining biblical teachings on wealth and providing examples of how wealth can be used for good.

Clarifying 1 Timothy 6:10

1. Misinterpretation of the Verse: The verse 1 Timothy 6:10 is often quoted incorrectly as "Money is the root of all evil." However, the correct wording is, "For the love of money is a root of all kinds of evil." This distinction is

significant. The verse emphasizes that it is not money itself that is problematic but the excessive desire for it and the unethical actions that may follow.

2. The Love of Money: The love of money refers to placing wealth above God and moral principles. This can lead to various negative behaviors, such as greed, dishonesty, and exploitation. When wealth becomes an idol, it can corrupt one's values and priorities. Matthew 6:24 warns, "No one can serve two masters. Either you will hate the one and love the other, or you will be devoted to the one and despise the other. You cannot serve both God and money."

1. Wealth is Neutral: Wealth, in itself, is neither good nor evil. It is a resource that can be used in different ways depending on the intentions and actions of the person who possesses it. Like any tool, its moral value depends on how it is utilized.

2. Biblical Examples of Righteous Wealth: The Bible provides numerous examples of individuals who were wealthy and used their resources for righteous purposes. These examples demonstrate that wealth can be a blessing when managed with integrity and generosity.

- Abraham: Abraham was a wealthy man blessed with many possessions, yet he remained faithful to God. His wealth was seen as a sign of God's favor, and he used his resources to support his family and others in need. Genesis

13:2 states, "Abram had become very wealthy in livestock and in silver and gold."

- Job: Job was another wealthy individual who is described as "blameless and upright" (Job 1:1). Despite his great wealth, he was known for his generosity and care for the poor and needy. Job 29:12-16 describes his charitable actions: "because I rescued the poor who cried for help, and the fatherless who had none to assist them. The one who was dying blessed me; I made the widow's heart sing. I put on righteousness as my clothing; justice was my robe and my turban. I was eyes to the blind and feet to the lame. I was a father to the needy; I took up the case of the stranger."

- Solomon: King Solomon was renowned for his immense wealth and wisdom. His wealth was a blessing from God, and he used it to build the temple and strengthen his kingdom. 1 Kings 3:13 records God's promise to Solomon: "Moreover, I will give you what you have not asked for—both wealth and honor—so that in your lifetime you will have no equal among kings."

1. Wealth as a Blessing: The Bible also portrays wealth as a blessing from God when it is used according to His will. Proverbs 10:22 states, "The blessing of the Lord brings wealth, without painful toil for it." This suggests that wealth,

when received as a blessing, comes with a sense of peace and purpose.

2. Stewardship of Wealth: Wealth comes with the responsibility of stewardship. Believers are called to manage their resources wisely and use them to advance God's kingdom and help others. 1 Timothy 6:17-19 provides instructions for the wealthy: "Command those who are rich in this present world not to be arrogant nor to put their hope in wealth, which is so uncertain, but to put their hope in God, who richly provides us with everything for our enjoyment. Command them to do good, to be rich in good deeds, and to be generous and willing to share."

1. Charity and Generosity: Wealth can be used to support charitable causes and help those in need. Acts of generosity reflect God's love and bring joy to both the giver and the recipient. 2 Corinthians 9:6-7 emphasizes the importance of cheerful giving: "Remember this: Whoever sows sparingly will also reap sparingly, and whoever sows generously will also reap generously. Each of you should give what you have decided in your heart to give, not reluctantly or under compulsion, for God loves a cheerful giver."

2. Building and Supporting Communities: Wealth can be used to build and support communities by funding infrastructure, education, healthcare, and other essential

services. This creates a positive impact and improves the quality of life for many people.

3. Investing in God's Kingdom: Wealth can be invested in ministries, missions, and church projects that spread the Gospel and support spiritual growth. By using resources to advance God's kingdom, believers fulfill their calling and make a lasting impact.

The misconception that wealth is inherently evil is based on a misinterpretation of biblical teachings. Wealth, in itself, is neutral and can be used for good or ill depending on the intentions and actions of the person who possesses it. The Bible provides numerous examples of wealthy individuals who used their resources for righteous purposes, highlighting that wealth can be a blessing and a tool for doing good when managed with integrity and generosity.

By understanding that it is the love of money, not money itself, that leads to harmful outcomes, believers can embrace the responsibility of stewardship. Wealth can be a powerful force for good, supporting charitable causes, building communities, and advancing God's kingdom. Recognizing the true nature of wealth and its potential for positive impact allows believers to manage their resources in ways that honor God and contribute to the well-being of others.

CHAPTER 34

MISCONCEPTION 2: POVERTY IS A SIGN OF RIGHTEOUSNESS

Another common misconception is that poverty is inherently a sign of righteousness. While the Bible does commend humility and reliance on God, it does not equate financial poverty with spiritual superiority. This chapter explores the biblical perspective on poverty and righteousness, emphasizing that while God calls His followers to humility and compassion, financial poverty is not inherently more virtuous than wealth. Instead, the Bible encourages believers to support the poor and address social injustices, reflecting God's love and justice in their actions.

1. The Beatitudes and Spiritual Poverty: In the Beatitudes, Jesus says, "Blessed are the poor in spirit, for theirs is the kingdom of heaven" (Matthew 5:3). This verse emphasizes spiritual poverty—the recognition of one's need for God—rather than material lack. Spiritual poverty involves humility, acknowledging one's dependence on God, and

seeking His guidance and grace. It is a heart posture that recognizes human limitations and the need for divine intervention.

2. Misinterpretation of Poverty and Righteousness: While the Bible highlights the importance of humility and reliance on God, it does not suggest that financial poverty is a prerequisite for righteousness. Material wealth or poverty, in themselves, do not determine one's spiritual standing. What matters is the attitude of the heart and the way resources are managed and used.

1. Supporting the Poor: The Bible contains numerous exhortations to support the poor and address social injustices. God calls His people to act with compassion and justice, caring for those in need. Isaiah 58:6-7 says, "Is not this the kind of fasting I have chosen: to loose the chains of injustice and untie the cords of the yoke, to set the oppressed free and break every yoke? Is it not to share your food with the hungry and to provide the poor wanderer with shelter—when you see the naked, to clothe them, and not to turn away from your own flesh and blood?" These verses emphasize the responsibility to care for the needy rather than glorifying poverty itself.

2. Jesus' Ministry to the Poor: Jesus' ministry included a strong focus on helping the poor and marginalized. In Luke 4:18-19, Jesus quotes Isaiah, saying, "The Spirit of the Lord is on me, because he has anointed me to proclaim good news to the poor. He has sent me to proclaim freedom for the prisoners and recovery of sight for the blind, to set the oppressed free, to proclaim the year of the Lord's favor." Jesus' actions demonstrated God's love and concern for the poor, and His followers are called to continue this mission.

3. Principles of Generosity and Justice: The Bible advocates for generosity and justice as key principles in dealing with wealth and poverty. Proverbs 19:17 states, "Whoever is kind to the poor lends to the Lord, and he will reward them for what they have done." This verse underscores the importance of generosity and the promise of divine reward for those who help the needy. Similarly, Micah 6:8 calls believers to "act justly and to love mercy and to walk humbly with your God," emphasizing the ethical and compassionate use of resources.

1. Economic Inequality and Oppression: The Bible speaks against economic inequality and oppression, urging believers to work towards justice and equity. In Amos 5:24, the prophet calls for justice to prevail: "But let justice roll on like a river, righteousness like a never-failing stream!" This call

to action emphasizes the need to address systemic injustices and create a fair society.

2. Advocating for the Vulnerable: Believers are called to advocate for the vulnerable and marginalized, ensuring that their needs are met and their rights are protected. Proverbs 31:8-9 advises, "Speak up for those who cannot speak for themselves, for the rights of all who are destitute. Speak up and judge fairly; defend the rights of the poor and needy." Advocacy and action on behalf of the vulnerable are essential aspects of biblical justice.

1. Using Wealth for Good: Wealthy believers have a responsibility to use their resources for the good of others, particularly the poor and marginalized. 1 Timothy 6:17-19 instructs, "Command those who are rich in this present world not to be arrogant nor to put their hope in wealth, which is so uncertain, but to put their hope in God, who richly provides us with everything for our enjoyment. Command them to do good, to be rich in good deeds, and to be generous and willing to share. In this way, they will lay up treasure for themselves as a firm foundation for the coming age, so that they may take hold of the life that is truly life."

2. Stewardship and Generosity: Wealthy believers are called to be good stewards of their resources, using them to support charitable causes, address social injustices, and help

those in need. Generosity is a reflection of God's love and a practical way to demonstrate faith. Acts 20:35 quotes Jesus, saying, "It is more blessed to give than to receive."

1. Charitable Giving: Financial donations to charitable organizations and causes that support the poor and address social injustices are practical ways to make a positive impact. Supporting local food banks, shelters, and international relief efforts can help meet immediate needs and promote long-term development.

2. Volunteering and Advocacy: Volunteering time and skills to support organizations that help the poor is another way to demonstrate compassion and justice. Additionally, advocating for policies and programs that address economic inequality and protect the rights of the vulnerable can create systemic change.

3. Ethical Consumption and Investment: Making ethical choices in consumption and investment can also support the poor. This includes buying fair trade products, supporting businesses that pay fair wages, and investing in companies that prioritize social and environmental responsibility.

The misconception that poverty is inherently a sign of righteousness is based on a misunderstanding of biblical teachings. While the Bible commends humility and reliance on God, it does not equate financial poverty with spiritual superiority. Instead, the Bible encourages believers to support the poor and address social injustices, reflecting God's love and justice in their actions.

By recognizing the distinction between spiritual poverty and material poverty, believers can embrace their responsibility to care for the needy and use their resources ethically. Wealth can be a powerful tool for good when managed with integrity and generosity, and addressing social injustices is an essential aspect of living out one's faith. By supporting charitable causes, volunteering, advocating for the vulnerable, and making ethical choices, believers can demonstrate the true meaning of biblical righteousness and contribute to a more just and compassionate world.

CHAPTER 35

MISCONCEPTION 3: WEALTH IS ALWAYS A SIGN OF DIVINE FAVOR

Conversely, the idea that wealth is always a sign of divine favor is another misconception. While the Bible does show that God can bless individuals with wealth, it also warns against assuming that material prosperity equates to spiritual favor or righteousness. This chapter explores the biblical perspective on wealth and divine favor, emphasizing that wealth should not be seen as a definitive indicator of God's approval. Instead, it highlights the importance of prioritizing one's relationship with God over material wealth.

1. Wealth as a Potential Blessing: The Bible does indicate that wealth can be a blessing from God. For example, in Deuteronomy 8:18, it is written, "But remember the Lord your God, for it is he who gives you the ability to produce wealth, and so confirms his covenant, which he swore to your ancestors, as it is today." This verse acknowledges that God

can provide the means to acquire wealth as part of His blessings.

2. Warning Against Misinterpretation: However, the Bible also warns against interpreting wealth as a sure sign of divine favor. Wealth can come through various means, not all of which align with God's will or reflect His blessing. Therefore, it is essential to discern the true source and purpose of wealth, recognizing that it can be a test of character and faithfulness.

1. A Lesson in Priorities: The story of the rich young ruler, found in Mark 10:17-22, illustrates the challenges wealth can pose to spiritual growth. Despite his wealth and adherence to the commandments, Jesus challenged the young man to sell his possessions and give to the poor. The young man's reluctance to part with his wealth revealed that his attachment to material possessions hindered his relationship with God.

2. Jesus' Teaching on Wealth: Jesus' teaching in this passage underscores that wealth can become a stumbling block if it takes precedence over one's relationship with God. In Mark 10:23-25, Jesus said to His disciples, "How hard it is for the rich to enter the kingdom of God! The disciples were amazed at his words. But Jesus said again, 'Children, how hard it is to enter the kingdom of God! It is easier for a camel to

go through the eye of a needle than for someone who is rich to enter the kingdom of God.'" This teaching highlights the spiritual dangers of wealth when it becomes an idol.

1. Righteousness Over Wealth: The Bible emphasizes that righteousness and a right relationship with God are more important than material wealth. Proverbs 11:4 states, "Wealth is worthless in the day of wrath, but righteousness delivers from death." This verse reminds believers that material wealth cannot save or justify a person; only righteousness can.

2. Warnings Against Wealth's Temptations: Throughout the Bible, there are warnings about the temptations and dangers associated with wealth. 1 Timothy 6:9-10 cautions, "Those who want to get rich fall into temptation and a trap and into many foolish and harmful desires that plunge people into ruin and destruction. For the love of money is a root of all kinds of evil. Some people, eager for money, have wandered from the faith and pierced themselves with many griefs." These verses highlight that the pursuit of wealth can lead to spiritual peril if it becomes an overriding desire.

1. Ananias and Sapphira: The story of Ananias and Sapphira in Acts 5:1-11 serves as a cautionary tale about the misuse of wealth. They sold a piece of property and lied about the proceeds, keeping some for themselves while pretending to donate the full amount to the apostles. Their deceit and

greed led to their sudden deaths, demonstrating the severe consequences of dishonesty and the misuse of wealth.

2. King Solomon's Downfall: Although King Solomon was blessed with immense wisdom and wealth, his later years were marked by a departure from God's ways. His accumulation of wealth, wives, and idolatry led him astray, illustrating that even divinely granted wealth can become a snare if it leads one away from God. 1 Kings 11:1-4 recounts Solomon's downfall: "King Solomon, however, loved many foreign women besides Pharaoh's daughter... As Solomon grew old, his wives turned his heart after other gods, and his heart was not fully devoted to the Lord his God, as the heart of David his father had been."

1. Stewardship and Accountability: The Bible teaches that wealth comes with significant responsibilities. Luke 12:48 states, "From everyone who has been given much, much will be demanded; and from the one who has been entrusted with much, much more will be asked." Wealthy individuals are called to use their resources wisely and for the benefit of others, reflecting God's justice and generosity.

2. Generosity and Compassion: Wealth should be used to support charitable causes, help those in need, and promote justice. 1 Timothy 6:17-19 instructs, "Command those who are rich in this present world not to be arrogant

nor to put their hope in wealth, which is so uncertain, but to put their hope in God, who richly provides us with everything for our enjoyment. Command them to do good, to be rich in good deeds, and to be generous and willing to share. In this way, they will lay up treasure for themselves as a firm foundation for the coming age, so that they may take hold of the life that is truly life."

1. Spiritual Fruit: The true indicators of divine favor are found in the fruits of the Spirit and a life that reflects God's love and righteousness. Galatians 5:22-23 lists the fruits of the Spirit: "But the fruit of the Spirit is love, joy, peace, forbearance, kindness, goodness, faithfulness, gentleness and self-control. Against such things there is no law." These qualities are the evidence of a life aligned with God's will, regardless of material wealth.

2. Faithfulness and Obedience: Faithfulness to God and obedience to His commandments are more significant indicators of divine favor than material wealth. John 14:15 records Jesus' words, "If you love me, keep my commands." A life marked by obedience to God's word and faithfulness to His calling is a true sign of His favor.

The misconception that wealth is always a sign of divine favor is based on a misunderstanding of biblical teachings. While God can bless individuals with wealth, material prosperity should not be seen as a definitive indicator of God's approval or righteousness. The Bible warns against the spiritual dangers of wealth when it takes precedence over one's relationship with God.

True indicators of divine favor are found in spiritual fruit, faithfulness, and obedience to God. Wealth, whether it is seen as a blessing or a responsibility, should be managed with integrity, generosity, and a heart aligned with God's purposes. By prioritizing their relationship with God over material wealth, believers can navigate the challenges and responsibilities of wealth, using their resources to reflect God's love and justice in the world.

CHAPTER 36

MISCONCEPTION 4: GENEROSITY IS ONLY FOR THE WEALTHY

There is a misconception that only wealthy individuals are called to be generous. However, the Bible teaches that generosity is a virtue for all believers, regardless of their financial status. This chapter explores the biblical perspective on generosity, emphasizing that it is an attitude of the heart and a responsibility for all Christians. Through the story of the widow's offering and other biblical examples, we see that generosity is measured by the intention and sacrifice behind the giving, not the amount.

1. The Widow's Offering (Mark 12:41-44): The story of the widow's offering is a powerful testament to the principle that generosity is not about the amount given but the heart and sacrifice behind it. Jesus observed the people putting money into the temple treasury and noted a poor widow who gave two small coins. He said, "Truly I tell you,

this poor widow has put more into the treasury than all the others. They all gave out of their wealth; but she, out of her poverty, put in everything—all she had to live on."

2. Heart and Intention: Jesus commended the widow not because of the monetary value of her offering, but because of the heart and intention behind it. She gave all she had, demonstrating her deep trust in God and her willingness to sacrifice for His purposes. This story highlights that true generosity is about the willingness to give sacrificially, regardless of the amount.

1. Biblical Teachings on Generosity for All: The Bible consistently teaches that generosity is a virtue for all believers, not just the wealthy. In 2 Corinthians 9:7, Paul writes, "Each of you should give what you have decided in your heart to give, not reluctantly or under compulsion, for God loves a cheerful giver." This instruction is for everyone, regardless of financial status, encouraging all believers to give with a willing and joyful heart.

2. The Macedonian Churches (2 Corinthians 8:1-4): Paul commended the Macedonian churches for their generosity despite their extreme poverty. He wrote, "In the midst of a very severe trial, their overflowing joy and their extreme poverty welled up in rich generosity. For I testify that they gave as much as they were able, and even beyond their

ability. Entirely on their own, they urgently pleaded with us for the privilege of sharing in this service to the Lord's people." Their example shows that generosity is possible even in difficult circumstances and that it stems from a willing heart.

1. Giving Time and Talents: Generosity is not limited to financial giving. Believers can also be generous with their time and talents. Volunteering for church activities, helping neighbors, and offering skills to support community projects are valuable forms of generosity that contribute to the well-being of others.

2. Acts of Kindness: Simple acts of kindness, such as providing a meal for someone in need, offering a listening ear, or helping with household tasks, can have a significant impact. These acts demonstrate love and care, reflecting the heart of generosity.

3. Sharing Resources: Sharing resources, such as food, clothing, and household items, is another practical way to practice generosity. Donating to local shelters, food banks, and community organizations helps meet the needs of those who are less fortunate.

4. Hospitality: Practicing hospitality by opening one's home to others, whether for a meal, a gathering, or providing temporary shelter, is a meaningful way to show generosity.

Romans 12:13 encourages believers to "share with the Lord's people who are in need. Practice hospitality."

1. Blessing Others: Generosity has a profound impact on those who receive it. It can provide relief in times of need, offer encouragement, and demonstrate God's love in tangible ways. Acts of generosity can inspire hope and strengthen the faith of both the giver and the receiver.

2. Building Community: Generosity fosters a sense of community and connectedness. When individuals share their resources and time, it creates bonds of trust and mutual support. This sense of community reflects the early church, where believers "were together and had everything in common" (Acts 2:44).

3. Spiritual Growth: Practicing generosity contributes to spiritual growth by developing qualities such as selflessness, compassion, and trust in God's provision. Jesus taught that "it is more blessed to give than to receive" (Acts 20:35), highlighting the joy and fulfillment that come from generous living.

1. Fear of Scarcity: One common barrier to generosity is the fear of not having enough. Trusting in God's provision is key to overcoming this fear. Philippians 4:19 reassures believers, "And my God will meet all your needs according to the riches of his glory in Christ Jesus." Faith in God's

abundant provision enables believers to give generously, knowing that He will take care of their needs.

2. Cultural Pressures: Cultural pressures to accumulate wealth and prioritize personal gain can hinder generosity. Countering these pressures involves embracing biblical values and seeking to live counterculturally. Romans 12:2 encourages believers, "Do not conform to the pattern of this world, but be transformed by the renewing of your mind."

3. Materialism: Materialism, or the excessive focus on acquiring and possessing material goods, can stifle generosity. Cultivating a heart of contentment and gratitude helps combat materialism. Hebrews 13:5 advises, "Keep your lives free from the love of money and be content with what you have, because God has said, 'Never will I leave you; never will I forsake you.'"

1. Teaching and Preaching: Church leaders and teachers can encourage a culture of generosity by teaching biblical principles and sharing examples of generosity from Scripture and contemporary life. Regular messages on the importance of giving and stewardship help foster a generous spirit within the congregation.

2. Modeling Generosity: Leaders and mature believers can model generosity by their actions. Seeing others practice generosity can inspire and motivate others to do the same.

Leading by example demonstrates the joy and impact of generous living.

3. Community Initiatives: Organizing community initiatives and service projects provides practical opportunities for individuals to practice generosity. These initiatives can address local needs and involve members in collective acts of giving, strengthening the sense of community and shared purpose.

The misconception that generosity is only for the wealthy is based on a misunderstanding of biblical teachings. The Bible teaches that generosity is a virtue for all believers, regardless of their financial status. The story of the widow's offering and other examples in Scripture highlight that true generosity is measured by the heart and intention behind the giving, not the amount.

Generosity is an attitude of the heart and a responsibility for all Christians. By practicing generosity through giving time, talents, resources, and hospitality, believers can make a significant impact on the well-being of others and build a sense of community. Overcoming barriers to generosity involves trusting in God's provision, countering cultural pressures, and cultivating contentment. Encouraging a culture of generosity through teaching, modeling, and community initiatives helps foster a generous spirit within the church and beyond.

Generosity reflects God's love and compassion, bringing joy and fulfillment to both the giver and the receiver. By embracing the call to generosity, believers can contribute to a more compassionate and just world, demonstrating the heart of God in their actions.

CHAPTER 37

MISCONCEPTION 5: FINANCIAL SUCCESS EQUALS SPIRITUAL SUCCESS

Another common misconception is that financial success equates to spiritual success. While financial prosperity can be a sign of hard work and wise stewardship, it does not necessarily reflect one's spiritual health or relationship with God. This chapter explores the biblical perspective on financial and spiritual success, emphasizing that true spiritual success is measured by faith, character, and obedience to God's commandments. The fruit of the Spirit, as described in Galatians 5:22-23, are indicators of spiritual health, not material wealth.

1. Storing Up Treasures in Heaven: In Matthew 6:19-21, Jesus cautioned against equating wealth with spiritual favor: "Do not store up for yourselves treasures on earth, where moths and vermin destroy, and where thieves break in and steal. But store up for yourselves treasures in heaven,

where moths and vermin do not destroy, and where thieves do not break in and steal. For where your treasure is, there your heart will be also." Jesus emphasized that true value lies in heavenly treasures, which are eternal, rather than earthly wealth, which is temporary.

2. The Rich Fool (Luke 12:16-21): Jesus also told the parable of the rich fool, who amassed great wealth but failed to recognize his spiritual poverty. In the parable, the rich man planned to store his surplus grain and live a life of ease, but God said to him, "You fool! This very night your life will be demanded from you. Then who will get what you have prepared for yourself?" Jesus concluded, "This is how it will be with whoever stores up things for themselves but is not rich toward God." This parable underscores the futility of relying on wealth for security and the importance of being "rich toward God."

1. Faith and Obedience: True spiritual success is measured by one's faith and obedience to God's commandments. In John 14:15, Jesus said, "If you love me, keep my commands." Faithful adherence to God's word and a life lived in accordance with His will are the hallmarks of spiritual success.

2. The Fruit of the Spirit: Galatians 5:22-23 describes the fruit of the Spirit, which are indicators of a healthy spiritual life: "But the fruit of the Spirit is love, joy, peace,

forbearance, kindness, goodness, faithfulness, gentleness and self-control. Against such things there is no law." These attributes reflect a transformed character and a life led by the Holy Spirit.

3. Character and Integrity: Spiritual success is also reflected in one's character and integrity. Proverbs 11:3 states, "The integrity of the upright guides them, but the unfaithful are destroyed by their duplicity." A person of integrity lives in a manner consistent with God's principles, displaying honesty, humility, and righteousness.

1. Wealth as a Distraction: Wealth can become a distraction from spiritual growth and dependence on God. In Matthew 19:24, Jesus remarked, "Again I tell you, it is easier for a camel to go through the eye of a needle than for someone who is rich to enter the kingdom of God." Wealth can lead to self-reliance and a diminished sense of need for God, making it difficult to maintain a humble and dependent heart.

2. The Laodicean Church (Revelation 3:17-18): The church in Laodicea was rebuked for its complacency and self-sufficiency. Revelation 3:17-18 records Jesus' words to them: "You say, 'I am rich; I have acquired wealth and do not need a thing.' But you do not realize that you are wretched, pitiful, poor, blind and naked. I counsel you to buy from me gold

refined in the fire, so you can become rich; and white clothes to wear, so you can cover your shameful nakedness; and salve to put on your eyes, so you can see." This passage highlights the danger of equating material wealth with spiritual health and the need for true spiritual riches.

1. Wise Stewardship: Financial success can be a sign of wise stewardship, but it should be balanced with a focus on spiritual growth. 1 Timothy 6:17-19 advises, "Command those who are rich in this present world not to be arrogant nor to put their hope in wealth, which is so uncertain, but to put their hope in God, who richly provides us with everything for our enjoyment. Command them to do good, to be rich in good deeds, and to be generous and willing to share. In this way they will lay up treasure for themselves as a firm foundation for the coming age, so that they may take hold of the life that is truly life." This passage encourages believers to use their wealth responsibly and prioritize good deeds and generosity.

2. Spiritual Disciplines: Maintaining spiritual disciplines such as prayer, Bible study, worship, and fellowship helps believers stay focused on their relationship with God. These practices nurture spiritual health and ensure that material pursuits do not overshadow spiritual growth.

3. Generosity and Service: Using financial resources to serve others and support God's work reflects true spiritual

success. Acts 20:35 quotes Jesus, saying, "It is more blessed to give than to receive." Generosity and service align believers' hearts with God's purposes and contribute to their spiritual maturity.

1. Evaluate Priorities: Regularly evaluate your priorities to ensure that your pursuit of financial success does not overshadow your relationship with God. Reflect on Matthew 6:33, "But seek first his kingdom and his righteousness, and all these things will be given to you as well." Keep God's kingdom and righteousness at the forefront of your life.

2. Cultivate Humility: Cultivate humility by recognizing that all blessings, including financial success, come from God. James 1:17 reminds us, "Every good and perfect gift is from above, coming down from the Father of the heavenly lights, who does not change like shifting shadows." A humble heart acknowledges God's sovereignty and grace.

3. Engage in Community: Engage in a community of believers who can provide support, accountability, and encouragement. Hebrews 10:24-25 encourages believers to "consider how we may spur one another on toward love and good deeds, not giving up meeting together, as some are in the habit of doing, but encouraging one another—and all the

more as you see the Day approaching." Fellowship with other believers helps maintain spiritual focus and growth.

4. Practice Generosity: Regularly practice generosity by giving to those in need and supporting charitable causes. Proverbs 22:9 states, "The generous will themselves be blessed, for they share their food with the poor." Generosity reflects God's love and helps align your heart with His purposes.

The misconception that financial success equates to spiritual success is based on a misunderstanding of biblical teachings. While financial prosperity can be a sign of hard work and wise stewardship, it does not necessarily reflect one's spiritual health or relationship with God. True spiritual success is measured by faith, character, and obedience to God's commandments. The fruit of the Spirit—love, joy, peace, patience, kindness, goodness, faithfulness, gentleness, and self-control—are indicators of spiritual health, not material wealth.

Jesus' teachings and the examples in Scripture emphasize the importance of prioritizing one's relationship with God over material pursuits. Wealth can become a distraction and lead to spiritual complacency if not managed wisely. By balancing financial and spiritual pursuits, practicing wise stewardship, and maintaining spiritual disciplines, believers can foster true spiritual success.

Ultimately, true spiritual success is reflected in a life that seeks God's kingdom first, demonstrates the fruit of the Spirit, and uses financial resources to serve others and support God's work. By embracing these principles, believers can navigate the challenges of wealth and maintain a healthy, vibrant relationship with God.

CHAPTER 38

FOSTERING A BALANCED PERSPECTIVE

To foster a balanced perspective on wealth and spirituality, it is essential to integrate biblical principles and practical wisdom. This chapter outlines key points to consider in developing a healthy approach to wealth that aligns with God's purposes and promotes spiritual growth. By viewing wealth as a tool, practicing generosity, prioritizing spiritual growth, embracing stewardship, and avoiding comparisons, believers can navigate the challenges and responsibilities that come with financial resources.

1. Wealth as a Means to Fulfill God's Purposes: Wealth should be seen as a means to fulfill God's purposes and serve others, not as an end in itself. Proverbs 3:9-10 encourages honoring God with one's wealth: "Honor the Lord with your wealth, with the firstfruits of all your crops; then your barns will be filled to overflowing, and your vats will brim over with new wine." This perspective helps

believers focus on using their resources to advance God's kingdom and support those in need.

2. Avoiding Materialism: By viewing wealth as a tool rather than a goal, believers can avoid the pitfalls of materialism. Materialism prioritizes the accumulation of possessions over spiritual growth and can lead to a sense of emptiness and dissatisfaction. 1 Timothy 6:10 warns, "For the love of money is a root of all kinds of evil." Keeping wealth in its proper place helps maintain a balanced and healthy approach to financial resources.

1. Generosity Reflects God's Character: Regardless of financial status, believers are called to be generous. Generosity reflects God's character and helps build a compassionate and just society. 2 Corinthians 9:7 reminds us, "Each of you should give what you have decided in your heart to give, not reluctantly or under compulsion, for God loves a cheerful giver." By practicing generosity, believers demonstrate God's love and care for others.

2. The Joy of Giving: Generosity brings joy and fulfillment to both the giver and the receiver. Acts 20:35 quotes Jesus, saying, "It is more blessed to give than to receive." Giving helps foster a sense of purpose and connection with others, contributing to a vibrant and supportive community.

3. Practical Ways to Be Generous: Generosity can be practiced in various ways, including financial donations, volunteering time and talents, offering hospitality, and providing emotional support. These acts of kindness and compassion make a significant impact on the lives of others and reflect the heart of Christ.

1. Focus on Relationship with God: Spiritual growth should be prioritized over material pursuits. Developing a strong relationship with God involves regular prayer, Bible study, worship, and fellowship with other believers. Matthew 6:33 emphasizes the importance of seeking God first: "But seek first his kingdom and his righteousness, and all these things will be given to you as well."

2. Growing in Spiritual Maturity: Spiritual maturity involves developing the fruit of the Spirit—love, joy, peace, patience, kindness, goodness, faithfulness, gentleness, and self-control (Galatians 5:22-23). These qualities reflect a life transformed by the Holy Spirit and demonstrate true spiritual success.

3. Avoiding Distractions: Wealth should not distract from one's commitment to faith and obedience to God's commands. Regularly evaluating priorities and making intentional choices to focus on spiritual growth helps maintain a balanced perspective. Colossians 3:2 advises, "Set your minds on things above, not on earthly things."

1. Recognize God's Ownership: Embracing stewardship involves recognizing that all resources ultimately belong to God and that individuals are stewards entrusted to manage them wisely. This perspective fosters humility, responsibility, and gratitude. Psalm 24:1 states, "The earth is the Lord's, and everything in it, the world, and all who live in it."

2. Managing Resources Wisely: Good stewardship involves making wise decisions about how to use resources, including budgeting, saving, investing, and giving. Proverbs 21:20 highlights the importance of wise management: "The wise store up choice food and olive oil, but fools gulp theirs down." By managing resources responsibly, believers honor God and ensure that their wealth is used for His purposes.

3. Accountability and Transparency: Being accountable and transparent in financial matters is a key aspect of stewardship. Seeking counsel from trusted advisors and being open about financial practices helps maintain integrity and trustworthiness.

1. Focus on Individual Calling: Spiritual health and God's favor are not measured by financial status. Each person has a unique calling and set of circumstances. Avoid comparing your wealth with others, and instead, focus on how you can use your resources to honor God and help others.

John 21:22 records Jesus' words to Peter, "If I want him to remain alive until I return, what is that to you? You must follow me." This highlights the importance of focusing on one's own path and calling.

2. Contentment and Gratitude: Cultivating contentment and gratitude helps avoid the trap of comparison. Philippians 4:12-13 demonstrates Paul's contentment in all circumstances: "I know what it is to be in need, and I know what it is to have plenty. I have learned the secret of being content in any and every situation, whether well fed or hungry, whether living in plenty or in want. I can do all this through him who gives me strength." By focusing on God's provision and being thankful for what we have, we can maintain a balanced perspective.

3. Encouraging Others: Instead of comparing, seek to encourage and support others in their journey. Hebrews 10:24-25 encourages believers to "consider how we may spur one another on toward love and good deeds, not giving up meeting together, as some are in the habit of doing, but encouraging one another—and all the more as you see the Day approaching." Building each other up fosters a sense of community and shared purpose.

Fostering a balanced perspective on wealth and spirituality involves integrating biblical principles and practical wisdom. By viewing wealth as a tool rather than a goal, practicing generosity, prioritizing spiritual growth, embracing stewardship, and avoiding comparisons, believers can navigate the challenges and responsibilities that come with financial resources.

Wealth should be used to fulfill God's purposes and serve others, reflecting His character and building a compassionate society. True spiritual success is measured by one's faith, character, and obedience to God, not by material wealth. By focusing on a strong relationship with God and growing in spiritual maturity, believers can maintain a balanced perspective that honors God and benefits others.

Ultimately, fostering a balanced perspective on wealth and spirituality leads to a life of purpose, joy, and fulfillment, aligned with God's will and reflecting His love in the world. By embracing these principles, believers can navigate the complexities of wealth and spirituality with wisdom and grace, contributing to a just and compassionate society.

PART VIII

SPIRITUAL PRINCIPLES OF PROSPERITY

CHAPTER 39

PRINCIPLE 1: FAITH AND TRUST IN GOD

At the core of spiritual prosperity is unwavering faith and trust in God. Proverbs 3:5-6 advises, "Trust in the Lord with all your heart and lean not on your own understanding; in all your ways submit to him, and he will make your paths straight." Trusting God involves believing that He will provide for our needs and guide us in making wise financial decisions. This chapter explores the importance of faith and trust in God, emphasizing that true faith is not just passive belief but active trust that manifests in our actions and decisions.

1. Defining Faith: Faith is the foundation of a believer's relationship with God. Hebrews 11:1 defines faith as "confidence in what we hope for and assurance about what we do not see." Faith involves trusting in God's character, promises, and providence, even when circumstances are uncertain.

2. Trusting God's Provision: Trusting God means believing that He will provide for our needs. Philippians 4:19 reassures us, "And my God will meet all your needs according to the riches of his glory in Christ Jesus." This trust allows believers to rest in God's care and provision, freeing them from anxiety about material needs.

3. Active Trust: True faith is not passive; it involves active trust that manifests in our decisions and actions. James 2:17 states, "In the same way, faith by itself, if it is not accompanied by action, is dead." Active trust means seeking God's guidance, making decisions that align with His will, and stepping out in faith even when the path is unclear.

1. Prayer: Prayer is a crucial aspect of seeking God's guidance. Philippians 4:6 encourages believers, "Do not be anxious about anything, but in every situation, by prayer and petition, with thanksgiving, present your requests to God." Through prayer, believers can seek God's wisdom and direction in financial matters, asking for His help in making wise decisions.

2. Studying God's Word: The Bible provides timeless principles and guidance for managing finances. Psalm 119:105 declares, "Your word is a lamp for my feet, a light on my path." By studying Scripture, believers can gain insights into God's will and apply biblical principles to their financial decisions.

3. Listening to the Holy Spirit: The Holy Spirit plays a vital role in guiding believers. John 16:13 promises, "But when he, the Spirit of truth, comes, he will guide you into all the truth." Being attentive to the leading of the Holy Spirit helps believers discern God's will and make decisions that align with His purposes.

1. Surrendering Control: Trusting God involves surrendering control of financial matters to Him. Proverbs 3:5-6 instructs, "Trust in the Lord with all your heart and lean not on your own understanding; in all your ways submit to him, and he will make your paths straight." Surrendering control means acknowledging that God knows what is best and relying on His wisdom rather than our own.

2. Making Ethical Choices: Faith and trust in God lead to making ethical financial decisions. Proverbs 10:2 warns, "Ill-gotten treasures have no lasting value, but righteousness delivers from death." By prioritizing integrity and righteousness in financial matters, believers honor God and reflect their trust in His provision.

3. Generosity and Stewardship: Trusting God also involves being generous and practicing good stewardship. Proverbs 11:25 states, "A generous person will prosper; whoever refreshes others will be refreshed." By giving generously and managing resources wisely, believers

demonstrate their faith in God's provision and commitment to His purposes.

1. Dealing with Fear and Anxiety: Financial challenges can cause fear and anxiety, but trusting God involves casting these cares on Him. 1 Peter 5:7 advises, "Cast all your anxiety on him because he cares for you." Believers can overcome fear by focusing on God's faithfulness and promises.

2. Facing Uncertainty: Life is often uncertain, and financial situations can change unexpectedly. Trusting God means having faith that He is in control, even when circumstances are unclear. Isaiah 26:3-4 provides comfort: "You will keep in perfect peace those whose minds are steadfast because they trust in you. Trust in the Lord forever, for the Lord, the Lord himself, is the Rock eternal."

3. Resisting Temptation: Trusting God also involves resisting the temptation to take shortcuts or compromise ethical standards for financial gain. 1 Corinthians 10:13 encourages, "No temptation has overtaken you except what is common to mankind. And God is faithful; he will not let you be tempted beyond what you can bear. But when you are tempted, he will also provide a way out so that you can endure it." By relying on God's strength, believers can remain faithful and make righteous choices.

1. Peace and Contentment: Trusting God brings peace and contentment, knowing that He will provide and guide.

Philippians 4:6-7 promises, "Do not be anxious about anything, but in every situation, by prayer and petition, with thanksgiving, present your requests to God. And the peace of God, which transcends all understanding, will guard your hearts and your minds in Christ Jesus." This peace is a profound reward of trusting God.

2. Spiritual Growth: Faith and trust in God lead to spiritual growth, as believers learn to depend on Him and align their lives with His will. James 1:2-4 encourages believers to see trials as opportunities for growth: "Consider it pure joy, my brothers and sisters, whenever you face trials of many kinds, because you know that the testing of your faith produces perseverance. Let perseverance finish its work so that you may be mature and complete, not lacking anything."

3. Blessings and Provision: God promises to bless and provide for those who trust in Him. Malachi 3:10 invites believers to test God's faithfulness: "Bring the whole tithe into the storehouse, that there may be food in my house. Test me in this," says the Lord Almighty, "and see if I will not throw open the floodgates of heaven and pour out so much blessing that there will not be room enough to store it." God's provision and blessings are tangible rewards of faith and trust.

1. Daily Prayer and Devotion: Cultivate faith and trust by setting aside time for daily prayer and devotion. This

practice strengthens your relationship with God and helps you rely on His guidance.

2. Meditate on Scripture: Regularly meditate on Scripture that reinforces trust in God's provision and faithfulness. Verses such as Proverbs 3:5-6 and Philippians 4:6-7 can provide encouragement and strength.

3. Join a Faith Community: Being part of a faith community provides support and encouragement. Engage in fellowship with other believers who can offer wisdom, pray with you, and share their experiences of God's faithfulness.

4. Keep a Gratitude Journal: Keep a gratitude journal to record instances of God's provision and answered prayers. Reflecting on these moments can strengthen your faith and remind you of God's faithfulness.

5. Act in Faith: Step out in faith by making decisions that reflect your trust in God. Whether it's giving generously, making ethical choices, or pursuing a calling that requires faith, act on your belief that God will provide and guide.

At the core of spiritual prosperity is unwavering faith and trust in God. Proverbs 3:5-6 advises, "Trust in the Lord with all your heart and lean not on your own understanding; in all your ways submit to him, and he will make your paths straight." Trusting God involves believing that He will provide for our needs and guide us in making wise financial decisions. True faith is not just passive belief but active trust that manifests in our actions and decisions.

By seeking God's guidance through prayer, studying His Word, and being attentive to the Holy Spirit, believers can make decisions that align with God's will. Trusting God in financial matters means surrendering control, making ethical choices, practicing generosity, and embracing stewardship. Overcoming challenges to faith and trust involves dealing with fear and anxiety, facing uncertainty, and resisting temptation.

The rewards of faith and trust include peace, contentment, spiritual growth, and God's blessings and provision. By cultivating faith and trust through daily prayer, meditation on Scripture, engaging with a faith community, keeping a gratitude journal, and acting in faith, believers can navigate financial matters with confidence and align their lives with God's purposes.

CHAPTER 40

PRINCIPLE 2: OBEDIENCE OF GOD'S COMMANDS

Obedience to God's commands is a fundamental principle of prosperity. Deuteronomy 28:1-2 promises blessings for obedience: "If you fully obey the Lord your God and carefully follow all his commands I give you today, the Lord your God will set you high above all the nations on earth. All these blessings will come on you and accompany you if you obey the Lord your God." This chapter explores the importance of obedience, emphasizing that living a life of integrity, honesty, and righteousness is essential for true prosperity.

1. Biblical Promises: Throughout the Bible, God promises blessings for those who obey His commands. Deuteronomy 28:1-2 is a clear example, where God assures that obedience will lead to blessings that will "come on you and accompany you." These blessings encompass various aspects of life, including health, family, work, and community.

2. Holistic Prosperity: The blessings promised for obedience are not limited to material wealth but include holistic prosperity—well-being in all areas of life. This includes peace, joy, strong relationships, and spiritual growth. Psalm 1:1-3 describes the blessed person as one who delights in God's law, comparing them to a tree planted by streams of water that yields fruit in season and prospers in all they do.

1. Integrity in Financial Dealings: Integrity is a cornerstone of obedience to God's commands. Proverbs 10:9 states, "Whoever walks in integrity walks securely, but whoever takes crooked paths will be found out." In financial dealings, integrity involves being honest, transparent, and fair. It means avoiding deceit, fraud, and unethical practices.

2. Honesty in All Actions: Honesty is crucial in maintaining trust and building a good reputation. Proverbs 11:1 emphasizes the importance of honesty: "The Lord detests dishonest scales, but accurate weights find favor with him." Whether in business, personal finances, or everyday interactions, honesty reflects a commitment to God's standards.

3. Righteousness and Ethical Principles: Righteousness involves living according to God's standards and principles. This includes treating others fairly, practicing justice, and showing compassion. Micah 6:8 encapsulates this

call to righteousness: "He has shown you, O mortal, what is good. And what does the Lord require of you? To act justly and to love mercy and to walk humbly with your God."

1. Avoiding Dishonest Gain: God's commands clearly prohibit dishonest gain. Proverbs 13:11 warns, "Dishonest money dwindles away, but whoever gathers money little by little makes it grow." Believers are called to earn and manage their money ethically, avoiding practices such as fraud, exploitation, and bribery.

2. Fair Treatment of Others: Obedience to God's commands includes treating others fairly and with respect. James 5:4 condemns exploitation: "Look! The wages you failed to pay the workers who mowed your fields are crying out against you. The cries of the harvesters have reached the ears of the Lord Almighty." Fair wages, just treatment of employees, and ethical business practices are essential aspects of obedience.

3. Generosity and Compassion: Ethical financial dealings also involve generosity and compassion. Proverbs 19:17 states, "Whoever is kind to the poor lends to the Lord, and he will reward them for what they have done." Generosity towards those in need and a commitment to social justice are expressions of obedience to God's commands.

1. Aligning with God's Will: Obedience aligns believers with God's will and purposes. John 14:15 records

Jesus' words, "If you love me, keep my commands." Obedience is a response to God's love and an expression of our commitment to His will. It deepens our relationship with Him and aligns our actions with His desires.

2. Building Trust in God: Obedience builds trust in God. By following His commands, believers demonstrate their trust in His wisdom and goodness. Proverbs 3:5-6 advises, "Trust in the Lord with all your heart and lean not on your own understanding; in all your ways submit to him, and he will make your paths straight." Trusting and obeying God leads to guidance and blessings.

3. Experiencing God's Presence: Obedience fosters a deeper experience of God's presence. John 14:23 promises, "Jesus replied, 'Anyone who loves me will obey my teaching. My Father will love them, and we will come to them and make our home with them.'" Living in obedience brings believers closer to God and opens their lives to His presence and work.

1. Dealing with Temptations: Temptations to compromise integrity and honesty are common, but God provides strength to overcome them. 1 Corinthians 10:13 reassures, "No temptation has overtaken you except what is common to mankind. And God is faithful; he will not let you be tempted beyond what you can bear. But when you are tempted, he will also provide a way out so that you can endure

it." By relying on God's strength, believers can resist temptations and remain obedient.

2. Facing Opposition: Obedience to God's commands may sometimes lead to opposition or persecution. 2 Timothy 3:12 notes, "In fact, everyone who wants to live a godly life in Christ Jesus will be persecuted." Despite challenges, believers are called to remain steadfast in their commitment to God's commands, trusting in His justice and vindication.

3. Persevering in Difficult Circumstances: Obedience may be tested in difficult circumstances, such as financial hardship or moral dilemmas. James 1:12 encourages perseverance: "Blessed is the one who perseveres under trial because, having stood the test, that person will receive the crown of life that the Lord has promised to those who love him." Perseverance in obedience brings spiritual growth and eventual reward.

1. God's Favor and Blessings: Deuteronomy 28:1-2 promises that obedience brings God's favor and blessings. These blessings are comprehensive, covering various aspects of life and ensuring holistic prosperity. Experiencing God's favor is a profound reward of obedience.

2. Inner Peace and Joy: Obedience brings inner peace and joy, knowing that one is living according to God's will. Psalm 119:165 declares, "Great peace have those who love your law, and nothing can make them stumble." This peace

and joy are a deep-seated result of aligning one's life with God's commands.

3. Eternal Rewards: Obedience to God's commands also brings eternal rewards. Revelation 22:14 promises, "Blessed are those who wash their robes, that they may have the right to the tree of life and may go through the gates into the city." The eternal rewards of obedience include access to eternal life and fellowship with God.

1. Regularly Study God's Word: Cultivate obedience by regularly studying God's Word to understand His commands and principles. Psalm 119:105 says, "Your word is a lamp for my feet, a light on my path." Scripture provides guidance and clarity for living a life of obedience.

2. Pray for Strength and Guidance: Pray for strength and guidance to obey God's commands, especially in challenging situations. Philippians 4:6 encourages believers to present their requests to God with thanksgiving, trusting Him for help and direction.

3. Seek Accountability: Engage in accountability with other believers who can provide support and encouragement in your commitment to obedience. Proverbs 27:17 states, "As iron sharpens iron, so one person sharpens another." Accountability helps maintain integrity and faithfulness.

4. Reflect on God's Faithfulness: Reflect on God's faithfulness and past blessings as motivation to continue in obedience. Psalm 77:11 encourages remembrance: "I will remember the deeds of the Lord; yes, I will remember your miracles of long ago." Remembering God's faithfulness strengthens resolve to obey.

Obedience to God's commands is a fundamental principle of prosperity. Deuteronomy 28:1-2 promises blessings for obedience: "If you fully obey the Lord your God and carefully follow all his commands I give you today, the Lord your God will set you high above all the nations on earth. All these blessings will come on you and accompany you if you obey the Lord your God." Living a life of integrity, honesty, and righteousness is essential for true prosperity.

By embracing ethical principles in financial dealings, treating others fairly, and practicing generosity, believers can demonstrate their commitment to God's commands. Obedience aligns believers with God's will, builds trust, and fosters a deeper experience of His presence. Overcoming challenges to obedience involves dealing with temptations, facing opposition, and persevering in difficult circumstances.

The rewards of obedience include God's favor and blessings, inner peace and joy, and eternal rewards. By regularly studying God's Word, praying for strength and guidance, seeking accountability, and reflecting on God's faithfulness, believers can cultivate a life of obedience that leads to holistic prosperity and spiritual growth.

CHAPTER 41

PRINCIPLE 3: GENEROSITY AND GIVING

Generosity is a cornerstone of spiritual prosperity. Luke 6:38 emphasizes the reciprocal nature of giving: "Give, and it will be given to you. A good measure, pressed down, shaken together, and running over, will be poured into your lap. For with the measure you use, it will be measured to you." Generosity reflects God's character and opens the door to His blessings. This chapter explores the biblical principle of generosity, its various forms, and the understanding that all we have belongs to God, making us stewards of His blessings.

The Biblical Basis for Generosity

1. God's Generosity: God's nature is fundamentally generous. He gives abundantly and without reservation. John 3:16 highlights the ultimate act of divine generosity: "For God so loved the world that he gave his one and only Son, that whoever believes in him shall not perish but have eternal life." Reflecting God's character involves practicing generosity in our own lives.

2. The Principle of Reciprocity: Luke 6:38 underscores the reciprocal nature of generosity. When we give, we open ourselves to receive blessings from God. This principle encourages believers to give freely, knowing that their generosity will be met with God's abundant provision.

3. Blessings Through Giving: Proverbs 11:24-25 teaches, "One person gives freely, yet gains even more; another withholds unduly but comes to poverty. A generous person will prosper; whoever refreshes others will be refreshed." These verses emphasize that generosity leads to prosperity and refreshment, both for the giver and the recipient.

1. Tithing: Tithing involves giving a tenth of one's income to support the work of the church and God's ministry. Malachi 3:10 states, "Bring the whole tithe into the storehouse, that there may be food in my house. Test me in this," says the Lord Almighty, "and see if I will not throw open the floodgates of heaven and pour out so much blessing that there will not be room enough to store it." Tithing is an act of obedience and trust, acknowledging God's provision.

2. Offerings: Offerings are contributions given in addition to tithes. They can be directed towards specific causes, such as missions, building projects, or helping those in need. 2 Corinthians 9:7 encourages cheerful giving: "Each

of you should give what you have decided in your heart to give, not reluctantly or under compulsion, for God loves a cheerful giver."

3. Charitable Donations: Charitable donations extend beyond the church, supporting various humanitarian efforts and social causes. Proverbs 19:17 states, "Whoever is kind to the poor lends to the Lord, and he will reward them for what they have done." Supporting charitable organizations reflects God's compassion and justice.

4. Acts of Kindness: Generosity is not limited to financial giving. Acts of kindness, such as volunteering time, offering expertise, or providing emotional support, are powerful expressions of generosity. Galatians 6:10 encourages believers to do good to all people: "Therefore, as we have opportunity, let us do good to all people, especially to those who belong to the family of believers."

5. Sharing Talents and Compassion: Generosity includes sharing one's talents and showing compassion. 1 Peter 4:10-11 advises, "Each of you should use whatever gift you have received to serve others, as faithful stewards of God's grace in its various forms. If anyone speaks, they should do so as one who speaks the very words of God. If anyone serves, they should do so with the strength God provides, so that in all things God may be praised through

Jesus Christ." Using our abilities to serve others glorifies God and meets the needs of those around us.

1. Stewardship of God's Blessings: Recognizing that all we have belongs to God is fundamental to understanding generosity. Psalm 24:1 declares, "The earth is the Lord's, and everything in it, the world, and all who live in it." As stewards of God's blessings, we are called to manage and share our resources responsibly.

2. Joyful Giving: True generosity comes from a joyful heart. 2 Corinthians 9:7 emphasizes the importance of cheerful giving: "Each of you should give what you have decided in your heart to give, not reluctantly or under compulsion, for God loves a cheerful giver." Giving with joy and gratitude reflects our love for God and others.

3. Sacrificial Giving: Generosity often involves sacrifice. The widow's offering in Mark 12:41-44 is a powerful example of sacrificial giving. Despite her poverty, the widow gave all she had, demonstrating deep faith and trust in God. Jesus commended her, saying she had given more than the wealthy because she gave out of her poverty.

1. Meeting Needs: Generosity meets the needs of others, providing relief, support, and encouragement. Acts 2:44-45 describes the early church's generosity: "All the believers were together and had everything in common. They

sold property and possessions to give to anyone who had need." This collective generosity strengthened the community and ensured that no one was in need.

2. Building Community: Generosity fosters a sense of community and connectedness. By sharing resources and supporting one another, believers build strong, compassionate communities that reflect God's love. Hebrews 13:16 encourages, "And do not forget to do good and to share with others, for with such sacrifices God is pleased."

3. Witness to God's Love: Acts of generosity serve as a powerful witness to God's love and grace. John 13:35 states, "By this everyone will know that you are my disciples, if you love one another." Generosity demonstrates the transformative power of God's love in practical, tangible ways.

1. Fear of Lack: One common barrier to generosity is the fear of not having enough. Trusting in God's provision helps overcome this fear. Philippians 4:19 reassures, "And my God will meet all your needs according to the riches of his glory in Christ Jesus." By trusting in God's abundance, believers can give confidently and generously.

2. Materialism: Materialism, or the excessive focus on acquiring and possessing material goods, can stifle generosity. Cultivating a heart of contentment and gratitude helps combat materialism. Hebrews 13:5 advises, "Keep your lives

free from the love of money and be content with what you have, because God has said, 'Never will I leave you; never will I forsake you.'"

3. Selfishness: Selfishness can hinder generosity, as it focuses on personal gain rather than the well-being of others. Romans 12:10 encourages believers to be devoted to one another in love and to honor others above themselves. Developing a selfless attitude aligns with God's call to love and serve others.

1. Set Giving Goals: Setting specific giving goals helps prioritize generosity. Decide on a percentage of income to give regularly to the church, charitable organizations, and other causes. Regular giving fosters a habit of generosity.

2. Volunteer Time and Skills: Offer your time and talents to support community projects, church activities, and charitable organizations. Volunteering provides opportunities to serve and make a positive impact.

3. Practice Random Acts of Kindness: Look for opportunities to practice random acts of kindness, such as paying for someone's meal, helping a neighbor, or offering a listening ear. These small acts of generosity can make a significant difference.

4. Reflect on God's Blessings: Regularly reflect on God's blessings in your life and express gratitude. Keeping a

gratitude journal can help you recognize and appreciate God's provision, motivating you to share with others.

5. Engage in Community Giving Initiatives: Participate in community giving initiatives, such as food drives, fundraisers, and service projects. Engaging in collective acts of generosity strengthens the community and amplifies the impact of giving.

Generosity is a cornerstone of spiritual prosperity. Luke 6:38 emphasizes the reciprocal nature of giving: "Give, and it will be given to you. A good measure, pressed down, shaken together and running over, will be poured into your lap. For with the measure you use, it will be measured to you." Generosity reflects God's character and opens the door to His blessings.

Giving can take various forms, including tithing, offerings, charitable donations, and acts of kindness. It involves sharing not only financial resources but also time, talents, and compassion. The principle of generosity aligns with the understanding that all we have belongs to God, and we are stewards of His blessings.

By practicing generosity, believers meet the needs of others, build strong communities, and bear witness to God's love. Overcoming barriers to generosity involves trusting in God's provision, combating materialism, and developing a selfless attitude. Practical steps to cultivate generosity include setting giving goals, volunteering time and skills, practicing random acts of kindness, reflecting on God's blessings, and engaging in community giving initiatives.

Embracing the principle of generosity leads to spiritual growth, deeper relationships, and the joy of participating in God's work. As believers give generously and cheerfully, they reflect God's love and grace, contributing to a more compassionate and just world.

CHAPTER 42

PRINCIPLE 4: STEWARDSHIP AND RESPONSIBILITY

Stewardship is the responsible management of resources entrusted to us by God. It involves using wealth wisely, making prudent financial decisions, and planning for the future. The Parable of the Talents (Matthew 25:14-30) illustrates the importance of stewardship. The servants who wisely invested their master's money were rewarded, while the one who did nothing with his talent was punished. Stewardship also means avoiding wastefulness, living within one's means, and investing in ways that align with ethical and biblical values. It encompasses budgeting, saving, and seeking godly counsel in financial matters.

1. The Parable of the Talents: In Matthew 25:14-30, Jesus tells the Parable of the Talents, where a master entrusts his servants with different amounts of money before leaving on a journey. The servants who invested the money and made

a profit were praised and rewarded, while the servant who buried the money out of fear was reprimanded and punished. This parable underscores the importance of using God-given resources wisely and responsibly.

2. God's Ownership: Psalm 24:1 declares, "The earth is the Lord's, and everything in it, the world, and all who live in it." Recognizing that everything belongs to God is fundamental to stewardship. As stewards, we are called to manage His resources in ways that honor Him and further His purposes.

3. Accountability: Romans 14:12 reminds us, "So then, each of us will give an account of ourselves to God." Stewardship involves being accountable to God for how we use the resources He has entrusted to us. This accountability motivates us to make wise and ethical decisions.

1. Avoiding Wastefulness: Stewardship involves avoiding wastefulness and making the most of the resources we have. Proverbs 21:20 advises, "The wise store up choice food and olive oil, but fools gulp theirs down." Wise stewardship means using resources efficiently and avoiding unnecessary waste.

2. Living Within One's Means: Stewardship requires living within one's means and avoiding excessive debt. Proverbs 22:7 warns, "The rich rule over the poor, and the

borrower is slave to the lender." By managing expenses and avoiding unnecessary debt, believers can maintain financial stability and freedom.

3. Budgeting and Planning: Effective stewardship involves budgeting and planning for the future. Luke 14:28-30 illustrates the importance of planning: "Suppose one of you wants to build a tower. Won't you first sit down and estimate the cost to see if you have enough money to complete it? For if you lay the foundation and are not able to finish it, everyone who sees it will ridicule you, saying, 'This person began to build and wasn't able to finish.'" Creating and following a budget helps ensure that resources are used wisely and goals are met.

1. Ethical and Biblical Values: Stewardship involves investing in ways that align with ethical and biblical values. Proverbs 13:11 states, "Dishonest money dwindles away, but whoever gathers money little by little makes it grow." Investing in companies and projects that reflect godly principles and promote social good honors God and contributes to a just society.

2. Diversifying Investments: Ecclesiastes 11:2 advises, "Invest in seven ventures, yes, in eight; you do not know what disaster may come upon the land." Diversifying investments helps manage risk and ensure financial stability. By spreading

resources across different opportunities, believers can protect against potential losses and maximize returns.

3. Seeking Godly Counsel: Proverbs 15:22 highlights the importance of seeking advice: "Plans fail for lack of counsel, but with many advisers they succeed." Seeking godly counsel in financial matters helps ensure that decisions are made with wisdom and insight. Trusted advisors can provide valuable perspectives and guidance.

1. Saving for Future Needs: Proverbs 6:6-8 encourages preparation and saving: "Go to the ant, you sluggard; consider its ways and be wise! It has no commander, no overseer or ruler, yet it stores its provisions in summer and gathers its food at harvest." Saving for future needs, such as emergencies, education, and retirement, is a prudent aspect of stewardship.

2. Providing for Family: 1 Timothy 5:8 emphasizes the responsibility to provide for one's family: "Anyone who does not provide for their relatives, and especially for their own household, has denied the faith and is worse than an unbeliever." Ensuring that family needs are met through wise financial planning reflects godly stewardship.

3. Generosity in Planning: Stewardship also involves planning for generosity. 2 Corinthians 9:6-7 encourages cheerful giving: "Remember this: Whoever sows sparingly will

also reap sparingly, and whoever sows generously will also reap generously. Each of you should give what you have decided in your heart to give, not reluctantly or under compulsion, for God loves a cheerful giver." Setting aside resources for giving ensures that generosity remains a priority.

Practical Steps for Effective Stewardship

1. Create a Budget: Develop a budget that outlines income, expenses, and savings goals. A budget helps track spending, identify areas for adjustment, and ensure that resources are allocated according to priorities.

2. Set Financial Goals: Establish short-term and long-term financial goals, such as paying off debt, building an emergency fund, saving for education, and planning for retirement. Clear goals provide direction and motivation.

3. Monitor Spending: Regularly review and monitor spending to stay within the budget and make necessary adjustments. Tracking expenses helps maintain financial discipline and avoid overspending.

4. Invest Wisely: Research and choose investments that align with ethical and biblical values. Diversify investments to manage risk and seek advice from trusted financial advisors.

5. Save Regularly: Make saving a consistent habit by setting aside a portion of income for future needs. Automated

savings plans can help ensure regular contributions to savings accounts.

6. Seek Counsel: Consult with financial advisors, mentors, and trusted individuals for guidance on financial decisions. Seeking counsel provides valuable insights and helps avoid potential pitfalls.

Stewardship is the responsible management of resources entrusted to us by God. It involves using wealth wisely, making prudent financial decisions, and planning for the future. The Parable of the Talents (Matthew 25:14-30) illustrates the importance of stewardship. The servants who wisely invested their master's money were rewarded, while the one who did nothing with his talent was punished.

Effective stewardship requires avoiding wastefulness, living within one's means, budgeting, saving, and investing in ways that align with ethical and biblical values. By recognizing that all resources belong to God, believers can manage their finances responsibly and honor Him with their decisions.

Practical steps for effective stewardship include creating a budget, setting financial goals, monitoring spending, investing wisely, saving regularly, and seeking godly counsel. Embracing these principles leads to financial stability, fulfillment of responsibilities, and the joy of honoring God through wise stewardship.

CHAPTER 43

PRINCIPLE 5: HARD WORK AND DILIGENCE

The Bible emphasizes the value of hard work and diligence as pathways to prosperity. Proverbs 10:4 states, "Lazy hands make for poverty, but diligent hands bring wealth." Hard work, when combined with faith and trust in God, leads to success and fulfillment. This chapter explores the biblical principles of hard work and diligence, highlighting how these qualities contribute to prosperity and personal growth.

1. Proverbs on Diligence: The book of Proverbs contains numerous verses that extol the virtues of hard work and diligence. Proverbs 12:24 declares, "Diligent hands will rule, but laziness ends in forced labor." These verses emphasize that diligent efforts lead to leadership and success, while laziness results in subjugation and lack.

2. The Example of Industriousness: Ecclesiastes 9:10 encourages wholehearted effort: "Whatever your hand finds to do, do it with all your might, for in the realm of the dead,

305

where you are going, there is neither working nor planning nor knowledge nor wisdom." This verse underscores the importance of putting maximum effort into all tasks, and recognizing the limited time and opportunities we have.

3. New Testament Teachings: The New Testament also affirms the importance of hard work. Colossians 3:23-24 advises, "Whatever you do, work at it with all your heart, as working for the Lord, not for human masters, since you know that you will receive an inheritance from the Lord as a reward. It is the Lord Christ you are serving." This perspective elevates every task to an act of worship and service to God.

1. Proactive and Disciplined: Diligence involves being proactive and disciplined in all endeavors. Proverbs 6:6-8 uses the example of the ant to illustrate this principle: "Go to the ant, you sluggard; consider its ways and be wise! It has no commander, no overseer or ruler, yet it stores its provisions in summer and gathers its food at harvest." The ant's industriousness and foresight serve as a model for human diligence.

2. Committed to Excellence: Commitment to excellence is a hallmark of diligence. Ecclesiastes 9:10 and Colossians 3:23 both emphasize putting forth our best effort in every task. Striving for excellence reflects God's character and brings glory to Him.

3. Productivity and Improvement: Diligence involves continuous productivity and self-improvement. Proverbs 21:5 teaches, "The plans of the diligent lead to profit as surely as haste leads to poverty." Diligent individuals plan, work steadily, and seek ways to improve their skills and efficiency, leading to fruitful outcomes.

1. Financial Prosperity: Hard work often leads to financial prosperity. Proverbs 14:23 states, "All hard work brings a profit, but mere talk leads only to poverty." Consistent effort in one's profession or business typically results in increased income and financial stability.

2. Personal Fulfillment: Beyond financial gains, hard work brings personal fulfillment and satisfaction. Ecclesiastes 3:13 recognizes the joy of labor: "That each of them may eat and drink, and find satisfaction in all their toil—this is the gift of God." The sense of accomplishment from diligent work is a divine blessing.

3. Building Character: Hard work and diligence build character traits such as perseverance, discipline, and integrity. Romans 5:3-4 explains, "Not only so, but we also glory in our sufferings because we know that suffering produces perseverance; perseverance, character; and character, hope." Engaging in diligent work fosters these essential qualities.

1. Setting Goals: Effective diligence begins with setting clear, achievable goals. Proverbs 21:5 emphasizes

planning: "The plans of the diligent lead to profit as surely as haste leads to poverty." Setting specific goals provides direction and motivation.

2. Time Management: Managing time efficiently is crucial for productivity. Ephesians 5:15-16 advises, "Be very careful, then, how you live—not as unwise but as wise, making the most of every opportunity, because the days are evil." Prioritizing tasks and avoiding procrastination help maximize productivity.

3. Continuous Learning: Diligence involves a commitment to continuous learning and skill improvement. Proverbs 1:5 encourages growth in wisdom: "Let the wise listen and add to their learning, and let the discerning get guidance." Seeking knowledge and improving skills leads to greater effectiveness and opportunities.

4. Maintaining Focus: Staying focused on tasks and avoiding distractions are key components of diligence. Proverbs 4:25-27 advises, "Let your eyes look straight ahead; fix your gaze directly before you. Give careful thought to the paths for your feet and be steadfast in all your ways. Do not turn to the right or the left; keep your foot from evil." Focused effort leads to better outcomes.

1. Dealing with Fatigue: Fatigue can hinder diligent work, but finding rest in God provides renewal. Isaiah 40:31

promises, "But those who hope in the Lord will renew their strength. They will soar on wings like eagles; they will run and not grow weary, they will walk and not be faint." Balancing work with rest and relying on God's strength helps maintain diligence.

2. Facing Discouragement: Discouragement can affect diligence, but trusting in God's promises provides encouragement. Galatians 6:9 encourages perseverance: "Let us not become weary in doing good, for at the proper time we will reap a harvest if we do not give up." Keeping a long-term perspective helps overcome discouragement.

3. Managing Distractions: Distractions can impede diligent work. Setting boundaries and creating a conducive work environment helps maintain focus. Colossians 3:2 advises, "Set your minds on things above, not on earthly things." Prioritizing tasks and minimizing distractions lead to greater productivity.

1. Material Blessings: Proverbs 10:4 assures that "diligent hands bring wealth." Consistent hard work often results in material blessings and financial stability, providing for oneself and one's family.

2. Spiritual Growth: Hard work and diligence contribute to spiritual growth. 2 Peter 1:5-8 encourages adding virtues to faith, including perseverance and self-control, leading to a productive and effective Christian life.

Engaging diligently in God's work and personal growth fosters spiritual maturity.

3. Positive Influence: Diligence serves as a positive influence and testimony to others. Matthew 5:16 urges believers to "let your light shine before others, that they may see your good deeds and glorify your Father in heaven." Hard work and diligence in all areas of life reflect God's character and inspire others.

1. Set Clear Goals: Establish clear, achievable goals for various aspects of life, including work, personal development, and spiritual growth. Specific goals provide direction and motivation for diligent efforts.

2. Develop a Routine: Create a daily routine that prioritizes important tasks and allocates time for rest and recreation. A structured routine promotes consistency and productivity.

3. Pursue Continuous Improvement: Commit to continuous learning and skill enhancement. Attend workshops, read relevant materials, and seek feedback to improve performance and effectiveness.

4. Stay Accountable: Engage in accountability with trusted individuals who can provide support and encouragement. Accountability partners help maintain focus and motivation.

5. Reflect and Adjust: Regularly reflect on progress and make necessary adjustments to goals and strategies. Flexibility and willingness to adapt are essential for sustained diligence.

The Bible emphasizes the value of hard work and diligence as pathways to prosperity. Proverbs 10:4 states, "Lazy hands make for poverty, but diligent hands bring wealth." Hard work, when combined with faith and trust in God, leads to success and fulfillment. Diligence involves being proactive, disciplined, and committed to excellence in all endeavors, including seeking to improve one's skills, being productive, and striving to achieve one's best in every task.

Effective diligence requires setting clear goals, managing time efficiently, pursuing continuous learning, and maintaining focus. Overcoming challenges such as fatigue, discouragement, and distractions is essential for sustained hard work. The rewards of hard work and diligence include material blessings, personal fulfillment, spiritual growth, and positive influence.

By cultivating hard work and diligence, believers can honor God, achieve their goals, and contribute to a prosperous and fulfilling life. Embracing these principles leads to personal growth, success, and the joy of knowing that one's efforts reflect God's character and purpose.

CHAPTER 44

CONTENTMENT AND GRATITUDE

Contentment and gratitude are essential principles of spiritual prosperity. 1 Timothy 6:6-8 teaches, "But godliness with contentment is great gain. For we brought nothing into the world, and we can take nothing out of it. But if we have food and clothing, we will be content with that." Contentment involves finding joy and satisfaction in what God has provided, rather than constantly striving for more. Gratitude, on the other hand, involves recognizing and thanking God for His blessings. It shifts the focus from what we lack to what we have, fostering a positive and appreciative mindset. Philippians 4:6-7 encourages believers to present their requests to God with thanksgiving, promising peace that transcends understanding.

1. Godliness with Contentment: 1 Timothy 6:6-8 emphasizes the value of contentment combined with godliness. It teaches that material possessions are temporary and that true gain comes from a godly life marked by

contentment. This perspective encourages believers to focus on spiritual growth and eternal values rather than material accumulation.

2. Jesus' Teaching on Contentment: In Matthew 6:25-34, Jesus teaches about trusting God for our needs and not worrying about material things. He says, "Therefore I tell you, do not worry about your life, what you will eat or drink; or about your body, what you will wear. Is not life more than food, and the body more than clothes?" Jesus directs believers to seek first God's kingdom and righteousness, promising that all necessary things will be provided.

3. The Apostle Paul's Example: Paul exemplifies contentment in Philippians 4:11-13, where he writes, "I am not saying this because I am in need, for I have learned to be content whatever the circumstances. I know what it is to be in need, and I know what it is to have plenty. I have learned the secret of being content in any and every situation, whether well fed or hungry, whether living in plenty or in want. I can do all this through him who gives me strength." Paul's reliance on Christ for strength in all situations demonstrates the essence of true contentment.

1. Finding Joy in Provision: Contentment involves finding joy and satisfaction in what God has provided, rather than constantly striving for more. Hebrews 13:5 advises, "Keep your lives free from the love of money and be content

with what you have, because God has said, 'Never will I leave you; never will I forsake you.'" Trusting in God's presence and provision fosters a sense of peace and fulfillment.

2. Avoiding the Trap of Materialism: Contentment helps believers avoid the trap of materialism, which can lead to dissatisfaction and spiritual emptiness. Ecclesiastes 5:10 warns, "Whoever loves money never has enough; whoever loves wealth is never satisfied with their income. This too is meaningless." Recognizing the limitations of material wealth encourages a focus on spiritual riches.

3. Strengthening Relationships: Contentment enhances relationships by reducing envy and fostering gratitude for what one has. James 3:16 notes, "For where you have envy and selfish ambition, there you find disorder and every evil practice." Contentment promotes harmony and appreciation in relationships, contributing to a positive and supportive community.

1. Recognizing God's Blessings: Gratitude involves recognizing and thanking God for His blessings. James 1:17 reminds believers, "Every good and perfect gift is from above, coming down from the Father of the heavenly lights, who does not change like shifting shadows." Acknowledging God's provision fosters a sense of gratitude and dependence on Him.

2. Shifting Focus: Gratitude shifts the focus from what we lack to what we have, fostering a positive and appreciative mindset. Colossians 3:15 encourages, "Let the peace of Christ rule in your hearts, since as members of one body you were called to peace. And be thankful." Gratitude helps cultivate a peaceful and content heart.

3. Promoting Mental and Spiritual Health: Gratitude has been shown to promote mental and spiritual health. Philippians 4:6-7 encourages believers to present their requests to God with thanksgiving, promising peace that transcends understanding: "Do not be anxious about anything, but in every situation, by prayer and petition, with thanksgiving, present your requests to God. And the peace of God, which transcends all understanding, will guard your hearts and your minds in Christ Jesus." Gratitude reduces anxiety and fosters inner peace.

1. Practice Mindfulness: Be mindful of God's provision in daily life. Take time to appreciate the small blessings and recognize God's hand in every situation. Mindfulness fosters a sense of contentment and gratitude.

2. Simplify Your Life: Simplifying life by reducing unnecessary possessions and focusing on what truly matters can enhance contentment. Luke 12:15 warns, "Watch out! Be on your guard against all kinds of greed; life does not consist

in an abundance of possessions." Simplification leads to greater contentment and peace.

3. Set Realistic Goals: Set realistic goals that align with your values and priorities. Avoid the pressure to constantly achieve more and instead focus on what is meaningful and fulfilling. Ecclesiastes 4:6 advises, "Better one handful with tranquility than two handfuls with toil and chasing after the wind."

1. Keep a Gratitude Journal: Regularly write down things you are grateful for. This practice helps shift focus to positive aspects of life and fosters an attitude of thankfulness. Psalm 103:2 encourages, "Praise the Lord, my soul, and forget not all his benefits."

2. Express Thanks: Make it a habit to express thanks to God and others. Verbalizing gratitude strengthens relationships and reinforces a positive mindset. 1 Thessalonians 5:18 advises, "Give thanks in all circumstances; for this is God's will for you in Christ Jesus."

3. Serve Others: Serving others can foster gratitude by providing perspective and highlighting the blessings in your own life. Acts 20:35 quotes Jesus, saying, "It is more blessed to give than to receive." Serving others shifts focus from personal needs to the needs of others, cultivating gratitude.

1. Dealing with Envy: Envy can undermine contentment and gratitude. Proverbs 14:30 notes, "A heart at peace gives life to the body, but envy rots the bones." Overcoming envy involves focusing on personal blessings and trusting God's provision.

2. Combating Materialism: Materialism can hinder contentment and gratitude. Matthew 6:19-21 advises, "Do not store up for yourselves treasures on earth, where moths and vermin destroy, and where thieves break in and steal. But store up for yourselves treasures in heaven, where moths and vermin do not destroy, and where thieves do not break in and steal. For where your treasure is, there your heart will be also." Shifting the focus to eternal values combats materialism.

3. Addressing Discontent: Discontent can arise from unmet expectations and comparisons. Philippians 4:11-12 encourages learning contentment in all circumstances: "I have learned to be content whatever the circumstances. I know what it is to be in need, and I know what it is to have plenty. I have learned the secret of being content in any and every situation." Trusting in God's plan and timing fosters contentment.

1. Inner Peace: Contentment and gratitude lead to inner peace. Philippians 4:6-7 promises peace that transcends understanding to those who practice thanksgiving and trust in God. This peace guards the heart and mind.

2. Joy and Fulfillment: Contentment and gratitude bring joy and fulfillment, as they shift focus from lack to abundance. Psalm 16:11 declares, "You make known to me the path of life; you will fill me with joy in your presence, with eternal pleasures at your right hand." Recognizing and appreciating God's blessings brings joy.

3. Strengthened Faith: Practicing contentment and gratitude strengthens faith by fostering trust in God's provision and goodness. James 1:17 reminds believers that every good gift comes from God, reinforcing reliance on His faithfulness.

Contentment and gratitude are essential principles of spiritual prosperity. 1 Timothy 6:6-8 teaches, "But godliness with contentment is great gain. For we brought nothing into the world, and we can take nothing out of it. But if we have food and clothing, we will be content with that." Contentment involves finding joy and satisfaction in what God has provided, rather than constantly striving for more. Gratitude involves recognizing and thanking God for His blessings, shifting focus from what we lack to what we have.

By practicing mindfulness, simplifying life, setting realistic goals, keeping a gratitude journal, expressing thanks, and serving others, believers can cultivate contentment and gratitude. Overcoming barriers such as envy, materialism, and discontent fosters a positive and appreciative mindset.

The rewards of contentment and gratitude include inner peace, joy, fulfillment, and strengthened faith. Embracing these principles leads to a more prosperous and spiritually rich life, reflecting God's love and provision in every circumstance.

CHAPTER 45

PRINCIPLE 7: SEEKING FIRST THE KINGDOM OF GOD

Prioritizing God's kingdom is a fundamental principle of prosperity. Matthew 6:33 instructs, "But seek first his kingdom and his righteousness, and all these things will be given to you as well." This principle emphasizes that when we focus on God's purposes and righteousness, He will provide for our material needs. Seeking God's kingdom involves aligning our goals and actions with His will, participating in His work on earth, and promoting justice, mercy, and faithfulness. It means living a life that reflects God's values and advancing His mission.

1. Jesus' Teaching: Matthew 6:33 encapsulates Jesus' teaching on prioritizing God's kingdom: "But seek first his kingdom and his righteousness, and all these things will be given to you as well." Jesus assures that when we prioritize God's kingdom, our needs will be met. This teaching redirects our focus from material concerns to spiritual priorities.

2. The Lord's Prayer: In the Lord's Prayer, Jesus teaches us to pray, "Your kingdom come, your will be done, on earth as it is in heaven" (Matthew 6:10). This prayer reflects a desire for God's reign and righteousness to manifest on earth, guiding our actions and decisions.

3. Paul's Exhortation: Colossians 3:1-2 advises believers to focus on heavenly things: "Since, then, you have been raised with Christ, set your hearts on things above, where Christ is, seated at the right hand of God. Set your minds on things above, not on earthly things." Seeking God's kingdom involves a shift in perspective, prioritizing spiritual realities over earthly pursuits.

1. Understanding God's Will: To seek God's kingdom, we must understand His will as revealed in Scripture. Romans 12:2 instructs, "Do not conform to the pattern of this world, but be transformed by the renewing of your mind. Then you will be able to test and approve what God's will is—his good, pleasing and perfect will." Studying Scripture and seeking the Holy Spirit's guidance help us align our goals with God's will.

2. Setting Kingdom-focused Goals: Aligning our goals with God's kingdom involves setting objectives that reflect His values and purposes. This includes goals related to personal growth, ministry, community service, and social justice. Philippians 2:13 encourages, "For it is God who works in you to will and to act in order to fulfill his good purpose."

Allowing God to work through us ensures our goals align with His kingdom.

3. Living Out Kingdom Values: Seeking God's kingdom means living out values such as love, justice, mercy, and faithfulness. Micah 6:8 summarizes these values: "He has shown you, O mortal, what is good. And what does the Lord require of you? To act justly and to love mercy and to walk humbly with your God." Practicing these values in daily life advances God's kingdom on earth.

1. Evangelism and Discipleship: Participating in God's work includes sharing the gospel and making disciples. Matthew 28:19-20, known as the Great Commission, instructs, "Therefore go and make disciples of all nations, baptizing them in the name of the Father and of the Son and of the Holy Spirit, and teaching them to obey everything I have commanded you." Evangelism and discipleship are central to advancing God's kingdom.

2. Serving Others: Serving others is a tangible way to participate in God's work. Jesus modeled servanthood in John 13:14-15, washing His disciples' feet and teaching them to serve one another. Acts of service reflect God's love and compassion, promoting His kingdom values.

3. Promoting Justice and Mercy: Seeking God's kingdom involves advocating for justice and showing mercy.

Isaiah 1:17 urges, "Learn to do right; seek justice. Defend the oppressed. Take up the cause of the fatherless; plead the case of the widow." Promoting justice and mercy aligns our actions with God's heart and advances His kingdom on earth.

Living a Life That Reflects God's Values

1. Integrity and Honesty: Reflecting God's values includes living with integrity and honesty. Proverbs 11:3 states, "The integrity of the upright guides them, but the unfaithful are destroyed by their duplicity." Integrity in personal and professional life honors God and builds trust.

2. Compassion and Kindness: Demonstrating compassion and kindness is central to reflecting God's character. Colossians 3:12 encourages, "Therefore, as God's chosen people, holy and dearly loved, clothe yourselves with compassion, kindness, humility, gentleness and patience." These qualities enhance our witness and promote God's kingdom.

3. Faithfulness and Stewardship: Faithfulness in our responsibilities and stewardship of resources reflects God's values. 1 Corinthians 4:2 notes, "Now it is required that those who have been given a trust must prove faithful." Faithfulness in managing our time, talents, and resources advances God's kingdom.

1. Daily Devotion and Prayer: Prioritize daily devotion and prayer to seek God's guidance and align your heart with

His kingdom. Matthew 6:6 advises, "But when you pray, go into your room, close the door and pray to your Father, who is unseen. Then your Father, who sees what is done in secret, will reward you." Regular prayer strengthens your relationship with God and clarifies His will.

2. Study Scripture: Regularly study Scripture to understand God's kingdom values and principles. 2 Timothy 3:16-17 teaches, "All Scripture is God-breathed and is useful for teaching, rebuking, correcting and training in righteousness, so that the servant of God may be thoroughly equipped for every good work." Studying the Bible equips you to live according to God's purposes.

3. Engage in Community: Engage in a faith community that supports and encourages your commitment to God's kingdom. Hebrews 10:24-25 urges, "And let us consider how we may spur one another on toward love and good deeds, not giving up meeting together, as some are in the habit of doing, but encouraging one another—and all the more as you see the Day approaching." Community provides accountability and mutual support.

4. Serve and Give: Actively serve in your church and community, and practice generous giving. Acts 20:35 quotes Jesus, saying, "It is more blessed to give than to receive."

Serving others and giving generously reflect God's love and advance His kingdom.

5. Reflect and Adjust: Regularly reflect on your goals and actions, adjusting them to align more closely with God's kingdom. Psalm 139:23-24 encourages self-examination: "Search me, God, and know my heart; test me and know my anxious thoughts. See if there is any offensive way in me, and lead me in the way everlasting." Continual reflection and adjustment ensure your focus remains on God's kingdom.

Overcoming Barriers to Seeking God's Kingdom

1. Dealing with Distractions: Modern life is full of distractions that can divert attention from God's kingdom. Luke 10:41-42 records Jesus' words to Martha, "Martha, Martha," the Lord answered, "you are worried and upset about many things, but few things are needed—or indeed only one. Mary has chosen what is better, and it will not be taken away from her." Focusing on what truly matters helps overcome distractions.

2. Combating Materialism: Materialism can hinder the pursuit of God's kingdom. 1 Timothy 6:10 warns, "For the love of money is a root of all kinds of evil. Some people, eager for money, have wandered from the faith and pierced themselves with many griefs." Prioritizing spiritual values over material wealth combats materialism.

3. Facing Opposition: Seeking God's kingdom may lead to opposition or persecution. 2 Timothy 3:12 notes, "In fact, everyone who wants to live a godly life in Christ Jesus will be persecuted." Remaining steadfast in faith and trusting in God's ultimate justice helps overcome opposition.

1. Provision for Needs: Matthew 6:33 promises that God will provide for our needs when we seek His kingdom first. Trusting in this promise brings peace and security, knowing that God will take care of us.

2. Spiritual Fulfillment: Seeking God's kingdom leads to spiritual fulfillment and growth. John 15:5 explains, "I am the vine; you are the branches. If you remain in me and I in you, you will bear much fruit; apart from me you can do nothing." Abiding in Christ and focusing on His kingdom results in a fruitful and fulfilling life.

3. Eternal Rewards: Prioritizing God's kingdom brings eternal rewards. Matthew 25:34 speaks of the final judgment: "Then the King will say to those on his right, 'Come, you who are blessed by my Father; take your inheritance, the kingdom prepared for you since the creation of the world.'" Faithfulness in seeking God's kingdom leads to eternal blessings.

Prioritizing God's kingdom is a fundamental principle of prosperity. Matthew 6:33 instructs, "But seek first his kingdom and his righteousness, and all these things will be given to you as well." This principle emphasizes that when we focus on

God's purposes and righteousness, He will provide for our material needs. Seeking God's kingdom involves aligning our goals and actions with His will, participating in His work on earth, and promoting justice, mercy, and faithfulness. It means living a life that reflects God's values and advancing His mission.

By practicing daily devotion and prayer, studying Scripture, engaging in community, serving, giving, and regularly reflecting on and adjusting our goals, we can seek God's kingdom first. Overcoming distractions, materialism, and opposition ensures that our focus remains on God's purposes. The rewards of seeking first the kingdom of God include provision for our needs, spiritual fulfillment, and eternal blessings.

Embracing this principle leads to a prosperous and spiritually rich life, fulfilling God's purposes and reflecting His love and righteousness in the world.

CHAPTER 46

MODERN APPLICATIONS OF SPIRITUAL PRINCIPLES

Applying spiritual principles in modern contexts involves integrating faith into every aspect of life, including financial decisions. This chapter explores practical steps for incorporating spiritual principles into daily living, ensuring that faith guides actions and decisions in all areas, particularly in financial matters. These steps include regular prayer and devotion, ethical financial practices, generous living, financial planning, continuous learning, and community engagement.

1. Seeking God's Guidance: Regular prayer and devotion are essential for seeking God's guidance in financial matters. Philippians 4:6-7 advises, "Do not be anxious about anything, but in every situation, by prayer and petition, with thanksgiving, present your requests to God. And the peace of God, which transcends all understanding, will guard your hearts and your minds in Christ Jesus." By presenting financial concerns to God, believers can gain peace and clarity.

2. Meditation on God's Word: Meditating on Scripture provides wisdom and direction for financial decisions. Psalm 119:105 states, "Your word is a lamp for my feet, a light on my path." Studying biblical principles related to finances helps align actions with God's will and fosters wise stewardship.

3. Daily Devotion Time: Establishing a daily devotion time to pray, read the Bible, and reflect on God's teachings ensures that spiritual principles guide everyday decisions. This practice strengthens the relationship with God and reinforces faith-based living.

1. Honesty and Integrity: Ensuring honesty and integrity in all financial transactions is crucial. Proverbs 11:1 teaches, "The Lord detests dishonest scales, but accurate weights find favor with him." Maintaining ethical standards in business and personal finances honors God and builds trust with others.

2. Fairness and Justice: Ethical financial practices include treating others fairly and promoting justice. Micah 6:8 emphasizes, "He has shown you, O mortal, what is good. And what does the Lord require of you? To act justly and to love mercy and to walk humbly with your God." Upholding justice in financial dealings reflects God's character and fosters social equity.

3. Responsible Investments: Investing in alignment with ethical and biblical values ensures that financial growth

contributes to positive social outcomes. Proverbs 13:11 advises, "Dishonest money dwindles away, but whoever gathers money little by little makes it grow." Ethical investments support sustainable and responsible business practices.

Generous Living

1. Regular Giving: Committing to regular giving, such as tithing and supporting charitable causes, reflects God's generosity. Malachi 3:10 encourages, "Bring the whole tithe into the storehouse, that there may be food in my house. Test me in this," says the Lord Almighty, "and see if I will not throw open the floodgates of heaven and pour out so much blessing that there will not be room enough to store it." Regular giving fosters a spirit of generosity and trust in God's provision.

2. Supporting Charitable Causes: Actively supporting charitable organizations and initiatives helps address societal needs and demonstrates compassion. 2 Corinthians 9:7 emphasizes, "Each of you should give what you have decided in your heart to give, not reluctantly or under compulsion, for God loves a cheerful giver." Charitable giving reflects God's love and contributes to the well-being of others.

3. Helping Those in Need: Practicing generosity by helping those in need aligns with biblical teachings. Proverbs

19:17 states, "Whoever is kind to the poor lends to the Lord, and he will reward them for what they have done." Assisting the less fortunate demonstrates God's compassion and builds a supportive community.

Financial Planning

1. Creating a Budget: Developing and adhering to a budget ensures responsible financial management. Proverbs 21:5 advises, "The plans of the diligent lead to profit as surely as haste leads to poverty." Budgeting helps prioritize spending, save for future needs, and avoid unnecessary debt.

2. Saving Responsibly: Saving responsibly for emergencies, future goals, and retirement is a key aspect of financial stewardship. Proverbs 6:6-8 encourages preparation: "Go to the ant, you sluggard; consider its ways and be wise! It has no commander, no overseer or ruler, yet it stores its provisions in summer and gathers its food at harvest." Responsible saving ensures financial stability and readiness for unforeseen circumstances.

3. Ethical Investments: Investing in ways that align with ethical values supports responsible business practices and sustainable growth. Ecclesiastes 11:2 advises, "Invest in seven ventures, yes, in eight; you do not know what disaster may come upon the land." Diversified and ethical investments contribute to long-term financial security and social good.

Continuous Learning

1. Improving Skills and Knowledge: Continuously improving skills and knowledge enhances productivity and effectiveness in work and business. Proverbs 18:15 states, "The heart of the discerning acquires knowledge, for the ears of the wise seek it out." Lifelong learning ensures personal and professional growth.

2. Attending Workshops and Seminars: Participating in workshops, seminars, and courses related to one's field promotes skill development and keeps individuals updated on industry trends. Ecclesiastes 7:12 notes, "Wisdom is a shelter as money is a shelter, but the advantage of knowledge is this: Wisdom preserves those who have it." Investing in education and training enhances competence and opportunities.

3. Seeking Mentorship and Guidance: Seeking mentorship and guidance from experienced individuals provides valuable insights and advice. Proverbs 15:22 advises, "Plans fail for lack of counsel, but with many advisers they succeed." Mentorship supports growth and decision-making.

Community Engagement

1. Participating in Church Activities: Engaging in church activities and ministries fosters spiritual growth and community support. Hebrews 10:24-25 encourages, "And let us consider how we may spur one another on toward love and good deeds, not giving up meeting together, as some are in

the habit of doing, but encouraging one another—and all the more as you see the Day approaching." Active participation in church life strengthens faith and relationships.

2. Supporting Community Projects: Involvement in community projects promotes social good and reflects God's love. Acts 2:44-45 describes the early church's communal support: "All the believers were together and had everything in common. They sold property and possessions to give to anyone who had need." Community engagement fosters unity and addresses local needs.

3. Promoting Social Justice: Advocating for social justice and supporting initiatives that promote equality and fairness aligns with God's kingdom values. Isaiah 1:17 urges, "Learn to do right; seek justice. Defend the oppressed. Take up the cause of the fatherless; plead the case of the widow." Promoting justice reflects God's heart and advances His mission.

Applying spiritual principles in modern contexts involves integrating faith into every aspect of life, including financial decisions. Regular prayer and devotion, ethical financial practices, generous living, financial planning, continuous learning, and community engagement are practical steps that ensure faith guides actions and decisions.

By seeking God's guidance in financial matters through prayer and meditation on His Word, maintaining honesty and integrity in financial transactions, committing to regular giving and charitable support, creating and adhering to a budget, saving responsibly, and investing ethically, believers can honor God with their resources.

Continuous learning and skill improvement enhance productivity and effectiveness, while active participation in church and community activities promotes social good and reflects God's love. Embracing these modern applications of spiritual principles leads to a prosperous, fulfilling, and faith-centered life that honors God and advances His kingdom.

PART IX

SEEKING GOD IN ABUNDANCE AND SCARCITY

CHAPTER 47

BIBLICAL EXAMPLES OF ABUNDANCE AND SCARCITY

The Bible offers numerous examples of individuals who experienced both abundance and scarcity, providing valuable lessons on maintaining faith in all circumstances. These stories teach us how to navigate different seasons of life, highlighting the importance of unwavering faith and trust in God. This chapter explores the lives of Job and King Solomon, two prominent biblical figures who encountered both extreme scarcity and great abundance.

Job: Faithfulness in Scarcity

1. Job's Initial Abundance: Job was a man of great wealth and prosperity. He had a large family, numerous livestock, and extensive property. Job 1:3 describes his wealth: "He was the greatest man among all the people of the East." Job's initial abundance is depicted as a blessing from God, reflecting his upright and blameless character.

2. Job's Extreme Loss: Despite his righteousness, Job experienced severe trials. He lost his possessions, children, and health in rapid succession. Job 1:14-19 recounts the devastating news brought to Job by successive messengers, each reporting a new catastrophe. These events were not due to any wrongdoing on Job's part but were part of a divine test of his faith.

3. Job's Unwavering Faith: In the face of extreme loss, Job's faith remained steadfast. Job 1:21 captures his profound declaration of faith: "Naked I came from my mother's womb, and naked I will depart. The Lord gave and the Lord has taken away; may the name of the Lord be praised." Job's response to his suffering exemplifies seeking God and maintaining faith even in the direst circumstances.

4. Restoration and Abundance: After enduring his trials and remaining faithful, Job's fortunes were restored. Job 42:10-12 details his restoration: "The Lord restored his fortunes and gave him twice as much as he had before... The Lord blessed the latter part of Job's life more than the former part." Job's story highlights that faithfulness in scarcity can lead to renewed blessings and greater abundance.

Solomon: Wisdom in Abundance

1. Solomon's Great Wealth and Wisdom: King Solomon, the son of David, was known for his unparalleled wisdom and immense wealth. When God appeared to

Solomon in a dream and offered to grant him whatever he wished, Solomon asked for wisdom to govern his people. God was pleased and granted him not only wisdom but also riches and honor. 1 Kings 3:13 records God's promise: "Moreover, I will give you what you have not asked for—both wealth and honor—so that in your lifetime you will have no equal among kings."

2. Solomon's Prosperity: Solomon's reign was marked by peace, prosperity, and grand achievements, including the construction of the temple in Jerusalem. 1 Kings 10:23-24 describes his unparalleled status: "King Solomon was greater in riches and wisdom than all the other kings of the earth. The whole world sought audience with Solomon to hear the wisdom God had put in his heart." His prosperity was a testament to God's blessing and favor.

3. Reflections on Life and Faith: Despite his abundance, Solomon recognized the limitations of material wealth and the importance of seeking God. In Ecclesiastes, Solomon reflects on the meaning of life and the pursuit of God amidst his prosperity. Ecclesiastes 12:13 concludes his reflections: "Now all has been heard; here is the conclusion of the matter: Fear God and keep his commandments, for this is the duty of all mankind." Solomon's writings highlight that

true fulfillment comes from a relationship with God, not from material possessions.

4. Lessons from Solomon's Abundance: Solomon's story teaches that even in times of great wealth, seeking God and adhering to His commandments are paramount. Prosperity can be a blessing, but it should not distract from one's spiritual duties and relationship with God. Solomon's wisdom and reflections provide a valuable perspective on maintaining faith and integrity in abundance.

Other Biblical Examples

1. Joseph's Journey from Scarcity to Abundance: Joseph, sold into slavery by his brothers, experienced extreme scarcity and hardship. However, his faith and integrity led to his rise as the second-in-command in Egypt. Genesis 41:41-42 details his rise to power: "So Pharaoh said to Joseph, 'I hereby put you in charge of the whole land of Egypt.' Then Pharaoh took his signet ring from his finger and put it on Joseph's finger. He dressed him in robes of fine linen and put a gold chain around his neck." Joseph's journey from scarcity to abundance illustrates God's provision and faithfulness.

2. Ruth's Faithfulness and Provision: Ruth, a Moabite widow, faced severe scarcity but remained faithful and loyal to her mother-in-law, Naomi. Her faithfulness led to her marriage to Boaz, a wealthy kinsman-redeemer. Ruth 2:12 records Boaz's blessing: "May the Lord repay you for what

you have done. May you be richly rewarded by the Lord, the God of Israel, under whose wings you have come to take refuge." Ruth's story demonstrates that faithfulness in hardship can lead to divine provision and blessing.

3. The Widow's Mite: In Mark 12:41-44, Jesus observes a poor widow who gives two small coins, all she had, to the temple treasury. Jesus commends her sacrificial giving: "Truly I tell you, this poor widow has put more into the treasury than all the others." The widow's faith and generosity, despite her scarcity, are honored by Jesus, highlighting that true wealth is measured by the heart's intent and faithfulness.

Lessons from Abundance and Scarcity

1. Faith in All Circumstances: The stories of Job, Solomon, Joseph, Ruth, and the widow teach that faithfulness and trust in God are crucial in both abundance and scarcity. Philippians 4:12-13 reflects this principle: "I know what it is to be in need, and I know what it is to have plenty. I have learned the secret of being content in any and every situation, whether well fed or hungry, whether living in plenty or in want. I can do all this through him who gives me strength." Maintaining faith in all circumstances leads to true spiritual prosperity.

2. Dependence on God: Both abundance and scarcity highlight the need for dependence on God. In times of scarcity, dependence on God's provision and faithfulness is essential. In times of abundance, dependence on God's wisdom and guidance prevents material wealth from becoming a distraction. Proverbs 30:8-9 prays for balance: "Give me neither poverty nor riches, but give me only my daily bread. Otherwise, I may have too much and disown you and say, 'Who is the Lord?' Or I may become poor and steal, and so dishonor the name of my God."

3. Generosity and Stewardship: Whether in abundance or scarcity, generosity and good stewardship are vital. Acts 20:35 quotes Jesus, saying, "It is more blessed to give than to receive." Practicing generosity and responsibly managing resources honors God and reflects His character.

The Bible offers numerous examples of individuals who experienced both abundance and scarcity, providing valuable lessons on maintaining faith in all circumstances. The lives of Job and King Solomon illustrate that unwavering faith and trust in God are essential, regardless of material conditions. Job's steadfastness in extreme loss and Solomon's wisdom in great wealth highlight the importance of seeking God and adhering to His commandments.

Other biblical examples, such as Joseph, Ruth, and the widow with her mite, further emphasize that faithfulness, dependence on God, and generosity are key principles in navigating both abundance and scarcity. These stories teach us that true prosperity is found in a relationship with God and living according to His will, whether in times of plenty or want.

By applying these lessons to our own lives, we can maintain a balanced perspective, prioritize our faith, and trust in God's provision and guidance in all circumstances. Embracing these principles leads to a spiritually rich and fulfilling life, reflecting God's love and faithfulness in every season.

CHAPTER 48

SPIRITUAL PRACTICES IN TIMES OF ABUNDANCE

In times of abundance, it is crucial to remain humble and recognize God's provision. Prosperity can sometimes lead to complacency or a false sense of security, but spiritual practices can help maintain a focus on God. This chapter explores key spiritual practices that help believers navigate periods of prosperity, ensuring that their hearts and minds remain aligned with God's purposes.

Gratitude: Cultivating a Thankful Heart

1. Expressing Gratitude: Regularly expressing gratitude for God's blessings helps cultivate a heart of thankfulness. 1 Thessalonians 5:18 encourages, "Give thanks in all circumstances; for this is God's will for you in Christ Jesus." By consistently acknowledging God's goodness, believers can maintain a humble and appreciative mindset.

2. Gratitude Journal: Keeping a gratitude journal is an effective way to document and reflect on God's blessings. Writing down specific things for which you are thankful helps

reinforce a positive and thankful attitude. This practice can be especially powerful during times of abundance, as it highlights the continual flow of God's provision.

3. Sharing Testimonies: Sharing testimonies of God's goodness with others encourages mutual gratitude and builds community. Psalm 9:1-2 emphasizes the importance of declaring God's deeds: "I will give thanks to you, Lord, with all my heart; I will tell of all your wonderful deeds. I will be glad and rejoice in you; I will sing the praises of your name, O Most High." Testimonies inspire others and remind the community of God's faithfulness.

Generosity: Blessing Others with Abundance

1. Practicing Generosity: Abundance provides opportunities to bless others. Practicing generosity aligns with God's character and opens the door to further blessings. Acts 20:35 reminds us, "It is more blessed to give than to receive." Generosity can take many forms, including financial donations, acts of kindness, and volunteer work.

2. Tithing and Offerings: Regularly giving tithes and offerings is a practical way to honor God with your wealth. Malachi 3:10 encourages, "Bring the whole tithe into the storehouse, that there may be food in my house. Test me in this," says the Lord Almighty, "and see if I will not throw open the floodgates of heaven and pour out so much blessing that

there will not be room enough to store it." Faithful giving supports the church and its ministries, extending God's kingdom.

3. Acts of Kindness: Generosity is not limited to financial giving. Acts of kindness, such as helping a neighbor, volunteering at a local charity, or offering support to someone in need, reflect God's love. Galatians 6:9-10 encourages, "Let us not become weary in doing good, for at the proper time we will reap a harvest if we do not give up. Therefore, as we have opportunity, let us do good to all people, especially to those who belong to the family of believers."

Stewardship: Managing Resources Wisely

1. Wise Management: Managing resources wisely and ethically is a key aspect of seeking God in abundance. This includes budgeting, saving, and investing in ways that honor God. Proverbs 21:20 advises, "The wise store up choice food and olive oil, but fools gulp theirs down." Effective stewardship ensures that resources are used responsibly and for God's glory.

2. Budgeting: Creating and adhering to a budget helps manage expenses and prioritize spending. A budget ensures that resources are allocated wisely, allowing for savings, investments, and generosity. Luke 14:28 highlights the importance of planning: "Suppose one of you wants to build

a tower. Won't you first sit down and estimate the cost to see if you have enough money to complete it?"

3. Ethical Investments: Investing in ways that align with ethical values supports responsible business practices and promotes social good. Proverbs 13:11 teaches, "Dishonest money dwindles away, but whoever gathers money little by little makes it grow." Ethical investments contribute to sustainable growth and reflect God's principles.

Worship and Praise: Keeping Focus on God

1. Regular Worship: Regular worship and praise keep the focus on God rather than material possessions. Psalms 100:4 encourages, "Enter his gates with thanksgiving and his courts with praise; give thanks to him and praise his name." Worship fosters a deeper connection with God and reminds believers of His sovereignty and goodness.

2. Corporate Worship: Participating in corporate worship with other believers strengthens faith and builds community. Hebrews 10:24-25 urges, "And let us consider how we may spur one another on toward love and good deeds, not giving up meeting together, as some are in the habit of doing, but encouraging one another—and all the more as you see the Day approaching." Corporate worship provides encouragement and mutual support.

3. Personal Devotion: Personal devotion times, including prayer, Bible study, and singing praises, help maintain a personal relationship with God. Psalm 119:15-16 emphasizes the importance of personal devotion: "I meditate on your precepts and consider your ways. I delight in your decrees; I will not neglect your word." Personal worship keeps the heart aligned with God.

In times of abundance, it is crucial to remain humble and recognize God's provision. Prosperity can sometimes lead to complacency or a false sense of security, but spiritual practices can help maintain a focus on God. Gratitude, generosity, stewardship, and worship are key practices that keep believers grounded in their faith and aligned with God's purposes.

Regularly expressing gratitude for God's blessings helps cultivate a heart of thankfulness. Practicing generosity allows believers to bless others and reflect God's character. Managing resources wisely through budgeting, saving, and ethical investing ensures responsible stewardship. Regular worship and praise keep the focus on God rather than material possessions.

By embracing these spiritual practices, believers can navigate times of abundance with humility and faithfulness, honoring God with their resources and maintaining a deep, personal relationship with Him. These practices lead to a spiritually rich and fulfilling life, reflecting God's love and faithfulness in every season of abundance.

CHAPTER 49

SPIRITUAL PRACTICES IN TIMES OF SCARCITY

During times of scarcity, it is essential to trust in God's provision and remain steadfast in faith. Scarcity can test one's faith, but it can also lead to profound spiritual growth. This chapter explores key spiritual practices that help believers navigate periods of scarcity, emphasizing trust in God, contentment, community support, and hope in God's promises.

Prayer and Dependence on God

1. Leaning on God through Prayer: In challenging times, leaning on God through prayer strengthens faith and reliance on Him. Philippians 4:6-7 encourages, "Do not be anxious about anything, but in every situation, by prayer and petition, with thanksgiving, present your requests to God. And the peace of God, which transcends all understanding, will guard your hearts and your minds in Christ Jesus." Prayer allows believers to cast their anxieties on God and seek His guidance and comfort.

2. Consistent Prayer Life: Maintaining a consistent prayer life during scarcity fosters a deeper connection with God. 1 Thessalonians 5:16-18 advises, "Rejoice always, pray continually, give thanks in all circumstances; for this is God's will for you in Christ Jesus." Regular communication with God provides strength and clarity.

3. Prayers of Petition and Thanksgiving: Combining prayers of petition with thanksgiving shifts the focus from problems to God's provision. Colossians 4:2 instructs, "Devote yourselves to prayer, being watchful and thankful." Acknowledging God's past faithfulness builds confidence in His continued provision.

Contentment

1. Learning Contentment: Learning to be content with what one has, even in scarcity, reflects trust in God's provision. Philippians 4:12-13 states, "I know what it is to be in need, and I know what it is to have plenty. I have learned the secret of being content in any and every situation, whether well fed or hungry, whether living in plenty or in want. I can do all this through him who gives me strength." Contentment in all circumstances is a testimony of faith.

2. Focusing on Spiritual Wealth: Shifting focus from material to spiritual wealth fosters contentment. 1 Timothy 6:6-8 teaches, "But godliness with contentment is great gain.

For we brought nothing into the world, and we can take nothing out of it. But if we have food and clothing, we will be content with that." Recognizing the sufficiency of basic needs cultivates gratitude.

3. Practicing Gratitude: Regularly practicing gratitude for what one has, even if it is little, helps maintain a positive outlook. Hebrews 13:5 advises, "Keep your lives free from the love of money and be content with what you have, because God has said, 'Never will I leave you; never will I forsake you.'" Trusting in God's constant presence and provision brings peace.

Community and Support

1. Seeking Support from Faith Communities: Seeking support from faith communities can provide encouragement and practical help. Acts 2:44-45 describes the early church's communal support: "All the believers were together and had everything in common. They sold property and possessions to give to anyone who had need." Community support reflects God's love and care.

2. Sharing Burdens: Sharing burdens with fellow believers provides emotional and spiritual relief. Galatians 6:2 encourages, "Carry each other's burdens, and in this way you will fulfill the law of Christ." Mutual support strengthens the body of Christ.

3. Participating in Church Activities: Actively participating in church activities fosters a sense of belonging and support. Hebrews 10:24-25 emphasizes, "And let us consider how we may spur one another on toward love and good deeds, not giving up meeting together, as some are in the habit of doing, but encouraging one another—and all the more as you see the Day approaching." Engagement in the faith community offers encouragement and practical assistance.

Trust and Hope in God's Promises

1. Holding on to God's Promises: Holding on to God's promises can provide hope and strength in times of scarcity. Jeremiah 29:11 offers reassurance, "For I know the plans I have for you," declares the Lord, "plans to prosper you and not to harm you, plans to give you hope and a future." Believing in God's good plans fosters hope.

2. Trusting in God's Provision: Trusting in God's provision alleviates anxiety about material needs. Matthew 6:31-33 advises, "So do not worry, saying, 'What shall we eat?' or 'What shall we drink?' or 'What shall we wear?' For the pagans run after all these things, and your heavenly Father knows that you need them. But seek first his kingdom and his righteousness, and all these things will be given to you as well." Prioritizing God's kingdom assures provision.

3. Finding Strength in God's Faithfulness: Reflecting on God's past faithfulness strengthens trust in His continued care. Lamentations 3:22-23 affirms, "Because of the Lord's great love we are not consumed, for his compassions never fail. They are new every morning; great is your faithfulness." Trusting in God's steadfast love provides endurance.

Practical Steps to Cultivate Trust and Contentment

1. Daily Devotion and Reflection: Setting aside time for daily devotion and reflection on Scripture strengthens faith and trust in God. Psalm 119:105 declares, "Your word is a lamp for my feet, a light on my path." Regular engagement with God's Word provides guidance and reassurance.

2. Memorizing Scripture: Memorizing verses that emphasize God's promises and provision offers quick reminders of His faithfulness during challenging times. Psalm 119:11 states, "I have hidden your word in my heart that I might not sin against you." Scripture memorization fortifies faith.

3. Engaging in Service: Serving others, even in times of personal scarcity, shifts focus from self to others and reflects God's love. Acts 20:35 quotes Jesus, "It is more blessed to give than to receive." Acts of service cultivate contentment and gratitude.

4. Practicing Simplicity: Embracing simplicity and reducing material desires fosters contentment. Ecclesiastes

4:6 advises, "Better one handful with tranquility than two handfuls with toil and chasing after the wind." Simplified living enhances spiritual focus.

5. Building Support Networks: Establishing and nurturing support networks within the faith community ensures mutual encouragement and assistance. Proverbs 17:17 states, "A friend loves at all times, and a brother is born for a time of adversity." Strong support networks provide resilience.

During times of scarcity, it is essential to trust in God's provision and remain steadfast in faith. Scarcity can test one's faith, but it can also lead to profound spiritual growth. Prayer and dependence on God, learning contentment, seeking support from faith communities, and holding on to God's promises are key practices that help believers navigate periods of scarcity.

Leaning on God through prayer strengthens faith and reliance on Him. Learning to be content with what one has, even in scarcity, reflects trust in God's provision. Seeking support from faith communities provides encouragement and practical help. Holding on to God's promises fosters hope and strength.

By embracing these spiritual practices, believers can navigate times of scarcity with faith, trust, and resilience, growing closer to God and experiencing His provision and faithfulness. These practices lead to a spiritually rich and fulfilling life, even in the face of material challenges, reflecting God's love and faithfulness in every season.

CHAPTER 50

MAINTAINING SPIRITUAL BALANCE

Maintaining a spiritual balance between abundance and scarcity involves understanding that both are part of life's journey and God's plan. Recognizing that God is sovereign over all circumstances helps maintain faith and trust in Him. This chapter explores how to cultivate a balanced perspective, integrating faith into every aspect of life, and embracing both abundance and scarcity as opportunities for spiritual growth.

Understanding God's Sovereignty

1. God's Sovereignty Over Circumstances: Acknowledging God's sovereignty is crucial for maintaining spiritual balance. Romans 8:28 assures us, "And we know that in all things God works for the good of those who love him, who have been called according to his purpose." Believing that God is in control and has a purpose for every situation provides comfort and perspective.

2. Faith in God's Plan: Trusting in God's plan, even when it is not fully understood, is essential. Proverbs 3:5-6 advises, "Trust in the Lord with all your heart and lean not on your own understanding; in all your ways submit to him, and he will make your paths straight." Faith in God's wisdom and timing fosters peace and balance.

3. Embracing Life's Seasons: Ecclesiastes 3:1 reminds us, "There is a time for everything and a season for every activity under the heavens." Recognizing that life includes seasons of abundance and scarcity helps us navigate these periods with grace and trust in God's overarching plan.

Viewing Challenges as Opportunities for Growth

1. Spiritual Growth Through Trials: James 1:2-4 teaches, "Consider it pure joy, my brothers and sisters, whenever you face trials of many kinds, because you know that the testing of your faith produces perseverance. Let perseverance finish its work so that you may be mature and complete, not lacking anything." Trials and challenges are opportunities for spiritual growth and development.

2. Perseverance and Maturity: Trials build perseverance, which leads to spiritual maturity. Romans 5:3-4 states, "Not only so, but we also glory in our sufferings, because we know that suffering produces perseverance; perseverance, character; and character, hope." Embracing

challenges as refining processes strengthens our faith and character.

3. Learning Contentment: Both abundance and scarcity teach contentment. Philippians 4:12-13 emphasizes, "I know what it is to be in need, and I know what it is to have plenty. I have learned the secret of being content in any and every situation, whether well fed or hungry, whether living in plenty or in want. I can do all this through him who gives me strength." Contentment in all circumstances reflects a deep trust in God's provision.

Cultivating a Balanced Perspective

1. Gratitude in All Circumstances: Practicing gratitude in both abundance and scarcity maintains a balanced perspective. 1 Thessalonians 5:18 encourages, "Give thanks in all circumstances; for this is God's will for you in Christ Jesus." Gratitude shifts the focus from what is lacking to recognizing God's blessings.

2. Stewardship and Generosity: Effective stewardship of resources, whether in abundance or scarcity, promotes balance. 1 Peter 4:10 advises, "Each of you should use whatever gift you have received to serve others, as faithful stewards of God's grace in its various forms." Generosity, even in times of need, reflects trust in God's provision.

3. Focusing on Eternal Values: Maintaining a focus on eternal values rather than temporary circumstances fosters spiritual balance. Matthew 6:19-21 instructs, "Do not store up for yourselves treasures on earth, where moths and vermin destroy, and where thieves break in and steal. But store up for yourselves treasures in heaven, where moths and vermin do not destroy, and where thieves do not break in and steal. For where your treasure is, there your heart will be also." Prioritizing eternal treasures over material wealth ensures a balanced spiritual life.

Integrating Faith into Daily Life

1. Daily Devotion and Prayer: Consistent daily devotion and prayer keep the focus on God. Philippians 4:6-7 advises, "Do not be anxious about anything, but in every situation, by prayer and petition, with thanksgiving, present your requests to God. And the peace of God, which transcends all understanding, will guard your hearts and your minds in Christ Jesus." Regular communication with God fosters peace and spiritual stability.

2. Scripture Meditation: Meditating on Scripture provides wisdom and perspective. Psalm 1:2-3 describes the blessed person: "But whose delight is in the law of the Lord, and who meditates on his law day and night. That person is like a tree planted by streams of water, which yields its fruit in season and whose leaf does not wither—whatever they do

prospers." Scripture meditation roots believers in God's truth, promoting spiritual growth.

3. Community and Fellowship: Engaging in a supportive faith community provides encouragement and accountability. Hebrews 10:24-25 urges, "And let us consider how we may spur one another on toward love and good deeds, not giving up meeting together, as some are in the habit of doing, but encouraging one another—and all the more as you see the Day approaching." Fellowship with other believers strengthens faith and fosters a sense of belonging.

Practical Steps to Maintain Spiritual Balance

1. Set Spiritual Goals: Setting and pursuing spiritual goals ensures continuous growth and focus on God. 2 Peter 3:18 encourages, "But grow in the grace and knowledge of our Lord and Savior Jesus Christ. To him be glory both now and forever! Amen." Spiritual goals provide direction and purpose.

2. Balance Work and Rest: Balancing work and rest is essential for maintaining spiritual health. Exodus 20:9-10 commands, "Six days you shall labor and do all your work, but the seventh day is a sabbath to the Lord your God. On it you shall not do any work." Observing rest periods prevents burnout and fosters spiritual renewal.

3. Practice Generosity: Practicing generosity, even in times of scarcity, promotes a balanced perspective. Luke 6:38 teaches, "Give, and it will be given to you. A good measure, pressed down, shaken together and running over, will be poured into your lap. For with the measure you use, it will be measured to you." Generosity reflects trust in God's provision and love for others.

4. Maintain Accountability: Establishing accountability with trusted individuals helps maintain spiritual focus and balance. Proverbs 27:17 states, "As iron sharpens iron, so one person sharpens another." Accountability provides support and encouragement in the faith journey.

Maintaining a spiritual balance between abundance and scarcity involves understanding that both are part of life's journey and God's plan. Recognizing that God is sovereign over all circumstances helps maintain faith and trust in Him. James 1:2-4 teaches, "Consider it pure joy, my brothers and sisters, whenever you face trials of many kinds, because you know that the testing of your faith produces perseverance. Let perseverance finish its work so that you may be mature and complete, not lacking anything." Viewing challenges as opportunities for spiritual growth can transform how we approach both abundance and scarcity.

By practicing gratitude in all circumstances, effective stewardship, focusing on eternal values, integrating faith into daily life, and maintaining supportive relationships, believers can navigate life's ups and downs with faith and trust in God. These practices ensure a balanced spiritual life that honors God and reflects His love and faithfulness, regardless of material circumstances. Embracing both abundance and scarcity as opportunities for spiritual growth leads to a fulfilling and spiritually rich life, grounded in the unchanging nature of God's love and provision.

CHAPTER 51

MODERN APPLICATIONS

Applying spiritual principles in contemporary life involves integrating faith into daily practices, regardless of financial status. This chapter explores practical ways to maintain spiritual focus and balance in modern contexts, ensuring that faith guides actions and decisions. Key areas include regular devotional time, financial planning, service and volunteering, and practicing mindfulness and simplicity.

Regular Devotional Time

1. Setting Aside Time for Prayer and Bible Study: Regular devotional time helps maintain focus on God. Psalm 119:105 declares, "Your word is a lamp for my feet, a light on my path." Setting aside dedicated time each day for prayer, Bible study, and reflection strengthens the relationship with God and provides spiritual nourishment.

2. Creating a Devotional Routine: Establishing a consistent devotional routine fosters discipline and spiritual growth. Choose a specific time each day, such as early

morning or before bed, to spend with God. Following a structured Bible reading plan or devotional guide can provide direction and keep the focus on spiritual matters.

3. Journaling and Reflection: Keeping a journal to document prayers, insights from Scripture, and reflections on God's work in your life enhances devotional time. Philippians 4:8 encourages focusing on what is true, noble, right, pure, lovely, and admirable. Journaling helps internalize these values and track spiritual progress.

Financial Planning

1. Practicing Sound Financial Planning: Financial planning, including budgeting and saving, prepares for both times of abundance and scarcity. Proverbs 21:5 advises, "The plans of the diligent lead to profit as surely as haste leads to poverty." Developing a budget and sticking to it ensures responsible stewardship of resources.

2. Creating a Budget: A budget helps track income and expenses, ensuring that spending aligns with priorities and goals. Luke 14:28 highlights the importance of planning: "Suppose one of you wants to build a tower. Won't you first sit down and estimate the cost to see if you have enough money to complete it?" A well-constructed budget provides financial stability and preparedness.

3. Saving and Investing: Saving responsibly and investing wisely ensure financial security and growth. Proverbs 6:6-8 encourages preparation: "Go to the ant, you sluggard; consider its ways and be wise! It has no commander, no overseer or ruler, yet it stores its provisions in summer and gathers its food at harvest." Responsible saving and ethical investments align financial practices with biblical values.

Service and Volunteering

1. Engaging in Service and Volunteering: Serving others fosters a spirit of generosity and community support. Acts 20:35 quotes Jesus, saying, "It is more blessed to give than to receive." Volunteering and participating in service projects demonstrate God's love and compassion.

2. Finding Opportunities to Serve: Look for opportunities to serve within your community and church. Matthew 25:35-36 highlights the importance of serving others: "For I was hungry and you gave me something to eat, I was thirsty and you gave me something to drink, I was a stranger and you invited me in, I needed clothes and you clothed me, I was sick and you looked after me, I was in prison and you came to visit me." Service opportunities can include helping at food banks, mentoring youth, or visiting the elderly.

3. Building a Service-Oriented Mindset: Cultivating a mindset focused on serving others ensures that generosity

becomes a regular practice. Galatians 5:13 advises, "Serve one another humbly in love." Incorporating service into daily life, such as helping neighbors or offering support to those in need, reflects God's character.

Mindfulness and Simplicity

1. Practicing Mindfulness: Mindfulness involves being present and aware of God's presence in every moment. Psalm 46:10 encourages, "Be still, and know that I am God." Practicing mindfulness through prayer, meditation, and quiet reflection fosters a deeper connection with God.

2. Embracing Simplicity: Simplicity reduces the desire for material excess and promotes contentment. 1 Timothy 6:6-8 teaches, "But godliness with contentment is great gain. For we brought nothing into the world, and we can take nothing out of it. But if we have food and clothing, we will be content with that." Simplifying life by prioritizing what truly matters helps maintain spiritual focus.

3. Reducing Material Excess: Limiting material possessions and focusing on spiritual wealth aligns with biblical teachings. Matthew 6:19-21 advises, "Do not store up for yourselves treasures on earth, where moths and vermin destroy, and where thieves break in and steal. But store up for yourselves treasures in heaven, where moths and vermin do not destroy, and where thieves do not break in and steal. For

where your treasure is, there your heart will be also." Reducing material excess fosters a deeper reliance on God.

Practical Steps for Modern Applications

1. Establish a Devotional Space: Create a dedicated space for prayer and Bible study to facilitate regular devotional time. This space can be a quiet corner of your home where you can focus and reflect without distractions.

2. Utilize Financial Tools: Use financial tools such as budgeting apps and investment platforms to manage resources effectively. These tools help track expenses, save for future goals, and invest responsibly.

3. Join Service Groups: Participate in service groups or community organizations that align with your values. Engaging with like-minded individuals fosters a sense of community and shared purpose.

4. Practice Digital Detox: Regularly disconnecting from digital devices can help focus on God and reduce distractions. Set aside specific times each day to unplug from technology and engage in prayer, reflection, or meaningful conversations.

5. Adopt Minimalist Practices: Embrace minimalist practices by decluttering your living space and simplifying your lifestyle. Focus on meaningful experiences and relationships rather than accumulating possessions.

Conclusion

Applying spiritual principles in contemporary life involves integrating faith into daily practices, regardless of financial status. Regular devotional time, sound financial planning, service and volunteering, and practicing mindfulness and simplicity are key ways to maintain spiritual focus and balance.

By setting aside time each day for prayer, Bible study, and reflection, believers can deepen their relationship with God. Practicing sound financial planning, including budgeting and saving, prepares for both times of abundance and scarcity. Engaging in service and volunteering fosters a spirit of generosity and community support. Practicing mindfulness and simplicity helps maintain contentment and reduces the desire for material excess.

These practical steps ensure that faith guides actions and decisions, leading to a spiritually rich and fulfilling life that honors God in every circumstance. Embracing these modern applications of spiritual principles fosters a balanced perspective, reflecting God's love and faithfulness in every aspect of life.

PART X

THE UNIVERSAL LOVE OF GOD

CHAPTER 52

THE NATURE OF GOD'S UNIVERSAL LOVE

The Bible consistently affirms the universal and unconditional nature of God's love. In John 3:16, one of the most well-known verses in the Bible, it is written, "For God so loved the world that he gave his one and only Son, that whoever believes in him shall not perish but have eternal life." This verse underscores that God's love is for everyone, transcending all human distinctions. This chapter explores the nature of God's universal love, its steadfast and enduring qualities, and its implications for humanity.

The Universality of God's Love

1. Love for All People: God's love extends to every person, regardless of race, nationality, or status. John 3:16 clearly states that God loves the world, indicating that His love is not limited by human boundaries. This universal love invites everyone into a relationship with God through Jesus Christ.

2. Inclusivity in Scripture: The Bible repeatedly highlights the inclusivity of God's love. Galatians 3:28 emphasizes this point: "There is neither Jew nor Gentile, neither slave nor free, nor is there male and female, for you are all one in Christ Jesus." God's love breaks down barriers and unites all people under His grace.

3. God's Love for the Marginalized: Throughout the Bible, God shows special concern for the marginalized and oppressed. In Isaiah 58:6-7, God calls His people to act justly and care for the needy: "Is not this the kind of fasting I have chosen: to loose the chains of injustice and untie the cords of the yoke, to set the oppressed free and break every yoke? Is it not to share your food with the hungry and to provide the poor wanderer with shelter?" This demonstrates that God's love is particularly evident in His care for those who are often overlooked by society.

The Steadfast Nature of God's Love

1. Enduring Love: Psalm 136 repeatedly emphasizes, "His love endures forever." This enduring love is a fundamental aspect of God's nature, remaining constant through all of life's circumstances. God's love does not waver or diminish based on human actions or situations.

2. Unfailing Love: God's love is described as unfailing in many scriptures. Lamentations 3:22-23 declares, "Because of the Lord's great love we are not consumed, for his

compassions never fail. They are new every morning; great is your faithfulness." God's love is a source of continual renewal and hope.

3. Love Despite Human Failure: Romans 5:8 illustrates the depth of God's love, stating, "But God demonstrates his own love for us in this: While we were still sinners, Christ died for us." God's love persists despite human shortcomings and sin, highlighting its unconditional nature.

The Unconditional Nature of God's Love

1. Not Based on Merit: God's love is not earned by human merit or good works. Ephesians 2:8-9 clarifies, "For it is by grace you have been saved, through faith—and this is not from yourselves, it is the gift of God—not by works, so that no one can boast." God's love is a free gift, given regardless of human effort.

2. Love for All Circumstances: God's love remains constant through all of life's highs and lows. Romans 8:38-39 assures, "For I am convinced that neither death nor life, neither angels nor demons, neither the present nor the future, nor any powers, neither height nor depth, nor anything else in all creation, will be able to separate us from the love of God that is in Christ Jesus our Lord." This passage underscores that nothing can separate believers from God's love.

3. Parables of Unconditional Love: Jesus' parables often illustrate the unconditional nature of God's love. The Parable of the Prodigal Son (Luke 15:11-32) is a poignant example, showing a father's unconditional love and forgiveness for his wayward son. This parable reflects God's readiness to forgive and embrace those who return to Him.

Implications of God's Universal Love

1. Call to Love Others: Believers are called to reflect God's universal love in their relationships with others. John 13:34-35 commands, "A new command I give you: Love one another. As I have loved you, so you must love one another. By this everyone will know that you are my disciples, if you love one another." Demonstrating love and compassion to others is a fundamental aspect of Christian faith.

2. Empathy and Compassion: Understanding the universal nature of God's love fosters empathy and compassion for others. Colossians 3:12 encourages, "Therefore, as God's chosen people, holy and dearly loved, clothe yourselves with compassion, kindness, humility, gentleness and patience." Believers are called to embody these qualities in their interactions.

3. Evangelism and Outreach: Recognizing that God's love is for everyone motivates believers to share the gospel and engage in outreach. Matthew 28:19-20, known as the Great Commission, instructs, "Therefore go and make

disciples of all nations, baptizing them in the name of the Father and of the Son and of the Holy Spirit, and teaching them to obey everything I have commanded you." Sharing God's love is an integral part of the Christian mission.

Living in Response to God's Love

1. Gratitude and Worship: Living in response to God's love involves gratitude and worship. Psalm 100:4-5 invites, "Enter his gates with thanksgiving and his courts with praise; give thanks to him and praise his name. For the Lord is good and his love endures forever; his faithfulness continues through all generations." Regularly expressing gratitude and worshipping God acknowledges His love and goodness.

2. Trust and Obedience: Trusting in God's love leads to obedience and faithful living. John 14:15 states, "If you love me, keep my commands." Obedience is a natural response to understanding and accepting God's love.

3. Forgiveness and Reconciliation: Reflecting God's love includes practicing forgiveness and seeking reconciliation. Ephesians 4:32 instructs, "Be kind and compassionate to one another, forgiving each other, just as in Christ God forgave you." Emulating God's forgiveness fosters healing and unity in relationships.

The Bible consistently affirms the universal and unconditional nature of God's love. In John 3:16, it is written,

"For God so loved the world that he gave his one and only Son, that whoever believes in him shall not perish but have eternal life." This verse underscores that God's love is for everyone, transcending all human distinctions. God's love is described as steadfast, enduring, and unfailing. Psalm 136 repeatedly emphasizes, "His love endures forever." This enduring love is not based on human merit or material wealth but on God's nature and character.

God's universal love calls believers to reflect His love in their lives, demonstrating empathy, compassion, and forgiveness. Understanding and embracing God's love motivates evangelism and outreach, sharing the message of God's unconditional love with the world. Living in response to God's love involves gratitude, worship, trust, and obedience, leading to a fulfilling and spiritually rich life.

By recognizing the universal and unconditional nature of God's love, believers can navigate life's challenges and blessings with confidence, knowing that nothing can separate them from the love of God in Christ Jesus. Embracing and sharing this love transforms individuals and communities, reflecting the heart of God's character and His eternal plan for humanity.

CHAPTER 53

GOD'S LOVE FOR ALL, REGARDLESS OF WEALTH

One of the key messages of Jesus' ministry was the inclusivity of God's love. Jesus reached out to the marginalized, the poor, and the wealthy alike, demonstrating that God's love is not confined to any particular group. In Matthew 5:45, Jesus teaches, "He causes his sun to rise on the evil and the good, and sends rain on the righteous and the unrighteous." This teaching highlights that God's blessings and love are extended to all people, irrespective of their moral or financial status. This chapter explores the universal nature of God's love, illustrating through scripture and parables that His love transcends material wealth and social status.

God's Love for All

1. Inclusivity in Jesus' Ministry: Jesus' ministry was marked by inclusivity, reaching out to all individuals regardless of their social or economic status. He ministered to the poor, the sick, and the outcasts, as well as to the wealthy and powerful. Mark 2:17 records Jesus saying, "It is not the

healthy who need a doctor, but the sick. I have not come to call the righteous, but sinners." Jesus' mission was to bring God's love to everyone.

2. God's Blessings for All: In Matthew 5:45, Jesus teaches, "He causes his sun to rise on the evil and the good, and sends rain on the righteous and the unrighteous." This verse emphasizes that God's blessings are not limited by human distinctions. God's provision and care extend to all people, demonstrating His impartial love.

3. No Partiality with God: Romans 2:11 states, "For God does not show favoritism." God's love is impartial, reaching out to every individual regardless of their background or circumstances. This principle is central to understanding the nature of God's universal love.

The Parable of the Prodigal Son

1. Unconditional Love and Forgiveness: The parable of the Prodigal Son (Luke 15:11-32) is a powerful illustration of God's unconditional love and forgiveness. The father's acceptance of his wayward son, despite his reckless living and squandered wealth, reflects God's readiness to forgive and restore anyone who returns to Him. Luke 15:20 captures the father's reaction: "But while he was still a long way off, his father saw him and was filled with compassion for him; he ran to his son, threw his arms around him and kissed him." This act of compassion symbolizes God's boundless love.

2. Restoration Without Conditions: The father's willingness to restore his son without conditions or reproach demonstrates that God's love is not based on merit or material success. Luke 15:22-24 describes the father's response: "But the father said to his servants, 'Quick! Bring the best robe and put it on him. Put a ring on his finger and sandals on his feet. Bring the fattened calf and kill it. Let's have a feast and celebrate. For this son of mine was dead and is alive again; he was lost and is found.' So they began to celebrate." The son's restoration signifies God's joy in accepting those who repent, regardless of their past actions.

3. Equal Love for All Sons: The parable also highlights the father's equal love for both his sons, the prodigal and the elder. The father's reassurance to the elder son in Luke 15:31 32 shows that both sons are equally loved: "'My son,' the father said, 'you are always with me, and everything I have is yours. But we had to celebrate and be glad, because this brother of yours was dead and is alive again; he was lost and is found.'" This illustrates that God's love is not diminished by the repentance of the wayward but is abundant and inclusive.

Biblical Examples of God's Love for Different Individuals

1. Zacchaeus the Tax Collector: Zacchaeus was a wealthy tax collector, despised by society for his profession. However, Jesus reached out to him, demonstrating that God's love includes even those considered sinners. In Luke 19:9-10, Jesus declares, "Today salvation has come to this house, because this man, too, is a son of Abraham. For the Son of Man came to seek and to save the lost." Zacchaeus' transformation reflects God's love and grace extended to all, irrespective of their past.

2. The Rich Young Ruler: In Mark 10:17-27, Jesus encounters a rich young ruler seeking eternal life. Despite the man's attachment to his wealth, Jesus' interaction with him shows God's love and concern for his spiritual well-being. Jesus' instruction to sell his possessions and follow Him underscores the importance of prioritizing a relationship with God over material wealth. Jesus looked at him and loved him (Mark 10:21), indicating that God's love reaches out even to those who struggle with their attachments.

3. The Widow's Mite: In Mark 12:41-44, Jesus observes a poor widow giving two small coins at the temple treasury. Despite her meager offering, Jesus commends her generosity, highlighting that God values the heart behind the gift more than the amount. "Truly I tell you, this poor widow has put more into the treasury than all the others. They all gave out of their wealth; but she, out of her poverty, put in

everything—all she had to live on." This story demonstrates that God's love and approval are not based on wealth but on the sincerity and sacrifice of the giver.

Implications of God's Universal Love

1. Equality Before God: God's universal love affirms the equality of all people before Him. Galatians 3:28 emphasizes this: "There is neither Jew nor Gentile, neither slave nor free, nor is there male and female, for you are all one in Christ Jesus." This equality calls for believers to treat everyone with respect and love.

2. Breaking Social Barriers: Understanding God's love for all encourages breaking down social barriers and extending love and compassion to everyone, regardless of their social or economic status. James 2:1-4 warns against favoritism, urging believers to treat all people equally: "My brothers and sisters, believers in our glorious Lord Jesus Christ must not show favoritism... Have you not discriminated among yourselves and become judges with evil thoughts?"

3. Call to Love Others: Believers are called to reflect God's love in their interactions with others. John 13:34-35 commands, "A new command I give you: Love one another. As I have loved you, so you must love one another. By this everyone will know that you are my disciples, if you love one

another." Demonstrating love and compassion to all people is a testimony of God's love.

Living in Response to God's Love

1. Generosity and Compassion: Reflecting God's love involves practicing generosity and compassion towards others, regardless of their wealth or status. 1 John 3:17-18 challenges believers, "If anyone has material possessions and sees a brother or sister in need but has no pity on them, how can the love of God be in that person? Dear children, let us not love with words or speech but with actions and in truth." Acts of kindness and generosity demonstrate God's love in practical ways.

2. Forgiveness and Reconciliation: Emulating God's love includes practicing forgiveness and seeking reconciliation. Ephesians 4:32 instructs, "Be kind and compassionate to one another, forgiving each other, just as in Christ God forgave you." Forgiveness heals relationships and reflects God's unconditional love.

3. Trust and Obedience: Living in response to God's love involves trusting in His provision and obeying His commands. John 14:15 states, "If you love me, keep my commands." Obedience is a natural response to understanding and accepting God's love.

One of the key messages of Jesus' ministry was the inclusivity of God's love. Jesus reached out to the marginalized, the poor, and the wealthy alike, demonstrating that God's love is not confined to any particular group. In Matthew 5:45, Jesus teaches, "He causes his sun to rise on the evil and the good, and sends rain on the righteous and the unrighteous." This teaching highlights that God's blessings and love are extended to all people, irrespective of their moral or financial status.

The parable of the Prodigal Son (Luke 15:11-32) illustrates the depth of God's love and forgiveness. The father's unconditional love for his wayward son, regardless of his past actions and squandered wealth, reflects God's willingness to embrace and restore anyone who turns to Him. This parable emphasizes that God's love is not dependent on material wealth or success but on a relationship with Him.

By understanding and embracing God's universal love, believers can navigate life with a balanced perspective, treating everyone with compassion and respect, and living in a way that reflects God's inclusive and unconditional love. This approach fosters unity and demonstrates the heart of God's character, inviting others to experience His transformative love.

CHAPTER 54

LOVE AS THE GREATEST COMMANDMENT

Jesus summarized the essence of God's commandments with the call to love God and love others. In Matthew 22:37-40, Jesus said, "'Love the Lord your God with all your heart and with all your soul and with all your mind.' This is the first and greatest commandment. And the second is like it: 'Love your neighbor as yourself.' All the Law and the Prophets hang on these two commandments." This teaching emphasizes that love is the foundation of our relationship with God and with each other. This chapter explores the significance of love as the greatest commandment, its foundational role in Christian life, and practical ways to embody this love in our daily interactions.

The Greatest Commandment: Loving God

1. Wholehearted Love for God: Jesus commands us to love God with all our heart, soul, and mind. This comprehensive love involves total devotion and commitment to God. Deuteronomy 6:5, which Jesus quotes, emphasizes the depth and breadth of this love: "Love the Lord your God

with all your heart and with all your soul and with all your strength."

2. Expressing Love through Obedience: Loving God involves obeying His commandments. John 14:15 states, "If you love me, keep my commands." Obedience is a natural outflow of love for God, reflecting our commitment to His will and ways.

3. Worship and Devotion: Worship is a key expression of love for God. Psalm 95:6 invites, "Come, let us bow down in worship, let us kneel before the Lord our Maker." Regular worship and devotion deepen our relationship with God and reinforce our love for Him.

The Greatest Commandment: Loving Others

1. Loving Your Neighbor as Yourself: Jesus teaches that loving others is akin to loving God. Matthew 22:39 highlights the second commandment: "Love your neighbor as yourself." This command calls for empathy, compassion, and active care for others.

2. The Parable of the Good Samaritan: In Luke 10:25-37, Jesus illustrates the concept of loving one's neighbor through the Parable of the Good Samaritan. The Samaritan's compassion and care for a stranger in need exemplify true neighborly love. Luke 10:37 concludes, "Jesus told him, 'Go and do likewise.'"

3. Practical Acts of Love: Loving others involves practical acts of kindness and service. 1 John 3:18 advises, "Dear children, let us not love with words or speech but with actions and in truth." Genuine love is demonstrated through tangible actions that benefit others.

Love as the Fulfillment of the Law

1. The Law and the Prophets: Jesus asserts that all the Law and the Prophets hang on the commandments to love God and others (Matthew 22:40). This means that love fulfills the essence of God's instructions and moral requirements.

2. Paul's Teaching on Love: The Apostle Paul echoes Jesus' teaching in Romans 13:8-10: "Let no debt remain outstanding, except the continuing debt to love one another, for whoever loves others has fulfilled the law... Love does no harm to a neighbor. Therefore love is the fulfillment of the law." Paul reinforces that love encompasses and surpasses all other commandments.

3. The Primacy of Love: In 1 Corinthians 13, known as the "Love Chapter," Paul underscores the primacy of love. 1 Corinthians 13:13 concludes, "And now these three remain: faith, hope, and love. But the greatest of these is love." Love is the highest virtue and the core of Christian ethics.

Characteristics of Love

1. Attributes of Love: Paul describes the characteristics of love in 1 Corinthians 13:4-7: "Love is

patient, love is kind. It does not envy, it does not boast, it is not proud. It does not dishonor others, it is not self-seeking, it is not easily angered, it keeps no record of wrongs. Love does not delight in evil but rejoices with the truth. It always protects, always trusts, always hopes, always perseveres." These attributes define how love should manifest in our relationships.

2. Endurance of Love: Paul emphasizes that love never fails (1 Corinthians 13:8). Unlike other spiritual gifts or achievements, love endures forever. This enduring nature of love highlights its eternal significance and foundational role in the Christian faith.

3. Selfless and Sacrificial: True love is selfless and sacrificial, as demonstrated by Jesus. John 15:13 states, "Greater love has no one than this: to lay down one's life for one's friends." Jesus' sacrificial love is the ultimate example for believers to follow.

Practical Ways to Embody Love

1. Acts of Service: Serving others is a practical way to demonstrate love. Galatians 5:13 encourages, "Serve one another humbly in love." Volunteering, helping those in need, and offering support are tangible expressions of love.

2. Forgiveness and Reconciliation: Practicing forgiveness and seeking reconciliation are crucial aspects of

love. Colossians 3:13 instructs, "Bear with each other and forgive one another if any of you has a grievance against someone. Forgive as the Lord forgave you." Forgiveness heals relationships and reflects God's love.

3. Encouragement and Support: Offering encouragement and support strengthens others and fosters a loving community. Hebrews 10:24-25 urges, "And let us consider how we may spur one another on toward love and good deeds, not giving up meeting together, as some are in the habit of doing, but encouraging one another—and all the more as you see the Day approaching."

4. Generosity and Compassion: Being generous and compassionate towards others, especially those in need, embodies love. Proverbs 19:17 says, "Whoever is kind to the poor lends to the Lord, and he will reward them for what they have done." Acts of kindness and generosity demonstrate God's love in action.

Living in Love Daily

1. Daily Commitment to Love: Love should be a daily commitment and an integral part of a believer's life. Ephesians 5:2 advises, "And walk in the way of love, just as Christ loved us and gave himself up for us as a fragrant offering and sacrifice to God." Walking in love involves consistently choosing actions and attitudes that reflect Christ's love.

2. Prayer for a Loving Heart: Praying for a heart filled with love helps align one's actions with God's commandments. Philippians 1:9-10 expresses this prayer: "And this is my prayer: that your love may abound more and more in knowledge and depth of insight so that you may be able to discern what is best and may be pure and blameless for the day of Christ." Asking God to fill our hearts with love enables us to love others more fully.

3. Modeling Christ's Love: Jesus is the ultimate model of love. Following His example in daily life ensures that our love reflects His selflessness and compassion. 1 John 4:19 reminds us, "We love because he first loved us." Modeling Christ's love involves treating others with kindness, patience, and humility.

Conclusion

Jesus summarized the essence of God's commandments with the call to love God and love others. In Matthew 22:37-40, Jesus said, "'Love the Lord your God with all your heart and with all your soul and with all your mind.' This is the first and greatest commandment. And the second is like it: 'Love your neighbor as yourself.' All the Law and the Prophets hang on these two commandments." This teaching emphasizes that love is the foundation of our relationship with God and with each other.

The Apostle Paul, in 1 Corinthians 13, known as the "Love Chapter," further underscores the primacy of love. He writes, "And now these three remain faith, hope, and love. But the greatest of these is love" (1 Corinthians 13:13). Paul's message highlights that love surpasses all other virtues and is central to the Christian faith.

By understanding and embodying the greatest commandment, believers can navigate life with a balanced perspective, treating everyone with compassion and respect, and living in a way that reflects God's inclusive and unconditional love. This approach fosters unity and demonstrates the heart of God's character, inviting others to experience His transformative love. Embracing and sharing this love transforms individuals and communities, reflecting the heart of God's character and His eternal plan for humanity.

CHAPTER 55

IMPLICATIONS OF GOD'S LOVE FOR OUR LIVES

Understanding the universal love of God has profound implications for how we live our lives and relate to others. It calls us to reflect God's love in our actions, attitudes, and relationships. This chapter explores how embracing God's love transforms our lives, encourages inclusivity, promotes generosity, fosters forgiveness, prioritizes relationships, and cultivates humility.

Embracing All People

1. Inclusivity and Acceptance: Recognizing that God's love extends to everyone encourages us to embrace and value all individuals, regardless of their background, status, or wealth. Galatians 3:28 emphasizes, "There is neither Jew nor Gentile, neither slave nor free, nor is there male and female, for you are all one in Christ Jesus." This inclusivity reflects God's heart and promotes a spirit of unity and compassion.

2. Breaking Down Barriers: Embracing all people involves breaking down social, racial, and economic barriers. James 2:1 warns against favoritism: "My brothers and sisters, believers in our glorious Lord Jesus Christ must not show favoritism." Treating everyone with respect and love reflects God's impartiality and fosters a sense of belonging.

3. Acts of Kindness and Acceptance: Practical acts of kindness and acceptance demonstrate God's love. Romans 15:7 encourages, "Accept one another, then, just as Christ accepted you, in order to bring praise to God." Embracing others, especially those different from us, showcases God's inclusive love.

Living Generously

1. Generosity as an Expression of Love: The recognition of God's unconditional love motivates us to live generously, sharing our resources, time, and talents with others. 2 Corinthians 9:7 advises, "Each of you should give what you have decided in your heart to give, not reluctantly or under compulsion, for God loves a cheerful giver." Generosity is a tangible expression of God's love and helps meet the needs of those around us.

2. Supporting Those in Need: Generosity involves supporting those in need, reflecting God's care for the marginalized. Proverbs 19:17 states, "Whoever is kind to the poor lends to the Lord, and he will reward them for what they

have done." Acts of generosity provide practical help and show God's compassion.

3. Sharing Time and Talents: Besides financial resources, sharing time and talents is equally important. 1 Peter 4:10 encourages, "Each of you should use whatever gift you have received to serve others, as faithful stewards of God's grace in its various forms." Volunteering and using our skills to help others manifest God's love in action.

Practicing Forgiveness

1. Reflecting God's Forgiveness: Just as God's love is forgiving, we are called to forgive others. Colossians 3:13 instructs, "Bear with each other and forgive one another if any of you has a grievance against someone. Forgive as the Lord forgave you." Forgiveness fosters healing and reconciliation, reflecting the grace and mercy that we have received from God.

2. Healing Relationships: Forgiveness is crucial for healing relationships and restoring harmony. Matthew 18:21-22 highlights Jesus' teaching on forgiveness: "Then Peter came to Jesus and asked, 'Lord, how many times shall I forgive my brother or sister who sins against me? Up to seven times?' Jesus answered, 'I tell you, not seven times, but seventy-seven times.'" Practicing forgiveness helps rebuild trust and strengthens bonds.

3. Forgiveness as a Witness: Forgiving others serves as a powerful witness to God's love. John 13:35 emphasizes, "By this everyone will know that you are my disciples, if you love one another." Demonstrating forgiveness, especially in difficult situations, reflects the transformative power of God's love.

Prioritizing Relationships

1. Loving God and Others: The greatest commandment to love God and others places relationships at the center of our faith. Matthew 22:37-40 underscores this priority: "Jesus replied: 'Love the Lord your God with all your heart and with all your soul and with all your mind.' This is the first and greatest commandment. And the second is like it: 'Love your neighbor as yourself.' All the Law and the Prophets hang on these two commandments." Prioritizing relationships aligns with God's values and fosters a sense of community and belonging.

2. Investing in Relationships: Building and nurturing relationships requires intentional effort. Hebrews 10:24-25 encourages, "And let us consider how we may spur one another on toward love and good deeds, not giving up meeting together, as some are in the habit of doing, but encouraging one another—and all the more as you see the Day approaching." Spending quality time with loved ones and

participating in community activities strengthens relational bonds.

3. Relational Integrity: Maintaining integrity in relationships reflects God's love. Ephesians 4:2-3 advises, "Be completely humble and gentle; be patient, bearing with one another in love. Make every effort to keep the unity of the Spirit through the bond of peace." Treating others with kindness, patience, and honesty fosters healthy and enduring relationships.

Cultivating Humility

1. Recognizing God's Unconditional Love: Recognizing that God's love is not based on our achievements or wealth cultivates humility. Ephesians 2:8-9 reminds us, "For it is by grace you have been saved, through faith and this is not from yourselves, it is the gift of God—not by works, so that no one can boast." Understanding that our worth and identity are found in God's love and grace, not in material possessions, promotes humility.

2. Serving Others: Humility is expressed through serving others. Philippians 2:3-4 instructs, "Do nothing out of selfish ambition or vain conceit. Rather, in humility value others above yourselves, not looking to your own interests but each of you to the interests of the others." Serving others selflessly reflects Christ's humility and love.

3. Learning from Jesus' Example: Jesus is the ultimate example of humility. Matthew 11:29 invites, "Take my yoke upon you and learn from me, for I am gentle and humble in heart, and you will find rest for your souls." Following Jesus' example helps us embody humility in our daily lives.

Conclusion

Understanding the universal love of God has profound implications for how we live our lives and relate to others. It calls us to reflect God's love in our actions, attitudes, and relationships. Embracing all people, living generously, practicing forgiveness, prioritizing relationships, and cultivating humility are tangible ways to demonstrate God's love.

By embracing and valuing all individuals, regardless of their background, status, or wealth, we reflect God's inclusive heart and promote unity and compassion. Living generously with our resources, time, and talents is a tangible expression of God's love. Practicing forgiveness fosters healing and reconciliation, mirroring the grace and mercy we receive from God. Prioritizing relationships over material pursuits aligns with God's values and builds a sense of community and belonging. Cultivating humility reminds us that our worth and identity are found in God's love and grace, not in our achievements or possessions.

These principles, when lived out, not only transform our own lives but also positively impact those around us, reflecting the heart of God's character and His eternal plan for humanity. Embracing and sharing God's love in these ways leads to a fulfilling and spiritually rich life, grounded in the unchanging nature of God's love.

CHAPTER 56

GOD'S LOVE IN ACTION: SERVING OTHERS

Jesus' life and ministry provide the ultimate example of God's love in action. He served others selflessly, healed the sick, fed the hungry, and comforted the brokenhearted. As followers of Christ, we are called to emulate His example and serve others with love and compassion. In John 13:34-35, Jesus gives a new commandment: "A new command I give you: Love one another. As I have loved you, so you must love one another. By this everyone will know that you are my disciples, if you love one another." This command emphasizes that our love for others is a testimony to our faith and a reflection of God's love in the world. This chapter explores how we can put God's love into action through serving others.

Jesus' Example of Serving Others

1. Healing the Sick: Jesus' ministry was marked by numerous acts of healing. In Matthew 14:14, it is recorded,

"When Jesus landed and saw a large crowd, he had compassion on them and healed their sick." Jesus' compassion moved Him to serve others by addressing their physical needs.

2. Feeding the Hungry: One of the most well-known miracles of Jesus is the feeding of the five thousand. In Matthew 14:19-21, Jesus multiplied five loaves of bread and two fish to feed a large crowd. This act of service not only met their immediate need for food but also demonstrated God's abundant provision.

3. Comforting the Brokenhearted: Jesus comforted those who were grieving or in distress. In John 11:33-35, Jesus wept with Mary and Martha over the death of their brother Lazarus, showing deep empathy and compassion. His actions remind us that serving others includes providing emotional support and comfort.

The Call to Serve Others

1. Emulating Jesus' Example: As followers of Christ, we are called to emulate His example of selfless service. In Mark 10:45, Jesus states, "For even the Son of Man did not come to be served, but to serve, and to give his life as a ransom for many." Serving others is central to our discipleship and reflects Christ's love.

2. Loving One Another: Jesus' new commandment in John 13:34-35 emphasizes that our love for others is a testimony to our faith: "A new command I give you: Love one another. As I have loved you, so you must love one another. By this everyone will know that you are my disciples, if you love one another." Serving others with love demonstrates our commitment to following Christ.

3. Serving as a Reflection of God's Love: Serving others is a tangible expression of God's love. 1 John 4:19-21 reminds us, "We love because he first loved us. Whoever claims to love God yet hates a brother or sister is a liar. For whoever does not love their brother and sister, whom they have seen, cannot love God, whom they have not seen. And he has given us this command: Anyone who loves God must also love their brother and sister." Our service reflects the love we have received from God.

Practical Ways to Serve Others

1. Meeting Physical Needs: One of the most direct ways to serve others is by meeting their physical needs. This includes providing food, clothing, shelter, and medical care. James 2:15-16 highlights the importance of addressing physical needs: "Suppose a brother or a sister is without clothes and daily food. If one of you says to them, 'Go in peace; keep warm and well fed,' but does nothing about their

physical needs, what good is it?" Practical acts of service demonstrate God's love in action.

2. Offering Emotional Support: Providing emotional support and comfort to those who are hurting is another vital aspect of service. 2 Corinthians 1:3-4 encourages us, "Praise be to the God and Father of our Lord Jesus Christ, the Father of compassion and the God of all comfort, who comforts us in all our troubles, so that we can comfort those in any trouble with the comfort we ourselves receive from God." Listening, offering a kind word, and being present for others are powerful ways to serve.

3. Using Our Gifts and Talents: God has given each of us unique gifts and talents to serve others. 1 Peter 4:10 instructs, "Each of you should use whatever gift you have received to serve others, as faithful stewards of God's grace in its various forms." Whether it's teaching, cooking, building, or providing professional skills, using our talents to help others honors God.

4. Volunteering Time: Volunteering our time for causes and organizations that help those in need is a practical way to serve. Ephesians 5:15-16 advises, "Be very careful, then, how you live—not as unwise but as wise, making the most of every opportunity, because the days are evil."

Investing time in service activities reflects our commitment to living out our faith.

The Impact of Serving Others

1. Transforming Lives: Serving others can have a profound impact on their lives, providing hope and meeting critical needs. Matthew 25:35-36 describes the impact of service: "For I was hungry and you gave me something to eat, I was thirsty and you gave me something to drink, I was a stranger and you invited me in, I needed clothes and you clothed me, I was sick and you looked after me, I was in prison and you came to visit me." These acts of service make a tangible difference.

2. Building Community: Serving others fosters a sense of community and strengthens relationships. Acts 2:44-45 illustrates the early Christian community's commitment to serving one another: "All the believers were together and had everything in common. They sold property and possessions to give to anyone who had need." Serving together builds unity and mutual support.

3. Reflecting Christ's Love: Serving others reflects Christ's love to the world. John 13:35 emphasizes, "By this everyone will know that you are my disciples, if you love one another." Our acts of service become a powerful testimony of God's love and can draw others to Christ.

Overcoming Barriers to Serving

1. Overcoming Self-Centeredness: One of the biggest barriers to serving others is self-centeredness. Philippians 2:3-4 advises, "Do nothing out of selfish ambition or vain conceit. Rather, in humility value others above yourselves, not looking to your own interests but each of you to the interests of the others." Cultivating humility and prioritizing others' needs helps overcome this barrier.

2. Finding Time: In our busy lives, finding time to serve can be challenging. Ephesians 5:16 encourages us to make the most of our time. Prioritizing service, even in small ways, and integrating it into our regular routines can help overcome this challenge.

3. Addressing Fear and Insecurity: Fear and insecurity can prevent us from serving others. 2 Timothy 1:7 reassures us, "For the Spirit God gave us does not make us timid, but gives us power, love and self-discipline." Trusting in God's strength and stepping out in faith enables us to serve boldly.

Jesus' life and ministry provide the ultimate example of God's love in action. He served others selflessly, healed the sick, fed the hungry, and comforted the brokenhearted. As followers of Christ, we are called to emulate His example and serve others with love and compassion. In John 13:34-35, Jesus gives a new commandment: "A new command I give you: Love one another. As I have loved you, so you must love one another. By this everyone will know that you are my disciples if you love one another." This command emphasizes that our love for others is a testimony to our faith and a reflection of God's love in the world.

By emulating Jesus' example, meeting physical and emotional needs, using our gifts and talents, and volunteering our time, we can put God's love into action. Serving others transforms lives, builds community, and reflects Christ's love. Overcoming barriers to serving, such as self-centeredness, time constraints, and fear, allows us to fully embrace our call to serve.

Living out God's love through service is a powerful witness to the world, demonstrating the transformative power of His love. As we serve others with love and compassion, we fulfill Jesus' command and reflect the heart of God's character. Embracing a lifestyle of service leads to a fulfilling and spiritually rich life, grounded in the unchanging nature of God's love.

BIBLIOGRAPHY

1. The Holy Bible, New International Version (NIV). Grand Rapids, MI: Zondervan, 2011.

2. Carson, D. A., and Douglas J. Moo. An Introduction to the New Testament. Grand Rapids, MI: Zondervan, 2005.

3. Fee, Gordon D., and Douglas Stuart. How to Read the Bible for All Its Worth. Grand Rapids, MI: Zondervan, 2014.

4. Keller, Timothy. Generous Justice: How God's Grace Makes Us Just. New York, NY: Penguin Books, 2010.

5. Piper, John. Desiring God: Meditations of a Christian Hedonist. Sisters, OR: Multnomah Publishers, 2011.

6. Wright, N.T. Simply Christian: Why Christianity Makes Sense. New York, NY: HarperOne, 2010.

Articles and Essays

1. Carson, D. A. "The Love of God: The Love of God and the Love of Man." Themelios, vol. 25, no. 1, 1999, pp. 4-13.

2. Packer, J.I. "Knowing God." Christianity Today, vol. 17, no. 7, 1973, pp. 9-15.

3. Wright, N.T. "The Mission of God and the Missional Church." Journal of Missional Practice, vol. 1, no. 1, 2013, pp. 1-12.

Online Resources

1. "Bible Gateway." Accessed June 1, 2024. https://www.biblegateway.com/.

2. "Blue Letter Bible." Accessed June 1, 2024. https://www.blueletterbible.org/.

3. "Desiring God." Accessed June 1, 2024. https://www.desiringgod.org/.

4. "Got Questions Ministries." Accessed June 1, 2024. https://www.gotquestions.org/.

Sermons and Speeches

1. Keller, Timothy. "The Power of Generosity." Redeemer Presbyterian Church, New York, NY, November 21, 2010.

2. Piper, John. "The Great Commandment and the Great Commission." Bethlehem Baptist Church, Minneapolis, MN, February 14, 2006.

3. Wright, N.T. "Love as the Fulfillment of the Law." St. Andrews Church, Oxford, UK, March 5, 2012.

Additional References

1. Smith, Christian. The Bible Made Impossible: Why Biblicism Is Not a Truly Evangelical Reading of Scripture. Grand Rapids, MI: Brazos Press, 2012.

2. Yancey, Philip. What's So Amazing About Grace? Grand Rapids, MI: Zondervan, 2002.

3. Willard, Dallas. The Spirit of the Disciplines: Understanding How God Changes Lives. New York, NY: HarperOne, 1999.

This bibliography includes essential sources that have informed the exploration and discussion of God's love, its implications for our lives, and the call to serve others. The listed books, articles, online resources, and sermons provide a comprehensive foundation for understanding and living out the principles of Christian love and service.

SHIMBA
PUBLISHING